AMERICAN
SOCIAL REFORM MOVEMENTS

Their Pattern Since 1865

I AM NOT AN ADVOCATE FOR FREQUENT CHANGES IN LAWS AND CONSTITUTIONS. BUT LAWS AND INSTITUTIONS MUST GO HAND IN HAND WITH THE PROGRESS OF THE HUMAN MIND. AS THAT BECOMES MORE DEVELOPED, MORE ENLIGHTENED, AS NEW DISCOVERIES ARE MADE, NEW TRUTHS DISCLOSED, AND MANNERS AND OPINIONS CHANGE WITH THE CHANGE OF CIRCUMSTANCES, INSTITUTIONS MUST ADVANCE ALSO, AND KEEP PACE WITH THE TIMES. WE MIGHT AS WELL REQUIRE A MAN TO WEAR STILL THE COAT WHICH FITTED HIM WHEN A BOY AS CIVILIZED SOCIETY TO REMAIN EVER UNDER THE REGIMEN OF THEIR BARBAROUS ANCESTORS.

Thomas Jefferson

AMERICAN
SOCIAL REFORM MOVEMENTS

Their Pattern Since 1865

BY

THOMAS H. GREER

MICHIGAN STATE COLLEGE

NEW YORK

PRENTICE-HALL, INC.

1949

PRENTICE-HALL SOCIOLOGY SERIES

HERBERT BLUMER, EDITOR

PRINTED IN THE UNITED STATES OF AMERICA

To
Margarette

Contents

PART TWO: SINCE 1917

Illustrative Documents

Illustrative Documents

AMERICAN
SOCIAL REFORM MOVEMENTS
Their Pattern Since 1865

INTRODUCTION

Reform and Democracy

DURING the past century Americans have been concerned chiefly with the development and exploitation of the nation's physical resources. During this era, about once in each generation, the people have turned their attention seriously to social reform. They have paused to listen while the " new society " has been hopefully proposed—specific programs have ranged from the lowering of railroad rates to a complete revision of the existing order. In such periods, the last of which was called " the New Deal," the reformers have been given a chance to try their plans, to make mistakes, to produce remedies. In the initial stages, the public has demonstrated an enthusiasm bordering upon exhilaration. But reform measures disturb social habits and vested interests and, while changes may promote the general welfare, they become increasingly tiresome to the public and to the individuals and groups that are regulated or taxed. Eventually reaction sets in, the reformers are out, and the people return to " normalcy."

Reform comes spasmodically in a democratic society. Needed adjustments are postponed, just as individuals postpone changing their personal habits. Only when affairs become unbearable are people willing to make the effort required for reform. But the emotional tension, which appears to be a psychological requisite, does not last indefinitely, and reform stops when the people relax.

Efforts to bring about reform are more continuous than reform itself. They may go on when reform is forgotten by the people while some proposals, though never heeded, may be persistently urged by their sponsors. Although programs for reform rise and

3

fall in an emotional cycle, some cry for change is always to be heard.

Beneath the confusion which appears on the surface of reform movements lie solid principles of social action. Conditions of living are constantly changing. Machines are invented which may destroy old jobs or create new work hazards; markets are shut off, leaving farm and factory producers without means of livelihood. Monopolistic giants develop in industry, forcing small enterprisers from the field, while the growth of arbitrary power in labor unions endangers the rights of both workers and the public. As such changes take place, institutions must be adjusted to protect the individual and society. Affected groups organize to meet the problem; they seek relief through direct action or legislation. *The resultant adaptation is called social reform, and the efforts to achieve it are social reform movements.*

Even in a static society there would be some agitation for reform. No system of life is perfect; there are always some who can see a means of improvement for themselves or others. But if underlying changes did not occur in the elements of social living, human institutions would tend to become hard and inflexible. It is the impact of new conditions that upsets the old order and compels adjustment. In such instances peaceful adjustment is desirable, but if entrenched groups refuse to permit change, a resort to force may result. Such was the case in France in 1789 and in Russia in 1917. Violence not only destroys existing institutions but distorts the plan of reform itself. If men always acted rationally they would continuously adapt their institutions to changing conditions. Since they frequently do not, adjustments are delayed and resisted until they come in legislative torrents or explosions of force.

If the American people are to avoid the evils of hasty legislation or violence, they need to understand more thoroughly the processes of social reform movements. Such movements, unfortunately, are not self-explanatory, because they are beclouded by passion and propaganda. The aim of this book is to remove the confusing slogans and labels and to set forth the essential pattern of modern reform movements. In fulfilling this aim it will not be necessary to treat every effort which has been made to alter American society, but the more important movements of the past century will be analyzed to determine the basic elements of the reform pattern.

The structure and functioning of organized, broadly based movements will be the central object of this analysis. To compare the basic elements of major reform efforts, appropriate questions will be raised concerning each of those under consideration. Why did the demand for reform arise? What groups composed the movement and what kind of men became the leaders? How was each movement organized? What were the principal objectives, and what techniques were employed to secure them? To what extent did the movement achieve its aims? Were the ultimate results of the effort socially beneficial or detrimental? Answers to these basic questions and many minor ones will provide an understanding of social reform movements; from these answers a rationale or general pattern may be drawn.

The matter of selection of movements for the purpose of this analysis at once appears. There have been hundreds of reform efforts during the last century, but most of them have developed along narrow lines and have been supported by limited and incohesive groups. Particular objectives such as taxation and municipal reform, slum clearance, safety and health regulation, judicial and penal reform, abolition of child labor, and civil service reform are among the many which have been advanced. All these individual efforts could not be treated adequately in a single volume; an attempt to do so would fail to achieve the primary aim of this book. A more suitable approach, keeping in mind the objective of establishing the general pattern of social reform movements, is to limit the study to an examination of major organized efforts by the principal socio-economic groups of the country. Once the behavior outline for each main group has been determined, American reform movements as a whole may be synthesized. The resultant over-all pattern should be more meaningful to readers than the multitude of conclusions which might be drawn from studying hundreds of particular reform programs.

The main socio-economic groups that have participated in

reform movements are not difficult to discern. American industrial labor is one large group that has had to seek continual adjustments to changing economic conditions; while the main body of workers has generally favored moderate action, minority elements have agitated for more radical programs. Farmers comprise another important group that has struggled to maintain itself by bringing about institutional changes. And the so-called "middle class"—that shifting, ill-defined quantity—has, on two notable occasions since 1865, formed its lines and moved toward broad social reforms. The principal movements by each of these groups—workers, farmers, and the middle class—will be examined separately, though no group has acted alone. The nature of reform activities can best be understood in connection with the primary human forces behind them.

Time has proved a conditioning factor in the character of these movements. The close of the War Between the States ushered in a new era which had its impact upon all the major socio-economic groups. Participation by the United States in World War I was another important turning point. That upheaval and the sweeping developments which followed affected every group in the nation, and reform efforts were consequently shifted to a different key. World War II has forced upon the world staggering new problems, only dimly comprehended. This book will recognize the influence of important time lapses while tracing the course of continuously active forces.

Social reform movements are an integral part of American democracy. They provide the required momentum to overcome convention and inertia and generally represent a peaceful means of making social adjustments. Many proposals for change are, of course, neither desirable nor sound, and citizens face the task of distinguishing reasonable and necessary programs from the fantastic and perverted. This responsibility will be more wisely exercised as the people reach a deeper understanding of the major reform efforts of the recent past.

PART ONE
1865 TO 1917

CHAPTER ONE

The Workers Organize

POWERFUL forces transformed the pattern of American life in the years following the War Between the States. Changes so deep-rooted and far-reaching had never before occurred so rapidly in this country. The United States of 1865 had little in common with the United States of 1890, barely a generation later. The simple old ways of a life which was small, agrarian, and personal gave way to strange new forms; a new nation of steel and electricity emerged—huge, mechanized, and corporate.

The New Economic Setting After 1865

No one planned this change. Before the main features were firmly established, few realized it was taking place. Various energies were combined to produce the new pattern. People from the Old World arrived in large numbers to swell the home demand for goods and to provide cheap labor for factories. Newly built railroad lines expanded markets to national proportions and made available vast natural resources; the abundance of these resources made the United States largely self-sufficient in raw materials. Technical and business inventions created novel implements and methods of enterprise, and American producers were quick to abandon obsolescent equipment or ideas in favor of more efficient tools. The absence of a rigid social system, furthermore, gave ambitious men in all walks of life an incentive to strive for fortune and recognition. Manufactures and labor productivity increased by leaps and bounds; capital was accumulated and concentrated; in the crucible of competition small concerns were annihilated or consumed by giant trusts and mergers. From 1865 onward Americans strove to retain their balance in the brave new world.

Workers were especially confused. Unwieldy in numbers and separated in points of view, they found difficulty in making adjustments. Business leaders were relatively more compact and exerted the initiative. Labor's record in the period following the War Between the States is filled with groping, uncertainty, and divided leadership. There was no steady plan of aims or methods. Sweeping changes in the capitalist system were championed at first and then abandoned for more limited demands. Independent politics was supported, then discarded, as the principal means of gaining objectives. Organization of all laborers into one big union was pursued for a time, then given up for organization along separate craft lines.

Severe problems faced the workers immediately upon the close of the War Between the States. Some of these were temporary post-war difficulties; others resulted from long-run developments which were to compel continuous adaptations by labor. Local labor unions were unable to cope with growing national problems. As the railroads extended markets from the Atlantic to the Mississippi Valley and beyond, workers in one area came into competition with others. It was no longer possible for a local union to control wages and conditions because employers could switch operations to regions where labor was unorganized and cheap. National organization of producers in numerous industries also gave employers an advantage in dealing with local unions. It appeared that nothing short of national trade unions could successfully meet this situation.

Organized labor was also menaced by the introduction of machinery on an expanding scale. This not only threatened to reduce employment, but made it possible for employers to replace craftsmen with unorganized, unskilled workers at lower wages. Such long-run developments which worked against labor were accentuated by price inflation during and after the war. While money wages were steadily rising, basic retail prices soared still higher. This situation became acute when the two great armies began to demobilize and the streets were filled with ex-soldiers seeking jobs.

Formation of National Trade Unions

Rising unemployment crystallized the demand for labor action in 1865. The need for organization on a national basis was generally felt, but the means was very much disputed. The principal movement in the direction of strengthening labor's position was the formation of national trade unions. Local, isolated unions of each craft began to join in strong national groups to meet the new economic situation. While there were a few national unions in the country before 1864, twenty-six were formed in the following decade.[1] Pioneers in this significant move were the stove-molders, carpenters, cigar-makers, bricklayers, typographical workers, and machinists.

The general aim of the national unions, whose total membership approached 300,000 by 1872, was to present a solid front to employers in each trade. Uniform national labor policies were imperative in the face of national markets and sources of labor supply. The story of the Stove-molders' Union is typical. This group, organized in 1859, was one of the first to feel the depressing competition of producers in new areas of the national market, and it also faced a national association of employers in the industry. The final outcome of organization on both sides was a measuring of strength and development of the trade agreement system of collective bargaining. That result, however, was long in coming. In the 1860's the stove-molders sought higher wages and equalization of wage rates for a given type of work in each locality and in the country as a whole. They opposed piece-work payment systems and attempted to regulate the supply of molders through union control of apprentices and helpers. As a furtherance of job security they also favored restrictions on the employment of prison labor, Negroes, immigrants, and other sub-standard workers. But the Stove-molders' Union did not limit itself to job-and-pay objectives. It wanted a higher social status for workers and a recognition of the

---

[1] John R. Commons, *et al.*, *History of Labour in the United States*, II, 47–48. New York: The Macmillan Company, 1926, 2 vols. This work is the principal factual source for the early national trade unions.

dignity of manual labor; it joined with other unions of this period in a program for general labor reform and the establishment of workers' co-operatives.

The man chiefly responsible for the successful development of the Stove-molders' Union was William H. Sylvis. A former worker in an iron foundry, he was one of the first labor leaders to recognize the necessity of organizing on a national basis, and he proved the feasibility of the idea through his own union. Sylvis pioneered in solving the problems of dues assessment and distribution, union membership qualifications, and establishment of criteria for determining the legality and advisability of strikes. In addition to his ability as an organizer, Sylvis recognized the importance of public opinion. Until his death in 1869 he exercised a broad influence over the expanding national trade unions and the labor movement as a whole.[2]

National trade unions were supported in their growth by the appearance of a well-founded labor press. *Fincher's Trades' Review*, first published at Philadelphia in 1863, became the most influential of some one hundred labor papers started after the war. It was a true journal of the national union movement, keeping a careful check on the founding and development of each country-wide federation. Support of the paper came entirely from workers' subscriptions and donations. Jonathan C. Fincher, who published the *Review*, was a member of the Machinists' Union and the most consistent trade leader of the 1860's. He steadfastly opposed Utopian schemes and independent political action by labor, while favoring direct economic action by strongly organized crafts. Fincher was a prophet of the restricted American Federation of Labor philosophy that was to triumph a generation later.

The National Labor Union

National trade unions, however, represented only a part of the labor movement in this period. Workers everywhere, in reaction to the broad economic forces at work, sensed a need for some

---

[2] Jonathan P. Grossman, *William Sylvis, Pioneer of American Labor,* 120–151; 269–274. New York: Columbia University Press, 1945.

united national action. This action could not be provided by the trade unions alone, for the national unions were not yet the common or dominant units of labor organization. More important in 1865 were the local trades' assemblies. These were comparable to the present-day " city-central " trade bodies of the American Federation of Labor, and were organized in all industrial centers. Each local assembly comprised representatives of local unions in the community and had advisory and co-ordinating functions in the area. Most workers still considered their problems in terms of the local labor situation. A national point of view for each craft had not yet been established. It was natural for workers to think of united national action in terms of a federation of local assemblies.

Beginning in 1864, sporadic but persistent efforts were made to create some such national league of local assemblies. After considerable agitation, representatives from a number of local groups met in Louisville on September 21, 1864. They drafted a constitution, which failed to provide representation to the growing national trade unions, and called their organization the International Industrial Assembly of North America. They listed as objectives the orderly adjustment of capital-labor disputes, establishment of consumers' co-operatives, and favorable legislation for workers. In February of the next year a number of the local assemblies of New York State met at Albany. They invited assemblies in other states to send delegations to a proposed convention at New York City. These workers were especially interested in the move for the eight-hour day, which had already taken organized form in several states.

The growing national trade unions rivaled the local assemblies in this maneuvering toward a united national labor body. In February of 1866 William Harding, International President of the Coachmakers' Union, and William H. Sylvis, President of the Stove-molders' Union, issued a call for a national labor convention. The plan proposed a meeting at Baltimore of delegates from each national union and from each local assembly. Sylvis' name gave strength to the call because he was probably the most prominent labor leader of the 1860's. The local assemblies, nevertheless, repudiated the idea, for the call had been made solely by the national trade unionists without consulting them. A few months later a compromise between the two rival organizations was worked out. Representatives of the national unions joined the Baltimore Trades' Assembly in a convention invitation to all labor groups in the United States.

Delegates answering the call met at Baltimore on August 20, 1866, and constituted themselves a permanent National Labor Union. This new organization was a natural successor to various " industrial congresses " of the period preceding the War Between the States. It also seemed part of a current international effort to deal with growing labor problems, paralleling the establishment of Karl Marx' International Workingmen's Association in England two years earlier. Although never formally joining the " First International," the National Labor Union sent A. C. Cameron as a delegate to the International Congress at Basle in 1869 and pledged adherence to the principles of the I.W.A. in 1870.[3]

Members of the National Labor Union came at first from national trade unions and their locals, city trades' assemblies, and " Eight-hour leagues " that were agitating for legislation to compel the eight-hour day for labor. Representatives of the building trades were the most numerous, followed by the stove-molders, machinists, and ship carpenters. In the convention of 1867 at Chicago, farmers temporarily joined forces by sending delegates from " Anti-monopoly associations " and " Land and Labor leagues." In 1868 the farmers and " Eight-hour leagues " dropped out, but the tide of organization reached its height. All important labor leaders attended the national convention, which represented an estimated 600,000 workers. In addition, delegates appeared from various " Labor Reform leagues," composed largely of " intellectuals," and from working women's organizations. Susan B. Anthony, famous suffragist, was one of the first women delegates, as was Mrs. Mary Kellogg Putnam, daughter of a prominent labor reformer. When in 1871 the National Labor Union became engrossed in politics and the trade union

[3] Nathan Fine, *Labor and Farmer Parties in the United States, 1828–1928*, 95. New York: Rand School of Social Science, 1928.

14

men withdrew, these non-working " intellectuals " and politicians dominated the Union membership. This element caused the Union at last to be disparaged as ". . . led by labor leaders without organizations, politicians without parties, women without husbands, and cranks, visionaries, and agitators without jobs." [4]

Leaders of the National Labor Union represented all the participating groups. In addition to William H. Sylvis of the Stove-molders' Union, there was John Hinchcliffe of the Printers' Union. Hinchcliffe was a well-known labor figure who worked with various trade unions and published the *Weekly Miner* for the American Miners' Association. The eight-hour movement had a spokesman in C. William Gibson of the New Haven Eight-hour Association. Local trades' assemblies were represented by many outstanding leaders, such as J. C. C. Whaley, who was elected President of the Union in 1866, and Richard F. Trevellick. Trevellick was one of the most prominent reformers of the time. Born in England in 1830, he later went to Australia and joined the labor movement there. In 1860 he arrived in New Orleans as an experienced ship carpenter and became president of the local trade union. In a few years Trevellick moved once again, this time to Detroit, where he remained. Representing the Detroit Trades' Assembly, Trevellick attended practically every meeting of the National Labor Union and was three times chosen its president. Like most of the other leaders in the Union, he was not strictly and solely a trade unionist. He was the chief lobbyist in Washington for a federal eight-hour law, an ardent temperance advocate, and a " Greenbacker." This scattering of energy was typical of the labor reform movement and leaders in the 1860's.

The program of the National Labor Union reflected the groping of many elements for a solution of common problems. In the face of severe difficulties, organized workers and their sympathizers intuitively sought a national organization for coping with the situation. But the fulfillment of this national union

---

[4] Norman J. Ware, *The Labor Movement in the United States, 1860–1895,* 11. New York: D. Appleton-Century Company, Inc., 1929.

did not provide the necessary answers. Labor was very much divided on specific objectives.

The fanning out of ideas over a wide front, rather than concentration upon limited aims, was shown in the first Union Congress. The delegates favored national trade unions as the chief means of achieving gains for workers, but suggested arbitration as a substitute for strikes. There was a strong feeling for independent political action that would bring reform through legislation. Donation of the public lands to actual settlers was endorsed, and the co-operative movement approved. Additional matters were treated in the Union Congress of 1867. The trade apprentice system, strikes, female labor, and Negro labor were investigated. Meanwhile the dominant demands of the organization increased toward adoption of the eight-hour day and greenbacks.

Since the eight-hour-day idea played so important a part in the story of the National Labor Union and of all reform in the 1860's, a sketch of its development is in order. The movement owed its origin mainly to Ira Steward, a Boston machinist. Steward had worked the regular twelve hours daily as an apprentice. He began agitation during the War Between the States, working out an elaborate " philosophy " for the movement. He contended that his plan, whereby hours would be shortened by law without decrease in workers' pay, would relieve toil and in the end raise the standard of living through greater leisure. Steward was a zealous reformer and converted a local idea into a nation-wide demand. Some observers referred to him as that " eight-hour monomaniac."

With the help of other labor propagandists like George E. McNeill, and " intellectuals " like Wendell Phillips, Steward formed the Grand Eight-hour League of Massachusetts in 1865. Other " leagues " sprang up throughout the land, and many of them sent delegates to the National Labor Union conventions. Political pressure was exerted on legislatures; by 1867 six states had passed eight-hour laws. A seemingly important victory was won when Congress in 1868 passed a law requiring the eight-hour day for federal employees. Activity by the National Labor Union had greatly aided the success of this measure. Results,

however, proved disappointing. Private employers failed to
follow the government's example, as had been hoped. Some
years passed before the federal law worked without bringing pay
as well as hour reductions.[5]

After 1868 the dominant objective of the Union was issuance
of more greenbacks by the government. These were paper notes
issued during the War Between the States and backed only by
the government's promise to pay. A few years earlier the
Treasury began redeeming part of the greenbacks. The con-
traction of the currency caused a depressing fall in prices and
widespread unemployment. To meet this situation the Union
demanded that the retirement of greenbacks be stopped, and
Congress in February, 1868, halted redemptions. Some social
reformers, however, felt that it was not enough to keep in circulation the paper money already issued. A special type of greenback was proposed which would free " producers " from " capitalist domination " and thereby bring prosperity to the masses.
This idea captured and fired the imagination of the majority in
the National Labor Union.

The " Greenbackism " of this period is distinct from the pure
and simple inflationist program of the 1870's and later. The
Union espoused a scheme invented by a theorist, Edward
Kellogg, who felt that his idea would revolutionize production
and finance. The scheme was designed not just to lift prices
and make " easy money," but to make possible the creation of
government-financed, worker-owned, producers' co-operatives.
According to the plan, the federal government would lend money
on real estate security at an interest rate of one per cent. This
money would be in the form of greenbacks. Borrowers could
use the money themselves, supposedly to finance co-operative
enterprises, or re-lend it to others. In case they were unable to
do either, borrowers had the further privilege of returning the
greenbacks to the government in exchange for " interconvertible
bonds," bearing one per cent interest. This latter feature was
to prevent general interest rates from falling below one per cent.
If prevailing rates should rise above that figure, holders of the

---

[5] Selig Perlman, *History of Trade Unionism in the United States,* 47–49.
New York: The Macmillan Company, 1922.

"interconvertible bonds" could return them in exchange for greenbacks.[6]

If the objectives of the National Labor Union appeared scattered and shifting, the structure of the organization was hardly more stable. A reform group seldom can achieve results if its organization is weak. At first the Union appeared to be developing a sound structural basis. Annual Congresses were provided for, consisting of proportional representation of delegates from local unions, trades' assemblies, national unions, and "Eight-hour leagues." Permanent organization between the annual meetings was to consist of a president, vice-president, treasurer, secretaries, finance committee, and an executive board comprising the important officers. As the Union became increasingly concerned with legislation, it switched from this sound beginning to a weaker, politically oriented structure. After 1870 the affiliated local bodies were grouped into state-wide unions, and these became the principal units of organization. Under such an arrangement the Union could never become a significant economic power because states are not natural economic units. The idea of a federation based on strong national trade unions was abandoned for the legislative idea which worked along state lines.

What techniques were used by the Union to achieve its varied aims? No general plan of action was formulated. Beginning in 1868 William H. Sylvis, a vigorous president and skilled administrator, introduced systematic management of the elementary affairs of the organization. An extensive correspondence was established with all interested and sympathetic groups, and many pamphlets were distributed. At the same time Sylvis moved to establish a new technique for carrying out the program of the Union. He appointed a committee of five men to reside in Washington, D. C., as the first permanent labor lobby in the nation's capital. The committee was instructed " to watch over the interests of our Union, lay our plans and objects before Congressmen and Senators, and take advantage of every opportunity to help along the work." [7] Sylvis and Richard Trevellick,

[6] Commons, *op. cit.,* II, 119–122, describes this interesting scheme.
[7] Commons, *op. cit.,* II, 130.

18

his successor as president, took their program directly to the people in 1869 by means of a propaganda tour through the South. They used every opportunity to advertise the principles of the Union by speeches, letters, and interviews.

Such methods were soon overshadowed, however, by the move toward independent political action. The majority in the organization showed great faith in reform by way of legislation, and some of the extremists envisaged the creation of a strong political association that would dominate national and state legislatures. So alluring was this prospect of political power as the easy road to labor and social reform, that other devices were pushed aside. At first the move was restricted to lobbying activities and an attempt to pledge candidates of either major party to the program of the National Labor Union. Step by step the organization pressed on toward the establishment of an independent party.

In the convention of 1870, plans were laid to maintain the Union as a strictly economic organization and to set up a national labor party as a co-ordinate branch. This plan was carried out, and in the election year of 1872 the National Labor and Reform party met in Columbus for its first and last convention. Each state was invited to send delegates equal to the number of Congressmen from that state. Massachusetts, New York, New Jersey, Pennsylvania, Ohio, Michigan, Illinois, Iowa, Missouri, Mississippi, and Arkansas sent representatives. Judge David Davis of Illinois, a Justice of the U. S. Supreme Court and a well-known liberal, was nominated for the presidency. The regular platform of the National Labor Union was adopted, and the convention adjourned with enthusiasm for the campaign. Bright hopes were suddenly dashed, however, when candidate Davis withdrew. Davis apparently had accepted the nomination of the labor party as a possible stepping stone toward his selection by the Liberal Republicans and Democrats, who met shortly thereafter in their respective conventions. When Horace Greeley received the nomination of both those groups, Judge Davis quit the race. His withdrawal seriously embarrassed the National Labor and Reform party and had the effect of wrecking the Union as well as its political affiliate. The trade unionists had already withdrawn in protest against the dilution of membership and tendency toward politics. Only seven persons attended the Union Congress at Cleveland in September, 1872. The effort to unite workers in a strong national organization was broken by mixing with non-labor forces and by attempting independent politics.

Secrecy and the Knights of Labor

After the collapse of the National Labor Union, several of the national trade unions tried to revive the idea of a country-wide federation of strictly labor groups. In July, 1873, a National Industrial Congress composed of such elements convened. Whatever prospects this organization might have had were crushed by the Panic of 1873, which descended upon the nation in September. The Industrial Congress met again in 1874 and, for the last time, in 1875. By then it was clear that labor was too depressed to build a strong national movement.

This was, indeed, a critical period for labor. The old national trade unions either went to pieces or existed in name only. Employers, under pressure of hard times, worked to wipe out any gains made by wage-earners before the Panic. Widespread unemployment shattered the workers' bargaining power. It was a time of lockouts, blacklists, and legal prosecutions against the unions.

In face of such an attack, what remained of the labor movement was largely forced underground. The violent " Molly Maguires," a secret fraternal order in the anthracite coal regions, tried to gain demands by threat and murder. This organization was brought to light and crushed by the authorities in 1876. A fraternal order of distinctly another type, however, was gaining a foothold in the labor movement during these difficult times.

The Noble Order of the Knights of Labor had been founded a few years before the Panic, on December 26, 1869. It was largely the idea of one man—a Philadelphia garment-cutter named Uriah Smith Stephens. This man, who had been trained for the ministry, believed a secret, fraternal type of organization would be best suited to the needs of the workers. Secrecy served to shield the group from the indiscretion of individual members and to protect it from attack by hostile employers. Smith's order was limited to a single assembly, or lodge, until 1872. It then began to expand from its place of origin in Philadelphia. As adverse conditions drove labor underground, the membership of the Knights of Labor rose to about 5,000 by 1875. By 1881 it had become strong enough to discard the veil of secrecy and emerge as the dominant labor organization of the day.

In the early 1880's the Knights experienced a mushroom-like growth. Improving economic conditions nurtured the whole labor movement. The peak of power was reached in 1886, when the Order claimed 700,000 members. Due to the rapid turn-over in membership, perhaps a million or more men were made Knights at some time during this period. Such numbers are impressive, and the Knights of Labor was considered a mighty force in the 1880's. But its growth was too rapid, and a sound organization with trained members can not be developed on such a basis.

This new force in the labor movement was a further attempt, following the National Labor Union, to unite all workers to attack common problems. The national trade unions played a minor part and, in the end, withdrew. The Knights appealed to the whole working-class for membership, along lines of broad " producer " solidarity. This approach was to lead to the same mixture of groups and the same scattering of effort which proved fatal to the National Labor Union.

In order to guard against dilution of the movement by " intellectuals ", or opposition forces, the Knights ruled that at least three-fourths of the members of each local assembly must be workers. The remainder might consist of non-working labor sympathizers, but doctors, lawyers, and bankers were specifically barred. Individuals or unions could join the local assemblies, and many of the unions surviving the Panic entered the movement. But unskilled, unorganized workers dominated the membership and it was this element, in combination with idealistic theorists, that carried forward the program.

The name of Terence V. Powderly is closely associated with that of the Knights of Labor. He was by all odds the outstanding leader of the Order and seemed to embody the spirit of the whole movement. Chosen Grand Master Workman in 1878, Powderly held that post until 1893, when the Knights were floundering to an end. He was a skilled worker himself, a member of the Machinists' and Blacksmiths' Union, but he had the broader point of view of the whole "producing" class. Powderly carried on the outlook of the National Labor Union, was not a strict trade unionist, and leaned toward political action. His first prominence was gained in 1878, when he was elected Mayor of Scranton, Pennsylvania, on a labor ticket. He stood for class collaboration rather than antagonism. A mild, diplomatic, sensitive man, Powderly tried to please the general public as well as labor.

The general objectives of the Knights of Labor closely paralleled those of the Grand Master Workman. The Order called for union of all trades, "education" of the public to the needs of labor, and the establishment of producers' co-operatives. This last aim was paramount—the Knights were to lead the working class out of "wage-bondage" into a system of self-employment. The motto of the Order was "Co-operation of the Order, by the Order, and for the Order." [8] This organization clearly was not set up as an instrument of any Marxian "class-struggle." It was principally an association of idealistic co-operators.

Greenbacks, the crying demand of the National Labor Union, were largely ignored by the Knights. With the return of prosperity and the resumption of specie payments for greenbacks by the Treasury, the issue became dormant after 1879. Other varied aims of the 1860's were revived, however. The eight-hour day was one of these. Reservation of the public lands for actual settlers only was demanded. Legislation for safety and health measures in hazardous occupations, prohibition of child labor, weekly pay, and mechanics' lien laws were newer objectives. Equal pay for equal work of both sexes and extended use of arbitration in labor disputes were also approved by the Knights. This entire program, however, was perverted in the declining years of the organization. Failing as a labor movement, the Knights of Labor in 1889 agreed to abandon its

---

[8] Perlman, *op. cit.*, 71–72.

traditional objectives for the platform of the "Southern Alliance," a powerful farmers' group. This shift meant virtually the end of the Knights as a labor body.

Ultimate collapse of the Order was hastened by problems of internal organization. The basic unit was called the local assembly. In most cases these assemblies were composed of "mixed" workers, some representing local unions and others joining as non-union members. For a while national trade union locals were permitted to form separate assemblies, but in 1885 this practice was forbidden in favor of "mixed" groups. The national trade unions objected to being submerged in such units and began to withdraw. The Knights of Labor tried too late to stop the secession by reversing its policy and urging all units to re-form along the lines of local national trade union assemblies. Such an arrangement paralleled the "city-central" trade bodies of the American Federation of Labor, whose strict craft basis was proving superior in the industrial struggles of the late 1880's. Failure of the Knights to give a more important position to the national unions and to permit them to retain their identity within the organization drove the skilled workers into a new type of labor body.

Above the local assemblies the Knights of Labor established a highly centralized organization. The country was divided into districts, each of which had a district assembly. This body, composed of representatives from local assemblies, had complete power over membership in the district. Highest authority was exercised by a General Assembly, consisting of representatives from the districts. Sole right to issue charters to inferior assemblies and final jurisdiction over all questions pertaining to the Order were given to the General Assembly. The main work was carried on by the Grand Master Workman and the Executive Board. This concentration of power and lack of autonomy for the component units of the Order appeared in marked contrast to the loose organization of the rising American Federation of Labor.

Techniques used by the Knights to gain their broad objectives were ineffective. The methods which they favored were generally impracticable, and the leaders directed workable methods in a half-hearted manner. Most of the program of the Order could be achieved only through legislation, and the difficulty of this technique had been clearly demonstrated by the failure of the National Labor Union and its Reform party. Local and district assemblies were allowed discretion in the field of political action. Arbitration was regarded by the leaders as the chief means of industrial peace. But this device was generally disregarded by employers, and even by the unions if they felt strong enough. The principal weapon remaining was the strike. Most of the activity of the Knights was connected with strikes, but the leaders showed neither enthusiasm nor skill when forced to conduct them.

The strikes were, of course, not general strikes by the Knights of Labor. They were actions by individual unions, supported by the Knights. Boycotts were commonly imposed against employers whose workers were on strike. A special " Resistance Fund " of the Knights extended financial aid during prolonged disputes. But the actions were usually unsuccessful, notably the great railway conflicts of 1877 and the epidemic of strikes in 1886 and 1887. Failure was due mainly to the fact that the membership of the Knights was too heterogeneous. Many of the non-wage earning members directly opposed strikes. The large group of unskilled workers could win strikes only when supported by skilled workers, and the craftsmen were growing weary of the idea of sacrificing their own interests to raise the wages of unskilled brethren in the organization.

It is difficult to point to any tangible achievements of the Knights of Labor. The main objective of Powderly and the bulk of the membership was establishment of producers' co-operatives. A few enterprises of this type succeeded. But the attempt to erect a system of independent, worker-owned establishments failed. Practically all the co-operatives launched soon collapsed because of inefficient management, lack of capital, or discriminatory treatment instigated by private competitors.

After the wild-fire growth of the early 1880's, the Order quickly burned out in the closing years of the decade. By 1890 the membership had fallen to 100,000 and nearly all the trade unionists had left. The surviving shell was drawn into the farmers' movement and subjected to its program. When James R. Sovereign, a farmer-editor of Iowa, became Grand Master Workman in 1893, the last symbol of the old Order was removed. Terence V. Powderly, once the leader of a formidable labor power, retired beaten and embittered.

Reasons for the decline of the Knights have already been suggested. The leadership was too preoccupied with idealistic notions and too little prepared to manage practical realities. Overcentralization of power contributed to internal jealousies, and the inclusion of unskilled workers reduced striking power. Employers weakened the Order by attacks with strong counter-weapons. But, finally, it was failure to achieve results that drove the Knights down the road of oblivion.

Triumph of Craft Unionism and the American Federation of Labor

With the disappearance of the Knights of Labor as a power, a new force began to rise among labor groups. Perceiving the fatal weaknesses in the attempt to unite all labor in one big organization, practical leaders in the trade unions moved toward a different type of association. The new idea was a loose federation of national trade unions, an idea which was to rule the philosophy of organized labor for over a generation.

The most important effort to form an organization of the new type was made on November 13, 1881. At that time a number of representatives from the national unions met in Pittsburgh and established a Federation of Organized Trades and Labor Unions. This association was to include both skilled and unskilled workers, as the time did not yet seem ripe for an organization of craftsmen exclusively. Annual conventions were held for several years afterward, until the group merged with the founders of the American Federation of Labor in 1886. The Federation of Organized Trades, however, is usually considered as the beginning of the A.F. of L.[9]

The growing power of the Knights of Labor in the early 1880's was the immediate cause of the formation of the American

---

[9] Commons, *op. cit.*, II, 318–331.

Federation of Labor. The Knights, aiming to increase the prosperity of all workers, wanted to bring the skilled workers into their organization and so boost their economic power. They attempted to break up the national craft unions by forming local assemblies of Knights with a nucleus of trade union men, hoping to draw away members of the craft unions. This was naturally resented by the trade union leaders and a majority of the skilled workers. They felt that in " one big union," such as the Knights of Labor, their interests would be subordinated to the masses of unskilled. They did not care to fight economic battles to raise wages for the masses, but preferred to maintain separate identities and work for their own gain alone.

With their organizations threatened by the activity of the Knights, trade union leaders reached out for a closer union of forces. When Samuel Gompers was sent out by the Cigar Makers' Union in the spring of 1886, his appeal for a federation met with ready response. Action was speeded up when the Knights in convention that year declared strongly against the trade unions. On December 8, 1886, a conference of union officials in Columbus, Ohio, declared itself the first convention of the American Federation of Labor.

The foundation of the Federation was largely the work of Samuel Gompers. He had helped to establish the Federation of Organized Trades in 1881, which was later merged with the A.F. of L. Gompers strove constantly for a closer union of crafts and finally led the way to the launching of the A.F. of L. itself, becoming its first President. He held that office continuously, except for one year, until his death in 1924. Gompers' life and that of the Federation were closely intermingled. The Federation was, of course, the product of forces larger than any one man, but Samuel Gompers left his stamp on the organization.

Born in England of Dutch-Jewish parentage, Gompers came to America in 1863 at the age of thirteen years. A cigar maker by trade, he joined the international union and came into contact with men of socialist beliefs, for this was the period of Marx' International Workingmen's Association. So enthusiastic was the youthful Gompers that he studied German for the sole purpose of reading Marx in the original. From this experience he developed a strong class-consciousness and idealism. He never lost this feeling of class-consciousness and he fought his whole lifetime for the improvement of organized labor. His idealism, however, died abruptly when he came into control of the Federation. He grew to detest socialism, to forget his earlier concern for the ills of humanity at large, and to concentrate in a realistic way upon the immediate benefits available for his unions.

Gompers possessed two of the qualities indispensable for the position he held—intelligence and energy. His motivation came from his extreme ambition and a love for power. He did not seek the applause of the general public, however, but enjoyed acclaim only as a labor leader. He was an astute politician, with an ability to hand out " headquarters " jobs and other favors to please all factions. He was a shrewd bargainer and master of practical psychology. Honesty was one of his essential characteristics. His minor attributes included speaking power and an ability to be a good " mixer " while remaining dignified.[10] His leadership was largely responsible for the success of the Federation. The growth of a strong organization is impossible without wise and energetic direction.

Although the Knights of Labor continued its attack upon the trade unions after 1886, the membership of the A.F. of L. grew rapidly. Failure of the Knights in important strikes caused practically all craftsmen to switch allegiance to the Federation, and in 1888 the A.F. of L. struck back at the Knights by forbidding any of its members to belong to that organization. After 1890 the Knights had practically passed from the labor scene, and the Federation began to enjoy a commanding position in the field of organized labor. In the late 1890's membership expanded, principally among the upper semi-skilled workers, but others less skilled were not entirely excluded. However, the totally unskilled and partially skilled foreign workers were ignored.

General prosperity favored the A.F. of L. after the turn of the century. In spite of some ups and downs, membership reached over 1,600,000 in 1904 and over 2,300,000 in 1917. Union-

---

[10] Herbert Harris, *American Labor,* 362–365. New Haven: Yale University Press, 1938.

ization of formerly unorganized trades was one of the main causes of this persistent growth. The effect of America's entry into World War I upon the development of the Federation will be examined in a later chapter.

In contrast with the earlier idealistic objectives of the Knights of Labor and the National Labor Union, the aims of the A.F. of L. were narrow and immediate. Gompers and his followers dreamed of no workers' paradise, and were frankly not interested in trying to aid all groups through Utopian schemes. The Federation suppressed visionaries and starry-eyed prophets. It was not concerned with " all men " or in " long shots." In fact, it absolutely refused to gamble. The leaders began with the " here " and " now." They stood for such immediate proposals as would directly benefit organized labor. They accepted the capitalist system as a going concern and did not oppose it, since they wanted only to get more out of it for organized labor. This objective came to mean more pay, fewer hours of work, job security, and better conditions. In order to achieve these ends the unions wanted to gain a monopoly over the supply of skilled jobs and workers.

Adolph Strasser, for years President of the Cigar Makers' Union and a leading developer of A.F. of L. philosophy, clearly stated the general attitude. Before a Senate investigating committee in 1883, Strasser said, " We have no ultimate ends. . . . We are all practical men. . . . We are going on from day to day." [11] This same philosophy was repeated over and over by Gompers until his death.

Specific objectives naturally changed from time to time. Each annual convention framed a program of objectives. A typical summary of early aims appeared in the original constitution of the Federation. Of peculiar interest is a first objective providing for legal incorporation of trade unions in order to free their members from prosecution under conspiracy laws. This objective was later reversed because corporate financial liability jeopardized the funds accumulated to hold the unions together. Compulsory education for children of school age was another

---

[11] Jacob B. Hardman, *American Labor Dynamics,* 99–101. New York: Harcourt, Brace & Company, Inc., 1928.

important aim, but not so idealistic as might appear. The chief interest of the Federation in this matter was to relieve organized adult labor from the wage-shattering competition of child labor. Legal prohibition of labor by children under fourteen was accordingly supported in the A.F. of L. constitution. A national eight-hour day was another important objective. The unions also called for the establishment of a national bureau of labor statistics, which later was realized in the Department of Labor. Immigration of contract-laborers was consistently opposed.

The chief strength in the organization of the Federation was the fact that it recognized and gave due place to the growing national trade unions. Only national unions were suited to deal with the problems of industry on an ever-increasing national scale. The A.F. of L. constitution provided that the basic units of the Federation should be not local assemblies of mixed workers, but national or international unions. Local trade organizations were given independent representation only where no national unit existed. Just one union in each craft could be recognized. " Dual unionism," or competing unions, was not tolerated. Later, the Federation gave representation to other labor groupings, such as state federations and " city-centrals," which are city-wide associations of union locals. However, the national unions have always dominated the A.F. of L. through their greater voting power in the National Convention.

The relationship between the independent national unions and the Federation was an important feature of the organization. The affiliated national unions were autonomous in almost all questions. Great moral power, however, was exercised by the Federation. Its annual convention passed recommendations that were usually followed by the member bodies. The convention, furthermore, had the power to expel any union by a two-thirds vote, and this threat kept dissenting factions in line. Large authority was invested in the Executive Council, which was chosen by the convention each year and whose members gave their full time to administration of the affairs of the Federation. This Council was composed of a president, several vice-presidents, a secretary, and a treasurer. Its functions were to publicize the aims of the Federation, watch legislation affecting labor, organize new unions, grant charters, pass upon boycotts started by affiliates, settle inter-union jurisdictional conflicts, and appeal for financial aid to help unions during industrial disputes.

The development of techniques for securing its limited reform program is an interesting part in the story of the A.F. of L. In the beginning only direct economic tactics were used, politics being shunned as a throwback to the unsuccessful efforts of the National Labor Union. Propaganda was, of course, a constant device. In 1890, during the campaign for a national eight-hour day, thousands of pamphlets were issued and salaried workers were employed for the first time. Mass meetings were held in the large cities. Strikes were the chief weapon of the national trade unions in this period, but the Federation rarely supported such tactics. Great confidence was held in the " union label " and the " boycott " as means of compelling employers to abide by union demands. Legal difficulties soon paralyzed the boycott as an effective technique. Federal courts were called upon by employers to issue injunctions against unions participating in boycotts. The basis for these injunctions and later damage suits was the Sherman Anti-trust Act of 1890, which forbade " illegal combinations in restraint of trade." In the famous Danbury Hatters' case,[12] the Supreme Court declared in 1908 that boycotts may constitute illegal restraint.

But long before the courts neutralized the strength of the boycott, many elements within the Federation tried to induce the membership to support direct political action. In 1892 the air was charged with politics and the temptation was great. A move in that direction was taken by the A.F. of L. convention when it openly endorsed two planks in the program of the People's party. These were the initiative and referendum, and government ownership of communications. Instructions were also given to the Executive Council to appoint organizers and lecturers for the purpose of strengthening the unions in politics.

Strike failures in 1892 and the Panic of 1893 lessened the effectiveness of labor's economic weapons. More and more members within the Federation began to lean toward direct political action and conversion of the A.F. of L. into a politico-

---

[12] Loewe vs. Lawlor, 208 U. S. 274.

economic body; socialist union members, in line with their philosophy, provided the spearhead for this drive toward politics. In the Federation convention in 1893 they offered a comprehensive political program which was adopted by the convention and submitted to the affiliated unions. This program described the entrance of English labor unions into politics and urged that American labor follow that example. It called for many of the things the Federation had consistently stood for, such as a legal eight-hour day, compulsory education, initiative and referendum, employers' liability laws, and government inspection of mines and workshops. The socialist mark was obvious in proposals for municipal ownership of public utilities, nationalization of telegraphs, telephones, mines, and railroads, and finally, collective ownership of the means of production and distribution.

Such proposals were a long way from the earlier policies of the A.F. of L. and naturally precipitated a bitter struggle between the original leadership and the socialist elements. The convention of 1894 debated the political platform all over again. Enthusiasm for political adventures was somewhat cooled by the general failure of many local unions to achieve election successes. The plank in the political platform favoring broad collective ownership was rejected. Other planks remained intact, but the convention defeated a motion to endorse the platform again as a whole. So angered were the socialists at this rebuff by the Federation leadership that they combined as a bloc with certain disgruntled factions to remove Samuel Gompers from the presidency of the A.F. of L. John McBride of the Miners' Union was elected and gave Gompers the only serious set-back he received in the Federation during his long career. In 1895 the old leadership regained control and restored Gompers.

The socialist union members persisted in their efforts to turn the Federation toward politics. In the heated campaign of 1896 many local labor leaders openly declared for Bryan, but Gompers remained officially non-partisan. Bryan's defeat disheartened many of the political reformers, and returning prosperity after 1898 put an end to the clamor for political action. The A.F. of L., by holding its ground against mixing in politics, avoided the pitfalls of earlier labor groups.

31

Although the Federation opposed direct political action, it did participate in lobbying activities. A special legislative committee urged upon each session of Congress the passage of favorable labor legislation. Bills calling for shorter working hours and restricted immigration were repeatedly supported. Affiliated state federations of labor carried on the same activity locally. In the 1900's this technique was extended to the practice of " questioning " political candidates and supporting those answering favorably. The slogan, " Reward our friends and punish our enemies," described this type of political pressure that the union put on candidates. But political activity of the A.F. of L. was definitely limited. The organization stressed its dependence upon trade union tactics. Political action and paternalistic legislation by government were out of favor. The Federation acted in politics chiefly against any legal threat to its freedom of economic action, like the right to strike.

As the dominant labor organization from 1886 to 1917, the A.F. of L. made solid achievements. It aided a number of crafts in winning the eight-hour day. One of its affiliates, the Stovemolders, in 1891 succeeded in writing a trade agreement with employers and gained recognition as sole bargaining representative of the trade, setting a precedent in industrial relations. Many national unions, encouraged by the A.F. of L., developed helpful benefit schemes. Federation efforts led to the establishment of a United States Department of Labor in 1913. Organized labor as a whole gained in strength, confidence, and general respect.

ILLUSTRATIVE DOCUMENTS

§1. ' The Address of the National Labor Congress to the Workingmen of the United States,' leaflet, Hazlitt and Quinton, Printers, Chicago, 1867. The committee on address was appointed at the Baltimore convention of the National Labor Union. Its chairman was Andrew C. Cameron.

FELLOW CITIZENS: On the twentieth of August, 1866, the first National Labor Congress ever convened in the United States, was ushered into existence in the city of Baltimore, Md., when sixty delegates representing a majority of the States of the Union, met for the purpose of effecting a permanent, systematic organization of the wealth-producing classes, and devising the best means by which their interests could be subserved and protected. Heretofore the highest form that labor associations had taken was the national union of some of the respective trades. Between these organizations, however, there was no sympathy or systematic correction; no co-operative effort; no working for the attainment of a common end, the want of which has been experienced for years by every craft and calling. As a matter of course the work there accomplished was of a preliminary character. While all present realized the importance and necessity of the undertaking, the magnitude and multiplicity of the interests involved were of such a nature, and the time for deliberation so limited, that little more could be effected than the adoption of a declaration of principles and the framing of a ground-work for future action. The number of subjects handled by the congress, and the enlightened judgment and moderation displayed in their discussion, even under these circumstances, was such as to elicit the commendation of all friends of the cause, which is certainly an augury of hope for the future.

At that convention the undersigned were appointed a committee to prepare, on behalf of the congress, an address to the workingmen of America, setting forth the objects sought to be attained, soliciting their co-operation in the premises, and their attendance at its next session, to be holden at Chicago, Illinois, on the nineteenth of August, 1867.

In the fulfillment of that task the first question which presents itself is the all-absorbing subject of Eight Hours.

The question of all others, which at present engrosses the attention of the American workman, and, in fact, the American people—is the proposed reduction of the hours of daily labor, and the substitution of the eight for the ten hour system, now recognized as the standard of a legal day's work. As might have been expected, the employing capitalists, aided by a venal press, have set up a howl of rage, and protested against the adoption of such a monstrous innovation, though it is worthy of note that the chief opposition comes from those who confessedly have given the subject the least consideration.

The committee do not intend, in this address, to enter into any lengthened defense of the measure, but prefer to present its claims, justice and necessity, upon a few single truths, which must commend themselves to the judgment of the public at large. In all the discussions of the partisan press—from the metropolitan journal to the village croaker—every moral consideration has been waived, every plea put forth by its advocates omitted, and every argument adduced has been based on a purely selfish, dollars and cents standpoint.

On the contrary, the producing classes assert that other and higher considerations than those heretofore advanced by its opponents should enter into the discussion of its merits or practicability. They insist it is a self-evident proposition that the success of our republican institutions must depend on the virtue, the intelligence and the independence of the working classes; and that any system, social or political, which tends to keep the masses in ignorance, whether by unjust or oppressive laws, or by over-manual labor, is injurious alike to the interests of the state and the individual. . . .

The plea urged that the laboring classes would not use the leisure time obtained to their own, and consequently, to the benefit of the community, is one which is disproved by the experience of the past. Every similar reformation, although ushered in with equally ominous prediction, has not only tended to the development of the resources and material prosperity of the country inaugurating it, but has been the means of improving the physical and intellectual condition of the laboring classes. . . .

The charge that workingmen, as a class, are ignorant and illiterate, instead of being an argument against, is one of the strongest reasons which could be urged in favor of its adoption. They are ignorant because they are over-worked; because they have been denied the privileges which others, more favored, have reaped. . . .

This question naturally leads us to the consideration of a subject which is intimately associated with its adoption, viz.: Co-operation.

The question of co-operative stores and co-operative associations for trading and manufacturing purposes has the widest bearing and effect upon the condition of the workingmen. . . .

The committee cannot urge too strongly upon the workingmen of this country the advantage—almost necessity even—of establishing co-operative stores.

TRADES' UNIONS. There are, probably, no organizations upon the nature of which so much real ignorance exists, even among workingmen, or against which such a persistent and systematic opposition has been urged, as trades' unions. Their aims and objects have been grossly misrepresented, and public prejudice has been aroused by those who only know enough to pander to popular ignorance. In spite of this opposition, however, they are daily increasing in numbers and influence, and the committee trust that the day is not far distant when every competent and honorable workman will be embraced within their folds. . . .

STRIKES. With regard to the question of strikes, the committee feel they cannot too strongly deprecate all appeals to such extreme measures, except as a *dernier* resort, believing that by the appointment, where practicable, of a conference committee, whose duty it would be to lay the nature of the grievance before the employer, and ask redress for the same, many, if not all, of the difficulties complained of could be satisfactorily removed. "An ounce of prevention is worth a pound of cure," and as a large majority of the strikes end in failure and disaster, our unions have everything to gain and nothing to lose by the adoption of such a course. . . .

POLITICAL ACTION. If there is one fact more than another which has impressed itself upon the attention of workingmen during the past year, it is the absolute necessity of cutting aloof from the ties and trammels of party, manipulated in the interests of capital, and using the advantages conferred by American citizenship—the ballot—to the furtherance of their own interests and welfare. . . .

The signs of the times are propitious. The working classes are fast rousing from the lethargy in which they have been sunk. They are realizing that, as the evils which weigh with crushing effect upon society are legislative in character, that the remedy must therefore be legislative. . . .

Fellow-citizens, your duty, under these circumstances, is plain and unmistakable. It is to discard the clap-trap issues of the past; select your representatives in the state and national councils from the ranks of labor; from men who acknowledge allegiance to no ism or party; from those whose welfare is your welfare, and who, when the conflict comes, as come it must, will be found nobly battling for your rights, and the recognition of human progress. . . .

We now extend a cordial invitation to all to participate in our deliberations. Come from the north and the south, from the east and west; come from the anvil and the loom; from the work-bench and the forge—every craft and every trade; come as the representatives of states' assemblies or trades' unions—singly or in delegations, all will be equally welcome. . . . Finally, brethren, come one and

35

all and help marshal those mighty forces of labor, which, when disciplined, will march to certain victory.

A. C. Cameron, Illinois, T. A. Armstrong, Pennsylvania, Wm. B. Iles, Georgia, Gilman Rand, Massachusetts, J. R. Bolan, New York, Committee.[13]

§2. 'Objectives of the Knights of Labor,' as declared in the preamble of the constitution of 1878.

The recent alarming development and aggression of aggregated wealth, which, unless checked, will invariably lead to the pauperization and hopeless degradation of the toiling masses, render it imperative, if we desire to enjoy the blessings of life, that a check should be placed upon its power and upon unjust accumulation, and a system adopted which will secure to the laborer the fruits of his toil; and as this much-desired object can only be accomplished by the thorough unification of labor, and the united efforts of those who obey the divine injunction that " In the sweat of thy brow shalt thou eat bread," we have formed the . . . with a view of securing the organization and direction, by co-operative effort, of the power of the industrial classes; and we submit to the world the object sought to be accomplished by our organization, calling upon all who believe in securing " the greatest good to the greatest number " to aid and assist us:—

I. To bring within the folds of organization every department of productive industry, making knowledge a standpoint for action, and industrial and moral worth, not wealth, the true standard of individual and national greatness.

II. To secure to the toilers a proper share of the wealth that they create; more of the leisure that rightfully belongs to them; more societary advantages; more of the benefits, privileges, and emoluments of the world; in a word, all those rights and privileges necessary to make them capable of enjoying, appreciating, defending, and perpetuating the blessings of good government.

III. To arrive at the true condition of the producing masses in their educational, moral, and financial condition, by demanding from the various governments the establishment of bureaus of Labor Statistics.

[13] J. R. Commons, Documentary History of American Industrial Society, Cleveland, 1910, IX 141–168.

IV. The establishment of co-operative institutions, productive and distributive.

V. The reserving of the public lands—the heritage of the people —for the actual settler;—not another acre for railroads or speculators.

VI. The abrogation of all laws that do not bear equally upon capital and labor, the removal of unjust technicalities, delays, and discriminations in the administration of justice, and the adopting of measures providing for the health and safety of those engaged in mining, manufacturing, or building pursuits.

VII. The enactment of laws to compel chartered corporations to pay their employes weekly, in full, for labor performed during the preceding week, in the lawful money of the country.

VIII. The enactment of laws giving mechanics and laborers a first lien on their work for their full wages.

IX. The abolishment of the contract system on national, State, and municipal work.

X. The substitution of arbitration for strikes, whenever and wherever employers and employes are willing to meet on equitable grounds.

XI. The prohibition of the employment of children in workshops, mines, and factories before attaining their fourteenth year.

XII. To abolish the system of letting out by contract the labor of convicts in our prisons and reformatory institutions.

XIII. To secure for both sexes equal pay for equal work.

XIV. The reduction of the hours of labor to eight per day, so that the laborers may have more time for social enjoyment and intellectual improvement, and be enabled to reap the advantages conferred by the labor-saving machinery which their brains have created.

XV. To prevail upon governments to establish a purely national circulating medium, based upon the faith and resources of the nation, and issued directly to the people, without the intervention of any system of banking corporations, which money shall be a legal tender in payment of all debts, public or private.[14]

---

[14] Terence V. Powderly, *Thirty Years of Labor*, Columbus, Ohio, 1889, 243–245.

CHAPTER TWO

Early Radical Efforts

W HILE the bulk of American workers sought to organize for moderate reforms, some were intent upon radical change. Radical change, as used here, means complete overthrow of the existing order, peacefully or by force. The small groups of laborers supporting such ideas were usually joined by non-working "intellectual" sympathizers. For the most part their efforts, however noisy, have had little in common with the main labor movement in America. But the public has not always believed this. Since their plans usually call for winning over the mass of workers, the radicals often work inside or in co-operation with moderate organizations. Such association is confusing to most people. In times of economic stress an apprehensive public may see Red in every labor group.

Sources of American Radicalism

Radical programs have appeared in the current of American reform movements like bubbles on a stream. Like other reform efforts they spring from conditions of distress. But since they appeal mainly to extremists, they have a restricted and peculiar following. So long as moderate paths of action remain open, people do not normally become radicals. That is why the "fringe" movements lack balance and general support. Without stability they may easily be perverted or wrecked by head-strong leaders.

Radical movements in the United States have been a strange complex of forces. Foreign theories and personalities have mingled with native reform elements. In the period just follow-

38

ing the War Between the States, foreign-born doctrines and workers dominated radical efforts, but large numbers of native-born workers joined in from time to time and, to some extent, modified the programs. The radical impetus has almost always come from abroad, although American conditions have generally fostered development. The fact of foreign influence and control has prejudiced the American public against these movements; the appeal of reform has quite naturally been darkened by the shadow of outside nationalisms.

The " First International " in the United States

The main labor movement in the United States after the War Between the States, as outlined in the preceding chapter, was chiefly a reflex from broad economic changes. Far-reaching industrial changes compelled the workers to seek protective reforms. Radical efforts, however, did not rise from native conditions, although the confusion of American workers furnished favorable soil for all kinds of reform theories. The radical movements of this period were imported and planted. They had no natural origin here, but were products of foreign economic and political systems.

The first radical movement to appear in America after the War Between the States was the International Workingmen's Association. This group, founded by Karl Marx and other radical European labor leaders, has been commonly called the " First International." It was begun on September 28, 1864, in London, where the socialist and trade union movements appeared stronger than on the Continent. French, German, Italian, and Polish workers and intellectuals were the chief organizers. They envisioned a world-wide effort against capitalism by affiliated trade unions and " political sections " in every country. The first section to be established here was the New York Communist Club, in October of 1867, and in the next few years German sections were set up in San Francisco, Chicago, and New York. Bohemian and French sections were also started. In 1870 a central committee for the American affiliates of the " International " was organized, with a corresponding secretary.

Over thirty sections were recognized by the committee in 1871.[1]

The " International " was obviously imported into this country and supported by foreign-born residents. The objectives of the American sections, like the affiliates elsewhere, were strictly Marxian. Overthrow of the capitalist system and " emancipation " of the working class was to be achieved by the workers themselves. " Class rule " was to be abolished and succeeded by equal rights and duties for all. The economic and political theories of Marx, developed in Europe, were followed parrot-like in the meetings of American sections.

As to techniques for achieving this revolutionary program, Marx and the " International " stressed the need for political power. That is why socialist movements have traditionally entered politics. Marx also called upon the whole working class for unity on an international front, in order to meet the essential problems of labor.

The " International " never took root here. Its program was incomprehensible to the masses of workers and ignored the facts of American life. The collapse of the organization, like its beginning, was due to European forces. Internal disputes among the founders, who represented varying schools of radicalism, and lack of a real labor movement on the Continent hastened the dissolution. The repression following the outbreak and defeat of the Paris Commune in 1871 at last made the " International " impossible in Europe. In 1876 it was officially declared dead in America, as well as abroad.

The Socialist Labor Party

The ideas of Marx were far from dead, however. Socialist groups in the United States, consisting largely of foreign-born members who brought their ideas here from Europe, persisted in various parts of the nation. A few days after the International Workingmen's Association was declared dissolved, an independent American socialist organization was established in

---

[1] Nathan Fine, *Labor and Farmer Parties in the United States, 1828–1928*, 93–97. New York: Rand School of Social Sciences, 1928. This work is the principal factual source of information on the early socialist movements.

Philadelphia. Meeting there on July 19, 1876, a unity convention representing several socialist groups accomplished this step. The name first given to the new national order was the Workingmen's party of the United States, but in the following year this was changed to the Socialist Labor party. The main element in the merger of socialist forces was the Social Democratic Workingmen's party that had been formed in New York City in 1874. Its membership was almost entirely German. Also merged was the Labor party of Illinois, representing a small group of Chicago socialists, and the Socio-Politico Labor Union of Cincinnati. In spite of all these imposing names, the total number in these combining groups was only about 3,000. Furthermore, it was concentrated among German-born residents of New York City.

The Socialist Labor party doubled its claimed membership in the first year of existence. It was soon to be split, however, by a bitter factional dispute. The majority favored political action as a means of achieving the ultimate end of socialism. A strong minority, composed of strict trade unionists, supported direct economic tactics and opposed politics. This latter group was influenced more by anarchist and syndicalist doctrines than by socialism. They believed in direct action to secure demands, with the use of force if necessary. Many of them, while still members of the Socialist Labor party, formed armed groups that drilled and practiced in a military fashion. These groups were called *Lehr* and *Wehr Vereine,* or Educational and Defensive Societies. The aim of this early variety of Storm Troopers was to compel respect for socialists and to protect party activities against police or militia. Leaders of these bodies within the party at last decided to break off from the more pacific, politically minded majority of the organization. On October 21, 1881, the anarchist-syndicalist element met in Chicago to form a separate body. The name of Revolutionary Socialist party was taken, and declarations were adopted against political action and in favor of armed defensive bodies.

In the following year the name of this secessionist group was changed to the International Working People's Association. It became a part of a world anarchist organization started in

London in 1881 by Johann Most, a German anarchist who had been expelled from the Socialist party in his native land and imprisoned in England. This organization was commonly known as the " Black International." When the International Working People's Association met in convention in 1883, Most was in attendance. He had arrived in this country in the previous year and had enjoyed a triumphal tour.

The influence of men like Johann Most was clear in the program adopted. A straightforward anarchist platform was outlined. It stated that trade unions were only a means of organizing the workers for revolutionary struggles. The " ruling class " was alleged to understand but one language—force. Destruction of " class rule " was urged by all means, through relentless, revolutionary, and international action. The ultimate goal, after smashing the existing order, was a " free society " based on co-operatives and a free exchange of goods among producers without use of " middle-men."

On May 4, 1886, leading members were present at an anarchist gathering in Haymarket Square, Chicago. A bomb was thrown into the ranks of policemen dispatched to the scene, and several of the patrolmen were killed. A famous trial followed, with the chief anarchists charged with murder. The true facts of the case were never established to the satisfaction of all, but the leaders were imprisoned or executed and the nation aroused and angered. The " Black International " in the United States was ended. It was blown up in the Haymarket bombing.

Meanwhile, the Socialist Labor party, deserted by the anarchist element in 1881, carried on. Its efforts in the 1880's seemed feeble, while the rival anarchist association held the spotlight in radical circles. The collapse of the " Black International " left the Socialist Labor party once again the main organization in the field. In 1890 Daniel De Leon became a member. He rose rapidly to a position of influence and soon gained control of party policy. De Leon gave fresh vigor to the organization and molded it to his personality.

This new leader of the party was a man of unusual background. He was born on the island of Curaçao, off Venezuela, in 1852. After early education in Germany, De Leon came to the United States and studied law. His first political experience was during the campaign for Henry George in New York City. Leaning more and more to the left, De Leon later joined the Socialist Labor party and became editor of its English-speaking organ, *The People*. After working his way to control of the party, he held a position of unquestioned authority until his death in 1914. His domineering personality, admitting of no compromise, drove many groups out of the organization.

The objectives of the Socialist Labor party after 1890 reflect chiefly the aims of De Leon. He despised the exclusive, craft-conscious attitude of the growing American Federation of Labor. He called for a " new trade unionism " which would discard petty, immediate demands for lofty, idealistic aims. The party platform criticized and opposed the whole " profit system " and looked to a complete overturn and the setting up of a co-operative workers' commonwealth. Under the industrial system contemplated by De Leon, all productive facilities would be owned collectively. The workers would elect their own foremen, superintendents, and higher industrial managers. The capstone of the system, which combined socialism with features of syndicalism, was to be the Industrial Union Congress. This top governing body would be chosen by the workers and would represent the working class alone. Before 1900 the party listed some " immediate aims," but after that year De Leon struck them from the platform, announcing that " sugar coating " of essential purposes was over and that the movement had emerged from " embryonic socialism."

Organization of the party was unique in the early years of its growth. Chief administrative power was at first vested in an Executive Committee that was elected by members residing in the Chicago area. To check on the Executive Committee and to hear appeals from them, a Board of Control was established. This Board was chosen by members residing in the New York area. The reason for this unusual arrangement was the early socialist practice of dividing elective power among various regions.

Changes were made in the organization after De Leon rose

to power. After 1900 the Executive Committee was selected by a referendum vote of the whole membership. The national secretary and the editor of the party paper were chosen in annual convention.

Socialists, like the labor organizations treated in the previous chapter, experimented with techniques. How was the broad, revolutionary program to be achieved? In the beginning, at the first convention in 1876, the Socialist Labor party decided to shun politics until greater strength had been reached. Education of trade unionists to socialism was considered the chief means at that time. In the late 1870's political action was attempted, with some local success. The issue of politics or direct action eventually caused a split in the organization which resulted in secession of the anarchist-syndicalist element and the formation of a separate International Working People's Association. The fate of that secession movement has already been considered.

The remaining membership in the Socialist Labor party continued to favor political methods. Militant, independent politics was begun in 1889, and three years later the organization nominated Simon Wing, the first presidential candidate to appear on a socialist ticket; he polled about 22,000 votes. The largest popular following showed in the Congressional elections of 1898, when candidates of the Socialist Labor party received a total of over 80,000 votes. In the following year an important factional split cut the membership of the party, and thereafter De Leon's organization proved feeble at the polls.

A technique more potent than politics was also tried by De Leon. It was the method of " boring from within," or capturing control of other organizations. After 1890 De Leon tried to gain control of the floundering Knights of Labor. The decentralized organization of the American Federation of Labor offered little chance for manipulation, but the Knights appeared vulnerable. His efforts within the Knights were detected, however, and he was ousted. De Leon became convinced that he would have to abandon socialism if he wanted to work inside the existing unions, because they refused to be converted by these methods. He decided to stay outside of them, form separate socialist unions, and try to attract the ordinary worker into them.

44

This was " dual unionism." Several such unions were started in 1895; a skeleton federation called the Socialist Trade and Labor Alliance was set up. The new unions were to work for the overthrow of private capitalism and, following the revolution, they would become primary organs of industrial management. This idea failed to draw any considerable following from the old trade unions. By 1898 the Alliance was in decline.

At its peak of strength in the 1890's the Socialist Labor party had no more than 6,000 members. Although these socialists were relatively few in numbers, they had difficulty in getting along even among themselves; constant quarrels within the Socialist Labor party occupied the chief attention of the members. The failure of the organization after 1900 was caused largely by the inability of De Leon and the other leaders to keep the various factions together. There were bitter quarrels over the centralization of power under De Leon, the party-owned press, doctrinal interpretation, and political tactics. Since he tolerated no opposition, De Leon solved these problems by expelling all groups refusing to support his point of view. This process simplified the internal problems of the party but whittled down the membership to an insignificant force.

Leadership in the socialist movement was soon to pass to other hands. De Leon died in 1914, and only a shadow of his party survived. The old Socialist Labor party could claim few achievements. As an organization it secured no foothold in the trade unions and no popular following at the polls; its program was too far beyond American realities, and its leadership failed to gain the confidence of party members or outside sympathizers.

Formation and Growth of the Modern Socialist Party

During the 1890's, all socialist thought in America was not confined to the Socialist Labor party. A number of independent socialist organizations had been started, and these were joined by members who had been forced out of De Leon's party. One of the most important of these groups was the Social Democratic party, founded in Chicago on June 8, 1898. Its platform declared that the trade union movement and independent political action were the chief means for " emancipating " the

45

working class. Public ownership of existing monopolies, public utilities, and mines was called for, along with a number of other "immediate demands." At the same time a group within the old Socialist Labor party were feeling the need for unity among all socialist thinkers—something impossible under De Leon. They decided to join forces with the Social Democratic party and met with leaders of that organization. At Indianapolis, on July 29, 1901, a consolidated socialist movement was launched by these pro-unity elements; it was called the Socialist party of the United States.

Three men were chiefly responsible for the formation of the modern Socialist party, which has continued to be the principal socialist effort in the United States. The leader whose name has been linked most often with the Socialist party was Eugene Victor Debs. During his lifetime he was the party candidate in every presidential campaign but one. He was the only outstanding socialist leader of the period to be a native American, born in Terre Haute, Indiana, in 1855. Debs was a grocer's son. He became a railroad worker, and after joining the Brotherhood of Locomotive Firemen in 1875, rose to a position of influence as secretary-treasurer of the national organization in 1880. His flair for writing made him an able editor of the union's journal. In 1885 Debs made a successful venture into politics and with labor support was elected to the Indiana Legislature on the Democratic ticket. He was strictly and whole-heartedly a labor man, however, and soon abandoned politics for union activity. In 1892 he attempted to unite all rail workers into a single American Railway Union.

The great Pullman strike led by Debs in Chicago in 1894 raised the young leader to national prominence. A nervous nation watched Debs and his union tie up railroad traffic until President Cleveland broke the strike by using federal troops to move United States mail. The American Railway Union collapsed, and Debs was jailed for violation of a court injunction issued during the conflict. It was in jail that this fearless leader was converted to socialism. Largely because of his experience with the Pullman strike, Debs became convinced that labor could win no substantial gains under capitalism. After his release from prison he openly declared himself a socialist and in 1898 helped found the Social Democratic party, which has already been mentioned. Debs later joined with other socialists seeking unity to establish the Socialist party in 1901. In spite of all his extreme words and deeds, Debs must be considered as an able and trust-worthy leader. While advocating a broader unionism and ultimate peaceful revolution, he abhorred sabotage, violence, and preparation for armed civil war.

The man usually credited with converting Debs to socialism and one of Debs' chief collaborators in founding the Socialist party was Victor L. Berger. He was born in Austria-Hungary in 1860 and was educated in Budapest and Vienna. He worked at various jobs after coming to America, but was not strictly a trade union man like Debs. Berger spent some time teaching and for several years edited a small radical journal in Milwaukee. He joined the old Socialist Labor party, but was one of the many to depart from it in later years. Becoming a close friend of Debs in the 1890's, he aided in launching a new and unified socialist organization. In 1910 Berger had the distinction of being the first Socialist elected to Congress.

Morris Hillquit led the pro-unity faction of the Socialist Labor party to join with Debs and Berger in 1901. Hillquit was a young man at the time but already enjoyed a national reputation. He was born in Riga, Russia, in 1870, and came to the United States in 1885. He worked briefly at various trades before entering law school. After completing his training Hill-quit made his living from law practice. He became a leading socialist thinker and joined the Socialist Labor party. Breaking at last with De Leon, Hillquit joined with leaders of the Social Democratic organization to form the new Socialist party. He was named its international secretary.

The Socialist party profited from the character of its leader-ship, in comparison with the leadership in other radical groups. It was also favored by a membership more largely composed of native-born persons; in the first convention of the party, although a number of the key leaders were of foreign birth, a large number of native Americans were present. German-Americans or Jewish-Americans did not dominate this organization, as was the case in most other socialist groups at that time. A survey in 1908 showed that seventy per cent of the members were native-born.

The party members were mainly urban, from New York and Chicago. Both skilled and unskilled workers belonged, as well as a considerable number of non-working "intellectuals." A few women took part, and there were many young people in the organization.

From 1901 to 1912 the growth of the Socialist party was rapid. The number of regular members increased from 10,000 to nearly 120,000. The number of votes received in national elections likewise increased about ten-fold, from 100,000 to 900,000. Many local election victories were won, and in 1912 the Socialist party claimed that over 1,000 of its members were in public office.

What was the program that gained this wide acceptance among native Americans? The growing success of the Socialist party suggested that its objectives must be more closely associated with the facts and needs of America than were the objectives of other radical movements. Socialists based their program on criticism of the capitalist system. Capitalism was indicted for waste. Socialists pointed out the wastes resulting from private business competition and advertising, from the exploitation of national resources, from the lack of protection for workers, and from unemployment. Capitalism was condemned for inequality in wealth and income, with its broad economic, social, political, intellectual, and moral consequences.[2]

Although all groups of the Socialist party united in attacking capitalism, there was a sharp cleavage in formulating positive objectives for the organization. The view of the majority remained fairly constant and became the party platform. But the aims of the powerful minority, which later merged with the Communist International, cannot be ignored.

The official platform of the majority was called "reformist" or "evolutionary," while the dissenting program was named

[2] Harry W. Laidler, *Socialism in Thought and Action,* ix–x. New York: The Macmillan Company, 1920. This writer is the main authority used for socialist aims.

"impossibilist" or "revolutionary." The latter was strictly
Marxian, while the former attempted to translate socialism into
a flexible program meeting special American conditions. The
Socialist party platform, written by the majority, therefore supported "immediate demands" to meet everyday needs of
American workers. Reduction of the hours of labor, inaugura-
tion of a system of public works to relieve unemployment, release
of inventions for free use by the public, social insurance, and
equality of the sexes were demanded. Greater democratization
in industry and more even distribution of income were also called
for.

While supporting immediate government ownership of existing
monopolies, public utilities, and means of transportation and
communication, the party hoped ultimately for collective ownership of all the basic productive industries. The majority group
insisted upon maintaining the independent, small, land-owning
farmer and opposing the "impossibilist" demand for collectivization of agriculture. Private ownership of consumers' goods
was upheld.

Socialist party organization recognized the states as key units.
The members in each state formed autonomous organizations.
This plan reflected the political character of the party, since the
states are the principal election units of the country. Co-
ordination for national activities was effected by an annual
National Convention of delegates from the states. The convention was organized in a most democratic fashion, permitting the
delegates themselves to elect a chairman and all regular committees. Between conventions administrative authority was
vested in a National Committee, composed of one member from
each state. All acts of this body were subject to a referendum
vote by the entire national membership. The secretary of the
national organization was the main active official. He was
aided in his work by a local "Supervisory Quorum" which was
chosen by the National Committee from Socialists living near
headquarters. Changes in organization have been made since
the original plans were adopted, but democratic control and
decentralization of power have been carefully respected.

As to methods for securing party objectives, the Socialists

relied mainly upon "education." Quantities of literature were published, including the works of Karl Marx, Friedrich Engels, Karl Kautsky, and other leading socialist writers. Thousands of dime pamphlets were issued. In 1906 the party established the Rand School of Social Science in New York City for the purpose of education in socialism and labor. It has been responsible for the publication of numerous books in this field. The party also aimed to reach the public through newspapers. In addition to the party-owned *American Socialist,* which was discontinued in 1917, many other journals carried the Socialist stamp. At the peak of Socialist party influence in 1912, nearly 300 papers were in active publication.

Socialist leaders recognized that their party appealed mainly to the working class. They knew also that effective means of action by the working class lay in the trade unions. One of their chief efforts, therefore, was to influence labor unions toward socialism. Daniel De Leon had unsuccessfully tried to do this in the 1890's, and his expulsion from the Knights of Labor resulted mainly from his impatient desire to "capture" the organization. The wiser leadership of the Socialist party attempted gradually to "educate" the trade unionists. By 1912 this technique seemed well on the way to success; in that year the Socialist leader, Max S. Hayes, received one-third of the total vote cast for president of the American Federation of Labor.

An innovation among radical groups was the Socialist party's appeal to young people. In 1905 the party formed an auxiliary called the Intercollegiate Socialist Society; this name was later changed to the League for Industrial Democracy. The purpose of this organization was to promote interest in socialism among men and women of college age. Harry W. Laidler and Norman Thomas, outstanding Socialist leaders of recent times, have had intimate connection with the work of the League.

The final means of achieving the Socialist program was, of course, through political power. Disagreement concerning the method of attaining this power created an interesting divergence between the "evolutionary" and "revolutionary" wings within the party. The "evolutionaries" were willing to seek voting support from sympathetic, non-Marxian groups, and tolerated a degree of flexibility in the dogma of their candidates. The " revolutionaries " insisted that party office-holders work strictly according to Marxian teachings. It was the old issue of moderation against " no compromise." The liberal view was supported by the majority, and in 1917 the disaffected " revolutionaries " seceded to join the Communist International.

Revolutionary Unionism and the Industrial Workers of the World

Almost from the beginning of the socialist movement, the followers of Marx were divided. The split first appeared in America in the ranks of the old Socialist Labor party. One group believed in politics and legal methods as the means of action. The other group, influenced by anarchism and syndicalism, favored direct economic action through strikes or violent tactics. The result of that first important cleavage has been discussed. The anarchist element quit the Socialist Labor party, formed an independent International Working People's Association, and became a part of a world movement called the " Black International." This violent effort was smothered in the United States by the aftermath of the Haymarket bombing, but the ideas of violence and direct action against the capitalist system were not extinguished.

In the early 1900's the ideas of anarchism and syndicalism once again came into the open. They were embodied this time not in a political party or association, but in a militant labor union. For more than a generation, Americans were to watch the rise and fall of this aggressive and rebellious organization— the I.W.W.

Although the ideology of the Industrial Workers of the World was imported, the actual nature of the union was a product of American conditions. Its founding was an outgrowth of a bitter strike by the Western Federation of Miners in 1903 and 1904. The Miners had already attracted national attention by earlier strikes at Cripple Creek, Colorado, in 1894, and at Coeur d'Alene, Idaho, in 1899. These conflicts were marked by militancy, violence, and bloodshed. The Miners strongly supported industrial unionism, the idea of organizing all the workers in each industry into one union, rather than into separate unions according to craft. They naturally disliked the American Federation of Labor, which was dominated by craft unions. After seceding from the A.F. of L. in 1897, the Miners led the launching of a rival labor movement, called the American Labor Union.

Following the end of their strike in 1904, the Miners made another bid for greater labor solidarity. On June 27, 1905, they were joined by sympathetic labor groups in establishing the Industrial Workers of the World. A large convention of delegates, representing about 90,000 workers and forty trades, participated in the founding. Eugene Debs, who was seeking a broader unionism to supplement the work of his Socialist party, was one of the leaders present. The founders looked to the development of " one big union," representing all workers and seeking broad reforms, which would supplant the more limited, opportunistic American Federation of Labor.

Many elements mingled in the I.W.W. In addition to skilled workers rebelling against trade union discipline, there were socialists, both " evolutionary " and " revolutionary," anarchists, syndicalists, and labor fakers. The principal groups appealed to, however, were the masses of immigrant and migratory workers. These unskilled thousands were not qualified for any craft affiliated with the A. F. of L. and were ignored by " respectable " labor leaders. The I.W.W. made substantial progress in winning them over, especially in the marine, metal, agricultural, iron, lumber, and railway fields. The character of the I.W.W. was naturally a reflection of this varied, unstable membership. Casual labor, used to bad conditions and low wages, comprised the bulk of the organization. Newly arrived, maladjusted foreigners were a large element. It is small wonder that this movement, strengthened by the roughness and violence of bitter labor disputes, struck fiercely against the capitalist system. One writer has suggested that the I.W.W. was largely a " symptom of a vicious economic situation." [3]

William D. Haywood, long feared by some Americans as Public Enemy Number One, was the outstanding leader of the

---

[3] Frederick E. Haynes, *Social Politics in the United States,* 220. Boston: Houghton Mifflin Company, 1924.

movement. He was born in Salt Lake City in 1869, the son
of a miner. For some sixteen years he worked as a miner himself,
and in 1901 he became Secretary-Treasurer of the Western
Federation of Miners. After that he devoted all his time to
organization work, aiding in the foundation of the Industrial
Workers of the World. Haywood was also a leading Socialist
of the left wing until he was forced out by the party in 1913.
He was daring and fought hard to organize the unskilled. The
public first became concerned about Haywood when he was on
trial in 1907 for the murder of ex-Governor Steuneberg of Idaho,
who had been killed during a strike. Haywood was acquitted.

The story of the I.W.W. is marked by internal disputes and
secessions. Such friction was natural, because of the variety of
elements in the organization. In 1908 the most important split
occurred when a minority wing favoring political action broke
off and declared itself the true I.W.W. This group was led by
Daniel De Leon, whose own Socialist Labor party had become
but a shadow. The majority, however, favoring direct economic
tactics, continued as the main force in the movement.

What was the program of the Industrial Workers? Most
Americans have been so shocked by their methods that they have
a biased picture of the I.W.W. as representing only hoodlums
and gangsters. The I.W.W. was formed as a reaction from harsh
economic conditions in the United States, and the program
adopted was an American mixture of anarchism and syndicalism.
Anarchism is a revolt against all authority over the individual;
syndicalism is a plan for a workers' co-operative commonwealth
without capitalists and politicians. The Industrial Workers
assumed that collaboration between workers and employers was
impossible and that class conflict was inevitable. They believed,
therefore, that the problem could be solved only by the workers'
organizing to abolish the wage system and to establish the
co-operative commonwealth. " Immediate demands " were
shunned as palliatives. There was only one, revolutionary cry—
" Abolition of the wage system! "

The I.W.W. was usually thought to be " one big union."
That was, indeed, the spirit of the movement, but technically it
was a kind of congress of industrial organizations. Its chief units

were called "departments," which were groupings of allied industries. The industrial unions within the "departments" had complete autonomy. The I.W.W. was not set up to foster "dual unionism," although it did aim to convert craft unions to the larger idea of industrial unionism. It was established primarily as a central body for the affiliation of existing labor organizations. In this sense it competed directly with the American Federation of Labor, which was the dominant central body of the labor world.

In spite of the broad power given to the industrial unions in their internal affairs, the I.W.W. provided for high centralization in matters affecting all workers. The National Convention and the General Executive Board wielded authority over all affiliated groups. The Executive Board, subject to a referendum vote by the whole membership, could call a strike in any field and order sympathetic action by other unions. This was a degree of centralized power higher than that exercised by any other important labor central body.

The policy toward members was most democratic. No workers were excluded; all were freely admitted to appropriate industrial unions. There were no closed books, benefit plans, or high dues and initiation fees. All this fitted perfectly the underlying purposes of the I.W.W. It was not a benefit organization. It did not, like the craft unions, attempt to restrict the labor supply in order to hold up wages. It was a workers' army organized for the ultimate object of overthrowing the capitalist system. Naturally it welcomed recruits!

Few Americans knew anything concerning the internal organization of the Industrial Workers. But they were nearly all familiar with its methods. These methods made excellent scare headlines, and the public was frightened. Americans gradually had become accustomed to the ways of the Socialist party. It had extreme objectives, but its methods were peaceful and legal. The I.W.W., on the other hand, appeared violent and lawless. Its defiant, revolutionary shouting brought public revulsion.

As a means of industrial peace, the craft unions of the A.F. of L. worked to negotiate wage contracts with employers. These contracts, stipulating that the workers stay at their jobs, prevented militant and sympathetic class action. Unions of the I.W.W. were forbidden to sign any such agreements. Indeed, industrial peace was not even an objective of the I.W.W.

Propaganda was considered a vital technique for securing the ultimate program of the organization, but this was not carried on through ordinary channels. Few books and pamphlets were printed, and there was only one official organ, the *Industrial Worker*. Most of the " education " was given out during isolated strikes of unskilled workers, which the I.W.W. provided with leadership. During these disputes organizers were sent in to manage strikes and advertise the aims of the Industrial Workers. In this fashion many thousands of laborers were exposed to their doctrines while under the stress of industrial conflict.

The strike was the principal method employed by the I.W.W. for the accomplishment of its program. Organization of unions was viewed chiefly as a means of forging this weapon. Political tactics were viewed with contempt because practical American experience showed that labor's political efforts had been futile, and the anarchist-syndicalist theory assumed that government was merely a means of coercion by the " ruling class." Workers could help themselves only by overthrow of the wage system, which was to be accomplished by continual war upon employers. Capitalists and the State were to be attacked, disabled, and weakened in every way possible. Sabotage was implicitly if not openly supported. The strike was the major instrument used, not primarily for improving working conditions, but as a weapon for strangling employers and the State. This was to be the key to power. Local tie-ups were viewed as training for later strikes in key industries. All this was directed toward the supreme act, the general strike, in which all workers would leave their jobs at a single command. Leaders of the I.W.W. believed that this weapon, or even the threat of it, would break all opposition and serve as the prelude to revolution.

Such dreams as these had a dramatic appeal to underpaid, overworked laborers. The fact that the general strike would paralyze and starve workers, as well as capitalists, was brushed aside; the idea of the mass power of labor was stimulating. It provided a following for the I.W.W., despite the fact that few tangible gains were achieved for labor.

The peak of strength was reached by the Industrial Workers about 1912. Its career thereafter was full of ups and downs, mostly downs. In 1917 it was to meet the wartime fate of other radical organizations, but that story will be told in a later chapter.

ILLUSTRATIVE DOCUMENTS

§3. *'First Appeal of the International Workingmen's Association to American Trade Unions,' as it appeared in the copy-book of the Central Committee of the North American Federation of the I.W.A., May 21, 1871.*

FELLOW WORKINGMEN! We take pleasure in notifying you that several Labor-societies of the United States, affiliated with the International Workingmen's Association, have formed the North American Central Committee of the I.W.A. . . .

The I.W.A. has spread over the entire civilized world and is planting its roots among the working classes of all countries, where modern industry reigns (England, Germany, France, Belgium, Austria, Switzerland, Spain, Italy, Russia, Holland, United States, etc.). Its central body or board of administration, the General Council of the I.W.A., is sitting at London and in its last official communication of March 14th distinctly recognizes and acknowledges the organization of the undersigned C. C. and " expresses its satisfaction with our activity." Every Trades Union or Labor Society of this country may affiliate with this Central Committee of the I.W.A. . . .

The principles of the I.W.A. may be condensed in the following extracts from its rules:

The emancipation of the working classes must be conquered by the working classes themselves.

The struggle for the emancipation of the working classes means not a struggle for class privileges and monopolies, but for equal rights and duties and the abolition of all class rule;

The economical subjection of the man of labor to the monopolizer of the means of labor, that is the sources of life, lies at the bottom of servitude in all its forms, of all social misery, mental degradation and political dependence;

The economical emancipation of the working classes is therefore the great end to which every political movement ought to be subordinate as a means.

All efforts aiming at that great end have hitherto failed from the want of solidarity between the manifold divisions of labor in each country and from the absence of a fraternal bond of union between the working classes of different countries. The emancipation of labor is neither a local, nor a national, but a social problem embracing all countries, in which modern society exists. . . .

A full and clear knowledge of the interests of our class will, we are satisfied, soon influence you in declaring your affiliation to that fraternal union of the laborers of all countries destined to break the yoke, under which the working classes languish—the wages-slavery.

Workingmen of all countries, unite! . . .

Theodore H. Banks, Conrad Carl, John Devoy, Edward Grosse, B. Hubert, Wilem Jantus, L. Ruppell, F. A. Sorge, Rud. Starke, — Weiss.[4]

§4. ' *Platform of the Socialist Labor Party,*' *adopted by its convention in New York City on July 8, 1896.*

The Socialist Labor party of the United States, in convention assembled, reasserts the inalienable right of all men to life, liberty, and the pursuit of happiness.

With the founders of the American republic, we hold that the purpose of government is to secure every citizen in the enjoyment of this right; but in the light of our social conditions, we hold, furthermore, that no such right can be exercised under a system of economic inequality, essentially destructive of life, of liberty, and of happiness.

With the founders of this republic, we hold that the true theory of politics is that the machinery of government must be owned and controlled by the whole people; but in the light of our industrial development we hold, furthermore, that the true theory of economics is that the machinery of production must likewise belong to the people in common.

To the obvious fact that our despotic system of economics is the direct opposite of our democratic system of politics, can plainly be

---

[4] J. R. Commons, *Documentary History of American Industrial Society,* IX, 356–359.

traced the existence of a privilege class, the corruption of government by that class, the alienation of public property, public franchises, and public functions to that class, and the abject dependence of the mightiest nations upon that class.

Again, through the perversion of democracy to the ends of plutocracy, labor is robbed of the wealth which it alone produces, is denied the means of self-employment, and, by compulsory idleness in wage slavery, is ever deprived of the necessaries of life. Human power and natural forces are thus wasted that the plutocracy may rule. Ignorance and misery, with all their concomitant evils, are perpetuated, that the people may be kept in bondage. Science and invention are diverted from their humane purpose to the enslavement of women and children.

Against such a system the Socialist Labor party once more enters its protest. Once more it reiterates its fundamental declaration, that private property in the natural sources of production and in the instruments of labor is the obvious cause of all economic servitude and political dependence.

The time is fast coming when, in the natural course of social evolution, this system, through the destructive action of its failures and crises on the one hand, and the constructive tendencies of its trusts and other capitalistic combinations on the other hand, shall have worked out its own downfall.

We therefore call upon the wage-workers of the United States, and upon all other honest citizens, to organize under the banner of the Socialist Labor party into a class-conscious body, aware of its rights and determined to conquer them by taking possession of the public powers; so that, held together by an indomitable spirit of solidarity under the most trying conditions of the present class struggle, we may put a summary end to that barbarous struggle by the abolition of classes, the restoration of the land, and all of the means of production, transportation, and distribution to the people as a collective body, and the substitution of the cooperative commonwealth for the present state of planless production, industrial war, and social disorder; a commonwealth in which every worker shall have the free exercise and full benefit of his faculties, multiplied by all the modern factors of civilization. . . .[5]

---

[5] *Proceedings of the Ninth Annual Convention of the Socialist Labor Party.* New York, 1896, 55–56. Pamphlet in Library of Congress.

§5. *'Program of the Industrial Workers of the World.'* Excerpts *from undated pamphlet published by the I.W.W. in Chicago, Illinois.*

THE PREAMBLE OF THE INDUSTRIAL WORKERS OF THE WORLD

The working class and the employing class have nothing in common. There can be no peace so long as hunger and want are found among millions of working people and the few, who make up the employing class, have all the good things of life.

Between these two classes a struggle must go on until the workers of the world organize as a class, take possession of the earth and the machinery of production, and abolish the wage system.

We find that the centering of management of the industries into fewer and fewer hands makes the trade unions unable to cope with the ever growing power of the employing class. The trade unions foster a state of affairs which allows one set of workers to be pitted against another set of workers in the same industry, thereby helping to defeat one another in wage wars. Moreover, the trade unions aid the employing class to mislead the workers into the belief that the working class have interests in common with their employers.

These conditions can be changed and the interest of the working class upheld only by an organization formed in such a way that all its members in any one industry, or in all industries if necessary, cease work whenever a strike or lockout is on in any department thereof, thus making an injury to one an injury to all.

Instead of the conservative motto, "A fair day's wage for a fair day's work," we must inscribe on our banner the revolutionary watchword, "Abolition of the wage system."

It is the historic mission of the working class to do away with capitalism. The army of production must be organized, not only for the everyday struggle with the capitalists, but also to carry on production when capitalism shall have been overthrown. By organizing industrially we are forming the structure of the new society within the shell of the old.

THE IMMEDIATE DEMANDS OF THE I.W.W.

. . . the first function of a labor union is to make immediate demands in regard to wages, hours and conditions and to fight for them, giving second place to the ultimate function of the I.W.W., i.e., to build industrial unions which are to serve as organs of production and distribution in a new society. . . .

59

Capitalism and its organs of production and distribution are breaking down in one country after another. . . . And it is well that the ultimate aim of the I.W.W. should thus be kept steadily in view. . . .

But—the realization of this ultimate program, which we should always keep in mind, is at the best several years off. Such a gigantic establishment as the world's economic mechanism cannot be revolutionized in a day, in a month, or in a year. . . . For that reason it is always well for the workers to keep their feet firmly on the ground of merciless reality. . . . Thus the two functions of the I.W.W.—the immediate and the ultimate—go hand in hand. They supplement each other and are equally necessary. . . .

The immediate demands for improved conditions, shorter hours and better pay are the rallying cries by means of which we can wake up the dormant mind of the average worker and get him with us so that we can educate him for efforts of a higher order, such as building the structure of a new society. . . .

Workers—get together and let your voice be heard. Make a set of immediate demands on the employers which will check the steady trend toward degradation. Take advantage of the situation thus arising to get your fellow workers into your industrial union, so that they may have power to enforce those demands and come with new ones. At the other end of that line of action lie industrial control through the union, abolition of wage slavery and a new society.

Go after the employers with an endless string of immediate demands.

Up and at them! [6]

---

[6] *The Immediate Demands of the Industrial Workers of the World* [I.W.W., Chicago, 19—]. Pamphlet in Library of Congress.

CHAPTER THREE

Farmers in Revolt

REFORM movements by organized labor and by the radicals
just described grew out of far-reaching industrial changes.
Workers, feeling the impact of new national economic forces,
sought adjustment through social reform. These new forces were
not restricted to industry, however. Another great body of
Americans felt the vast changes which marked the nation's
coming of age. This group was the largest single element in the
country's population—the farmers.

Before the War Between the States there had been little
organization of farmers as a special-interest group. But from
1870 to 1896, successive reform movements developed with
increasing power. They came as a result of revolutionary
changes in agriculture and world economy. Farmers, adversely
affected by these changes, moved to protect themselves. That
single motive was the common denominator of the varied efforts
which took form.

The "Agrarian Crusade," as the movement has been called,
was not radical in the true sense of the word. It struck fear into
the hearts of conservative financial interests and was, indeed,
rebellious. But it was not revolutionary. The farmers did not
wish to overthrow the existing economic, social, or political
system. They desired merely to compel modifications which
would protect and favor the interests of agriculture and the
" producing " classes. In this sense the movement was a struggle
for power with the industrial forces of the country, which had
emerged triumphant at the close of the War Between the States.
It was an attempt to wrest control of government from the
banking-manufacturing group, in order that adaptations could

61

be made for the benefit of agriculture. In 1896 the effort nearly succeeded, with Bryan as its champion. But in the final test of strength the forces of finance and industry won out; the election of McKinley signalized their victory and clinched their control over the direction of national development.[1]

The Farmers' Economic Dilemma

The farmers clamored for reforms in the existing system because of the precarious position in which they found themselves. Agriculture before the War Between the States had been largely self-sufficient. Food, clothing, and practically all the necessities of life were obtained from the farm or by simple barter. Money was not needed for most purposes, and the majority of farmers were not dependent upon distant markets for disposal of their produce. After the war, however, conditions changed rapidly. The expansion of industry developed growing centers of population near factories, and these centers called increasingly for agricultural products. Farmers found it profitable to concentrate on growing a cash crop, which provided income for purchasing more land and manufactured articles. Agriculture became a specialized production business, dependent upon the medium of exchange and upon other business. Farmers became small capitalists, engaged in commerce, and no longer self-sufficient.

The fact that farmers became businessmen in itself gave no special reason for complaint. Businessmen in industry during the same period were not complaining or crying for reform. The farmers were oppressed because as enterprisers they alone had no control over production, markets, or price. Enterprisers in manufacturing fields could more easily enlarge or decrease output in order to meet demands and avoid surpluses. Producers' agreements, " pools," and monopolistic controls were of special assistance. Advertising could be used in most industries to increase sales, and the protective tariff shut out foreign competi-

---

[1] Louis M. Hacker and Benjamin B. Kendrick, *The United States Since 1865*, third edition, 295–296. New York: F. S. Crofts & Co., 1939. This work is the main source used for the general background of the farmers' movement.

tion for manufacturers. But farmers had no such instruments for protection of their business. They were too numerous and scattered to co-operate closely for the control of production, and agricultural output was, by nature, less flexible than manufacturing. The farmers were not protected by a tariff and had to compete with producers everywhere. They were at the mercy of world forces beyond their control. Under such conditions security was impossible.

If the agrarian interests had been fortunate, they would not have suffered from lack of market control. If world forces had favored agricultural prices, farmers would have remained contented in spite of their economic impotence. Indeed, during the sprinkled years of farm prosperity, the cry for reform faded to a whisper. Neverthless, world forces and prices were generally adverse, and farmers lacked the power of other enterprisers to do anything about it.

In the whole period from 1870 to 1900 American farms were running at low profit, if any. The only sustaining factor was the increase in land values due to westward migration. Although falling prices for farm goods pressed the cultivators, they could meet losses by borrowing money on their land; as long as land values boomed, the amount they could borrow went up. But this was obviously an unsound situation. In the 1890's one-third of the total value of farm property in the " corn belt " was mortgaged. Many had passed the limit of borrowing and the crisis was near at hand.

The underlying cause of difficulty in agriculture was declining prices for produce. Average prices for wheat, corn, and cotton— the major staples—were cut nearly in half during the period from 1870 to 1896.[2] Increased total output compensated to a degree, but individual incomes fell. This development was especially severe on farmers who had borrowed when prices were good and money available, but who had to repay when prices were low and money hard to get.

Low farm prices were caused by world over-production of agricultural commodities. Output was increasing in many

---

[2] John D. Hicks, *Populist Revolt*, 54–58. Minneapolis: University of Minnesota Press, 1931. This book covers the later farmers' movements.

countries, but most of all in the United States. Broadening demand at home and in England stimulated the opening of new lands, and the tide of immigration from the Old World helped to provide hands to cultivate them. This development was aided by the liberal policy of the national government after the passage of the Homestead Act of May, 1862. Under this law genuine settlers were granted 160-acre plots in return for a minimum of five years' residence and work upon the soil. The total farm domain in the United States doubled in area from 1860 to 1900. Scientific research and the invention of farm machinery increased the output of all lands. It is no wonder that farm prices declined in face of this vast increase in the supply of produce.

Although low prices and incomes were the fundamental trouble, other factors increased the pressure on farmers. Many producers, in order to raise their earnings, borrowed money to expand or improve their lands. In the long run, the gain from larger crops thereby produced was wiped out by the continued fall in farm prices. In addition, the farmers had to pay a high rate of interest on the money borrowed, and as the total amount of mortgages on farm property steadily increased, the burden of interest payments grew heavier. There was also the matter of rising taxes. The westward movement of the population gave enhanced value to lands in the great farm areas. This rise in value raised the owners' ability to borrow money, but the higher valuation likewise increased the amount of real property taxes levied. The farmers were quite naturally chagrined; out of a falling income they had to pay constantly larger fixed amounts for interest and taxes.

Another reason for agricultural distress was the high charges by " middle-men " between the farm and market place. The railroads often set excessive freight rates and discriminated in favor of large producers. Owners of grain elevators, by collusive agreements, held up storage rates. The farmers believed that they might make a little profit, in spite of low commodity prices, if the " middle-men " didn't take it all in handling charges. As the margin of the farmers' profit melted away, cries against the railroads and warehouses grew ever louder.

Finally, farmers suffered from the fact that while they sold their goods at free, competitive prices, they had to buy in controlled, protected markets. Monopolies and price-maintenance agreements in industry, fortified by the tariff, kept prices for manufactured goods artificially high. When farmers bought agricultural implements, household furnishings, or ready-made clothing, they had to pay sums yielding good profits to manufacturers.

Agrarian movements in the latter nineteenth century aimed toward removing the causes of the "farm problem." Control over world production and prices was the real key to that problem, but farmers could not turn that key. World markets were mysterious and remote. American growers had no power over international commodity prices, and they found that such impersonal forces made poor targets. The farmers naturally struck out against the things they could hit. They convinced themselves that their difficulties must be caused by evil *men,* so they directed their efforts against those within reach who seemed responsible. This attack psychology, combined with lack of broad economic understanding, explains the nature of the agrarian programs during the period. The farmers fought the bankers and financiers in an effort to make money freer and to reduce interest charges. They put pressure on politicians to shift the tax burden from real property to income. They attacked the railroad and warehouse owners in order to lower transportation and storage costs. They fought the tycoons of industry in an attempt to break monopoly prices on articles the farmers bought.

Fraternalism and the National Grange of the Patrons of Husbandry

The first organization to give expression to the farmers' feelings was the National Grange of the Patrons of Husbandry. It was founded, strangely enough, not by "dirt farmers," but by government clerks in Washington, D. C. Oliver Hudson Kelley, a New Englander who had settled on a Minnesota farm before the War Between the States, was the originator of the Grange idea.[3] In 1864 he secured a government position. He was appointed two years later by the Agricultural Bureau to tour the southern states in order to gather information on farming. During this trip Kelley was so impressed with the social and economic needs of farmers that he determined to work for an organization that would help them. A Mason himself, Kelley felt that a fraternal order would be the best type of association.

With the aid of W. M. Ireland, a clerk in the Post Office Department, and William Saunders, another clerk in the Agricultural Bureau, Kelley worked out a careful plan of organization and ritual. On December 4, 1867, the first official meeting of the Grange was held. Membership was open to men and women engaged in agriculture who had no interest that conflicted with Grange purposes. The Order was to have social and intellectual functions, as well as economic and political. The broad nature of the Grange insured a wide response from the farmers of the country.

The growth of the Order was slow at first, because agriculture did not feel the full effect of post-war price deflation until several years after the end of hostilities. Beginning in 1872 the Grange expanded rapidly, mainly because it adopted special aims to secure cheaper railroad rates. In the early 1870's the farmers were in arms against transportation costs; they felt that those costs were eating away the narrow profit margin remaining after prices fell. When the Grange advocated lower rates, thousands flocked into the movement. The organization reached its greatest relative strength during the annual convention at St. Louis in 1874. Thirty-two states and territorial units were represented, claiming a total membership of nearly 500,000. Growth of the Order was really too rapid for sound development.

The program of objectives adopted by the National Grange in 1874 described the breadth of the movement and the needs of all farmers during that period. One aim was to help members increase the comfort and beauty of their homes. Reduction of living expenses, systematization of farm work, and diversification

---

[3] Solon J. Buck, *Granger Movement*, 41–42. Cambridge: Harvard University Press, 1913. This work is the chief authority on the National Grange.

of crops were other goals. Co-operative purchasing and marketing agencies were supported. Aside from aiming to help themselves through education and co-operation, the Grangers made important political demands. They wanted technical assistance from the government in the form of collection of statistics, establishment of state agricultural bureaus, and an independent federal Department of Agriculture. They called for the reduction of railroad rates through government regulation and the increase of other transportation facilities, such as waterways. Proposed currency and banking reforms were directed toward raising prices and lowering interest rates. Tax reform was also an objective, but many different points of view appeared on that subject. Changes in patent laws were urged which would reduce the cost of farm machinery.

The organization of the Grange began and continued as a fraternal order. The basic units were the local " subordinate " granges, established by regular organizers. There were also district or county granges, made up of local units for the administration of the educational and business interests of the order. The state granges were the next highest and were managed by representatives from subordinate granges in the respective states. At the top of the structure was the National Grange, which had two governing bodies, a National Council and a Senate, composed of men and women from the various states who had achieved higher degrees in the order. The permanent officers included a Master, Secretary, and Executive Committee.

Ritual and degrees of standing had a very strong appeal to Americans in the nineteenth century. Ceremony and color were particularly attractive in the midst of drab, isolated farm life. Taking these facts into consideration, the founders of the Grange provided for a series of seven degrees to be granted members upon the achievement of certain objectives. Local granges were empowered to grant the four lesser degrees, which for men were called Laborer, Cultivator, Harvester, and Husbandman; for women the corresponding degrees were called Maid, Shepardess, Gleaner, and Matron. The higher degrees had no gender. State granges had authority to confer the degree of Pomona (Hope).

The National Grange alone bestowed the degrees of Flora (Charity) and Ceres (Faith).

Education was professed to be the principal method used for the attainment of Grange objectives. In the field of home and farm improvement education was by all odds the chief device. When it came to winning political demands, however, education was often supplemented by lobbying. Resolutions and petitions regarding general programs or specific bills pending were sent to legislatures by local, state, and national granges. Sometimes meetings were held in state capitols while legislatures were in session. On important occasions, circular letters were sent to individual Congressmen. Candidates for public office were frequently questioned regarding their stand on farmers' demands.

Partisan politics was officially shunned as a means of securing the aims of the body. The Declaration of Purposes forbade all political and religious discussions within the organization, the calling of political conventions, or the nominating of candidates. But individual members, with members of local farm clubs, often participated in politics " outside of the Grange." They put up independent candidates under such party names as " Anti-monopoly " or " Reform." These candidates stood chiefly for curbing the railroads and were successful in passing restrictive railroad legislation in several states. Such laws, because of the unofficial Grange backing, were called " Granger laws." The power of the farmers in state politics was concentrated in the Middle-west and was at its peak from 1871 to 1876.

In addition to the passage of state laws regulating the rates and services of railroads and warehouses, the Grange was partly responsible for the ultimate enactment of the Interstate Commerce Act of 1887. This historic legislation came largely as a result of anti-railroad agitation carried on by the organization. The Grange also succeeded in having legal interest rates reduced in several states. One of the outstanding achievements was the hastening of the establishment of an independent Department of Agriculture, which was liberally provided for by Congress in 1889.

On the whole, however, local successes by the Grange were not accompanied by broad national legislation. This situation was due largely to the fact that agitation for national measures did not begin until after 1875, when the movement was starting downhill. Although the order revived slowly in the 1880's, other more vigorous groups came to the front as agencies of farmer action. United efforts for national measures were extremely difficult to obtain because the interests of different agricultural sections were often conflicting.

Membership in the Grange dropped sharply during the late 1870's, mainly as a reaction from over-rapid growth in preceding years. The general failure of the political ventures with which Grange members were associated worked against the organization. Collapse of many of the sponsored farmers' co-operatives proved especially discouraging. Finally, the ineffectiveness of railroad legislation disappointed the thousands who had joined the movement because of a desire to slash transportation charges.

After 1881 the Grange resumed its normal growth. The flood-tide of anti-railway agitation had swept over it and receded, but the sound basis of the organization remained. Although it served for a time as the spearhead of the agrarian drive for legislative reform, it was essentially an educational and social movement. The Grange was the first attempt at large-scale organization of farmers for their own welfare. Groups which followed showed the mark of its ideas and ideals.

Inflationary Demands and the National Greenback Party

When the influence of the Granger movement declined in 1875, the drive to curb the " middle-men " and insure farm salvation changed its course. Some favorable legislation had been gained in this direction, but railroad and storage charges still consumed a large slice of agricultural income. It appeared to farmers that the resistance to reform along those lines was too powerful. Spurred on by increased distress after the Panic of 1873, the farmers turned to another means of relief.

It has already been pointed out in this chapter that low farm prices were the primary cause of the agrarian problem. The growers felt unable to attack the root of this situation, which was world overproduction, but they began to believe they could raise prices in another way—by monetary inflation. It was felt that if large quantities of currency were injected into circulation, money would be freer, prices would go up, and farmers would receive larger dollar incomes, which would aid in paying off fixed debts. With money more plentiful, borrowing would be easier and interest rates would fall. Assured of a more comfortable profit margin, farmers would worry less about the high rates of the railroads.

How could this pleasant dream come true? How could more money be placed in circulation? By 1875 an answer was already in the air—" Greenbacks! " During the War Between the States the federal government had issued some $400,000,000 worth of promissory notes as a means of financing military expenditures. These paper bills, which specified no definite time for redemption, were called greenbacks because of their color. When the Treasury began to retire some of these notes after the close of the war, many groups throughout the country opposed the move. They declared that the removal of the greenbacks would reduce the outstanding currency, depress prices, and aggravate hard times. In response, Congress voted in February, 1868, to prohibit further redemptions. This step gave some men another idea. If it were unwise to withdraw the notes from circulation, why would it not be wise to increase the number in circulation? Samuel F. Cary, an Ohio politician, developed the notion. He proposed that the millions of dollars in federal bonds issued during the War Between the States be redeemed not in gold, as expected, but in greenbacks. Millions of paper dollars would thereby be added to the existing supply of gold and other currency. This idea became known as the " Ohio idea."

The " Ohio idea " was a part of the Democratic platform in 1868, but the party candidate, Horatio Seymour, did not support it. With both major parties cool toward the plan, its supporters began to establish independent parties. The Panic of 1873 accelerated this trend, and from 1873 to 1875 several minor state parties were won over to greenbackism. With a national election coming up in 1876, the greenback leaders decided to challenge the two major parties by forming an independent national organization. This development was characteristic of all reform movements in the early post-war period. They looked to politics as a quick and easy way to power.

On March 11, 1875, a convention of the farmer-advocates of monetary inflation met in Cleveland and formed the Independent party. Its program was greenbackism, and its name was later changed to the National Greenback party. The chief organizer was James Buchanan, an Indianapolis lawyer-editor. Another key figure was the colorful Ignatius Donnelly, who later became important as a leader in the People's party. A convention held in the following year nominated Peter Cooper of New York for President and Samuel Cary of Ohio for Vice-president. Cary was the inventor of the " Ohio idea "; Cooper was a well-known philanthropist who had made a fortune in manufacturing iron and later devoted himself to the education and uplifting of the working class. He was the founder of Cooper Union in New York City, which provided technical and general classes for workers and a free library. Cooper's age was his handicap. He was eighty-five years old and could take no part in the campaign of 1876. Although the ticket received considerable support in many middle-western states, it won a total of only 81,000 votes.

The leaders of the party were not discouraged. They considered their first bid for the presidency to be valuable mainly as advertising. Economic conditions continued bad. The idea of monetary inflation was winning wide support among workers as well as among farmers. In the Congressional elections of 1878 the party appeared at its greatest strength. Fully a million votes were cast for party candidates in California, Georgia, Maine, New York, and Pennsylvania, as well as in the Middle-west. Fourteen candidates were elected to Congress.

The components of the National Greenback party were predominantly agricultural. They came chiefly from the region of the Mississippi and Ohio valleys. Support in other states, however, was not lacking, as indicated in the by-elections of 1878. In that year a number of labor elements merged with the farmers. A special conference at Toledo, Ohio, united various labor groups with the organization and absorbed remnants of the National Labor and Reform party, which had grown out of the old National Labor Union in 1872. It was that meeting which changed the name of the party from Independent to National Greenback. By 1880, however, the workingmen had drifted away from their flirtation with the farmers and were moving into their own Knights of Labor. The 1880 Chicago convention of the Greenback party had 800 delegates, nearly all of whom were agrarian.

The aims of the party were rather narrowly limited to currency reform. With slight variations, each convention called for the substitution of greenbacks for national bank notes and complete control over the volume of money by the federal government, instead of by banks. The greenbackers demanded that all government bonds be redeemed in paper instead of gold. They supported unlimited coinage of silver as a supplementary means of increasing the currency. Subordinate planks favored measures independent of monetary reform. One called for a federal income tax and removal of tax exemption from government bonds. This plank aimed to shift some of the burden from the real property of farmers. Another plank was the reservation of all public lands for actual settlers only, to prevent exploitation of natural resources. Federal regulation of interstate commerce was proposed as a means of easing the transportation problems of agriculture. Political demands pointed toward extension of the franchise and democratization of Congressional procedure. Labor planks were inserted during the brief alliance with the workers in 1878, but were later omitted.

One of the techniques of the National Greenback party that attracted special attention was the formation of " greenback clubs " throughout the Middle-west; several thousands of these propaganda units were organized during the late 1870's. They had the appeal of social clubs, and the secrecy of their proceedings offered an additional lure. The members of these clubs studied the proposals of the Greenback party and planned local action. They were generally the most extreme elements in the movement and were opposed to fusion with any other party.

General James B. Weaver, who was sent to Congress by the party in 1878 and who carried the banner as presidential candidate in 1880, developed new campaign methods in politics. He was the inaugurator of the " whirlwind tour," which was later copied by such candidates as William Jennings Bryan, Theodore Roosevelt, Woodrow Wilson, and Franklin Roosevelt. Weaver toured most of the states in person, shaking the hands of nearly 30,000 people and reaching audiences of nearly half a million.

Independent political action was the principal method of the Greenback party in attempting to achieve its aims. The members did not try to force the major parties to adopt their demands. They wanted their whole program adopted quickly and without compromise, and this could be accomplished only by winning direct political power. The election of 1880, however, convinced most Greenbackers that they were fighting hopeless odds. Weaver's vote, in spite of his hard campaign, was less than the total vote cast for Greenback Congressional candidates in 1878. Many came to believe that future independent efforts would be a futile waste of votes on a candidate with no chance of winning. As a result, the party rapidly lost support after 1880. In 1884 General Benjamin F. Butler, supported by Greenback and fusion elements, received less than 200,000 votes for the presidency. A last stand was made by the party in 1888 when it joined with certain labor groups to support A. J. Streeter. This futile effort spelled the disappearance of the movement. Its decline was accelerated by the fact that bumper crops in 1880 brought temporary good times to agriculture, and the farmers repeatedly lost interest in reform when promising conditions returned. The National Greenback party would probably have disintegrated in any event; it was a one-track movement with a program too narrow to satisfy even a single economic group. Farmers gave it support for a while, but they were really waiting for the crystallization of a more comprehensive reform effort.

The Farmers' Alliance Movement

After the collapse of the " greenback interlude," a new movement appeared on the farmers' horizon. It had firm roots in the soil and grew up from the people. It was not planned in advance, like the National Grange, but came as the culmination of spontaneous local efforts in scattered parts of the country. The Farmers' Alliance Movement, as it came to be known, was

73

the second major attempt to organize all agriculture into a solid social, economic, and political front.

This movement is difficult to describe, because, unlike others of the period, it did not develop as a unified, symmetrical effort. It arose, instead, from several main sources. Gradually the various streams of action joined into two large currents, one in the South and one in the North. The Farmers' Alliance Movement must be considered in a broad way as a single phenomenon, but its structure can best be shown by tracing separately the southern and northern organizations.

The peculiar nature of conditions in the South after the War Between the States conditioned the alliance movement there.[4] The general causes of agricultural distress already mentioned were present, but southern farmers had other grievances as well. In the first place, they felt keenly their drop in relative political, economic, and social status as compared with the period before 1860. Furthermore, most of them were kept in constant debt by operation of the lien-law system in the South.

Practically all southern farmers had to take seed and supplies on credit before their staples were picked and sold. The merchants giving such credit charged high interest rates, and under the lien laws creditors had mortgage rights to debtors' property, including crops. If commodity prices fell sharply in any year, planters received insufficient income to pay off their debts and, through foreclosure, surrendered their lands and crops. Left on the soil as tenants with no ready cash, they had to borrow on the next year's crop in order to buy new seed and supplies. They seldom could get enough money ahead to avoid borrowing for each successive planting, and this bondage to creditors prevented them from regaining their lands and independence. The farmers hoped that through organization they could in some way break the intolerable cycle of debt.

Local frontier groups in Texas are credited with originating the alliance idea in the South.[5] After an earlier unsuccessful

---

[4] Benjamin J. Kendrick, " Agrarian Discontent in the South, 1880–1890," in *American Historical Association Reports,* Washington, 1920, 267. This article gives a clear picture of the situation.

[5] Hicks, *op. cit.,* 104.

effort in 1880, a number of scattered associations incorporated as the Grand State Farmers' Alliance of Texas. This alliance was a "secret and benevolent association," open to women as well as men, but closed to Negroes. The Alliance grew rapidly and by 1886 there were about 3,000 local lodges in the state. Aggressive leadership was given to the movement by C. W. Macune, who became chairman of the executive committee of the order.

Macune was to be a leading figure in the development of the alliance idea. His father had been a blacksmith and a preacher; the son seemed to inherit his evangelism. Macune had little education in his youth although he later read law and practiced medicine in Texas. Through various contacts he soon became influential in agricultural matters. He entered the alliance movement, gained control of it in Texas, and tried energetically to expand it. The man had a witty and magnetic personality. But, in spite of his abilities to attract, promote, and organize, Macune was an unsuccessful businessman.

Macune's first major achievement was to unite the Grand State Farmers' Alliance of Texas with the Farmers' Union of Louisiana in January, 1887. The Louisiana group had started in 1880 as an open farmers' society and was later transformed into a secret order modeled on the National Grange. Macune became president of the merged organization, which was called the National Farmers' Alliance. After this important step he sent organizers into most of the other southern states. Local units were established, grouped into state federations, and affiliated with the "national" organization. Nine states were represented in the Alliance convention of October, 1887.

Meanwhile, other farmers' groups were voluntarily joining with the Alliance. In South Carolina, for example, the "back-country" growers organized by Benjamin Tillman, one of the great southern farm leaders, decided to unite forces. The largest union occurred when the National Agricultural Wheel, a farmers' association organized in eight southern states and having 500,000 members, fused with the Alliance in 1889. The consolidation of the major agrarian groups in the South was completed by this step. Expansion of membership continued, and in 1890 the united "Southern Alliance," then officially called the National Farmers' Alliance and Industrial Union, claimed between one and three million members.

Only farmers and their "natural allies"—country preachers, farm editors, and teachers—were permitted to join. Special care was taken to safeguard the movement against infiltration of unfriendly groups. All lawyers, merchants, and financiers were specifically barred.

Objectives of the "Southern Alliance" evolved gradually. In the early days the chief purpose of the local farm groups in Texas was the rounding up of estrays. They also emphasized social features, education, and cultural development. For a while many of the organizations favored establishment of co-operatives, but early failures discouraged further experimentation along that line. Later aims included most of the things that farmers everywhere were demanding. Taxation of railroad property, issuance of greenbacks, reduction of the tariff, prohibition of alien land-ownership, and the imposition of an income tax were common objectives. In 1889 the Alliance convention in St. Louis adopted a special "sub-treasury plan," which captured the farmers' imagination for some time. It was introduced by the versatile C. W. Macune as a scheme for financing agricultural marketing and for providing short-term rural credits with government funds. Macune proposed that a sub-treasury office and government warehouse be set up in every county. Farmers could borrow on their non-perishable crops by bringing them to the warehouses and receiving warehouse receipts, which could be taken to sub-treasury offices as collateral for loans. This plan was similar to the commodity loan provisions of the New Deal agricultural program, some forty years later. The proposal called for direct first-aid from the national government.

The growth and final unification of the southern farmers' movement has been described; its internal organization was centralized and strong. The Alliance persisted as a secret fraternal order with headquarters at Washington, D. C., where much power over the local lodges was centered. The nature of the Alliance organization limited its methods of action. Since its membership was kept secret, open political efforts were not possible. As President Macune stated, " Let the Alliance be a business organization for business purposes, and as such, necessarily secret, and as secret, necessarily non-political." [6] In spite of this general policy, Alliance men secretly gained control of the Democratic party in several southern states.

Inability of the " Southern Alliance " to participate openly in politics proved the chief reason for its sudden decline after 1890. The farmers by that time had become carried away by the idea of independent political power. When the People's party was established in 1892, embodying the Alliance platform, the bulk of Alliance members deserted their organization to join in the swelling political expression. Other factors contributed to the rapid collapse of the Alliance movement in the South, but the main cause was the shift of farmers' interest from social to political organization.

There is some question about the beginnings of the farmers' alliance movement in the North. As in the South, scattered local groups sprang up before a centralized organization was developed. The earliest of these groups was founded in the State of New York on March 21, 1877, by some members of the National Grange who wanted to create a " political mouthpiece " for their order.[7] The first really effective organization of the alliance type was started in Cook County, Illinois, on April 15, 1880. Milton George, a Chicago editor, was the founder, and he planned to use the Cook County group as a central agency for establishing other alliances throughout the country. This idea of a national order of farmers caught hold. On October 14, 1880, several hundred delegates from scattered farmers' clubs, alliances, and local granges assembled in Chicago. This meeting, which was called the Farmers' Transportation Convention, is regarded as the first convention of the " Northern Alliance." [8]

By 1882 the number of local alliances in the North and Middle-west had grown remarkably, and some 2,000 units, with a total membership of 100,000 farmers, were claimed. The

---

[6] Solon J. Buck, *The Agrarian Crusade,* New Haven, 1920, 128.
[7] Hicks, *op. cit.,* 97.
[8] Hicks, *op. cit.,* 99.

following year brought a temporary lull in the movement, since improved farm conditions in 1883 and 1884 reduced enthusiasm for the organization. But in 1885 falling prices once again spurred activity. Hard times deepened during the ensuing years, and, favored by this turn of affairs, the movement gained nearly 1,000,000 members by 1889. Its official name became the National Farmers' Alliance, but its real influence was limited to the Mississippi Valley. It was generally known as the " Northern Alliance," to distinguish it from the separate alliance movement in the South.

The fundamental purposes of both major alliances were the same. The northerners called for the regulation of interstate commerce, more equitable taxation, and patent law reform. After 1887, with farm conditions in the Middle-west growing desperate, the " Northern Alliance " program became broader and more radical. First place was given to monetary inflation in the form of unlimited coinage of silver and the issue of paper money. This objective, directed toward raising prices, came more and more to be looked upon as a farmers' panacea. The " Northern Alliance " also demanded government ownership of the railroads and telegraphs.

In organization, the alliance of the North was sharply different from that in the South. It was not secret. It was open to Negroes. There was much less centralization of authority than in the " Southern Alliance." Chartered local units, concerned with social and educational affairs, were grouped into state alliances, and the state organizations were federated in a " national " alliance. In 1889 an elaborate governing structure was created for the national body, but central powers were limited and democratically exercised.

The " Northern Alliance " believed from the beginning in persistent, non-partisan, political activity. The organization platform was forwarded to federal and state officers and candidates. Lobbying was considered a foremost technique. By 1890 the zeal for independent political action swept aside these earlier practices. The Alliance as such refrained from forming a new party, but members in various states led in organizing independent minor parties pledged to the farmers' program. Such

party names as " People's," " Independent," and " Industrial,"
appeared on state ballots. The power of these efforts was
strengthened by a great popular reaction against the high
Republican tariff of 1890. Coalition with Democratic leaders
was sometimes effected. In the Congressional elections of 1890,
independent minor party candidates won eight seats in the
House and two in the Senate.

Leaders of the farmers' alliance movement in all parts of the
country believed that ultimately their forces would be united in a
single national effort. On December 3, 1889, the two great
sectional alliances convened simultaneously in St. Louis. Merger
between the two organizations was hoped for, and conferees
were appointed to arrange the basis for union. But in spite of
a general desire for welding the groups into a single movement,
certain obstacles could not be overcome. The southerners
wanted a complete merger, similar to those which Macune had
effected in building up his own organization. The northern
group might have agreed to this, but the southerners insisted also
that secrecy and Negro exclusion prevail in the unified order.
These features were incompatible with the principles of the
" Northern Alliance," which favored a federation of the two
groups that would not destroy their identities. There was also a
difference of policy regarding political action, and the survival
of sectional feeling occasionally raised friction. In the end,
offers of compromise failed; the movement faltered because its
leaders could not agree upon a unified program.

The " Southern Alliance " went to pieces soon after 1890, as
already noted. The northern organization lost its force, lived on
for a few years as an adjunct to the growing People's party, but
fell rapidly in membership and influence. The achievement of
the farmers' alliance movement in North and South was the complete awakening of agrarian consciousness. It taught the growers
about their problems and gave them experience in co-operation.
The nature of the farmers' march toward reform shifted suddenly in the early 1890's. It turned away from the socio-
educational methods of the alliance to the political methods of
the People's party. But the alliance movement was a necessary
prelude to the grand act of politics and Bryan.

FARMERS IN REVOLT

Populism and the People's Party

Direct political action came as a natural culmination of farm distress and upheaval in the period following the War Between the States. The immediate cause, however, was the calamity that fell over the middle-western states in the late 1880's.

Recovery from the depression which followed the Panic of 1873 developed into a land boom in parts of the Middle-west by 1880. The early years of the following decade, marked by abnormal rainfall in arid sections, became known as the " prosperous eighties." Immigration to the western borderlands of Kansas, Nebraska, and the adjoining states was encouraged by good crops, and a reckless speculation in land began. Settlers mortgaged their holdings to the limit in order to buy more property. As land values soared, the farmers in this area tried to invest every cent available, in the hope of reaping gains from further increments.

As usually happens in such speculative manias, the day of reckoning came. It struck suddenly in some places and gradually in others. The immediate reason for the boom's collapse was lack of rain in 1887 and for ten succeeding years. The whole mid-western region was visited by one of those cycles of drought which have become well known in the United States. The eastern sections of the Middle-west escaped serious damage, but settlers in the western areas had simply pushed too far into arid lands. In five out of the ten years of drought which ensued, there were practically no crops at all on the borderlands. Boom towns collapsed. Farmers, deprived of income, were unable to meet payments on mortgage debts and lost their properties. In western Kansas, where the collapse occurred most abruptly, about half of the inhabitants were forced off the land from 1888 to 1892. But the chief storm center of discontent and bitterness was the central portion of the Middle-west. Here most of the growers were able to stay on their farms, but they remained in precarious and desperate circumstances.

These conditions gave rise to a demand for immediate action. The farmers' alliance movement, with its social and educational

80

features, did not promise quick results. On the other hand, many felt that independent political organization might be unwise. Failure of the National Greenback party was fresh in memory and it was feared that partisan activity might cause internal disputes which would wreck the main objectives of the farmers' movement. For some time leading agrarian figures preferred to remain loyal to either of the major parties and to shun any separate political activity.

Continued disappointments brought a shift in outlook, however. In spite of promises, the major parties and politicians accomplished little for agriculture. By 1890 many of the farmers quit the old parties and looked toward independent politics as the only means of gaining their ends. It has already been mentioned that many alliance members, working outside of the organization, supported several successful independent candidates for Congress in that year. A number of colorful campaigners whipped the smoking plains into political fire. Best known among them was Mrs. Mary Elizabeth Lease. A woman lawyer of Irish birth, Mrs. Lease turned her talents and temperament upon the issues facing the farmers of Kansas, where discontent ran highest. She made over 150 speeches during the campaign, in spite of her duties as mother of four children. Her work attracted wide attention, and its effectiveness was probably enhanced by her attractive, though masculine, personality. She became a target of praise by her supporters and of censure by her opponents. Friends called her " refined, magnetic, witty." Enemies called her a " hard, unlovely shrew." Mrs. Lease's famous exhortation to Kansas farmers was to " raise less corn and more Hell! " [9]

Another unusual figure was Jerry Simpson, " populist " candidate for Congress in Kansas during the same campaign. Expressing the " people's " sentiment, Simpson called his dignified opponent, Col. James Hallowell, by the name of " Prince Hal." Simpson was in turn ridiculed for his rough, unconventional dress and called " Sockless Simpson," or " Sockless Socrates." [10] He was elected, however, and served competently in the House

[9] Buck, *The Agrarian Crusade,* 135–136.
[10] *Ibid.,* 136–137.

of Representatives. The whole political tone in the Middle-west in 1890 indicated that sharply opposing social and economic forces were moving into battle.

In May, 1891, the feeling for organized political action on a national scale came to a head. A convention of farmers, composed chiefly of " Northern Alliance " men in the Mississippi Valley, met and decided to form a People's party of the U. S. A. Appeals were made to all liberal groups in the country to join forces with the farmers and other " producers."

In response to invitations, 860 delegates from every agricultural order in the country and from many labor groups convened in St. Louis on February 22, 1892. Leaders of the " Southern Alliance," which was at last committed to independent political action, were present with farm leaders of all sections. Meeting on Washington's birthday, with much patriotic display, the assembly officially launched the People's party and called a national nominating convention for July 2, to meet at Omaha. This gathering of 1300 representatives from all parts of the Union nominated a liberal, Judge Walter Q. Gresham, for the presidency. Gresham, however, declined to accept, and the convention then named General James B. Weaver of Iowa to head the ticket. Another soldier, General James G. Field of Virginia, was chosen as running mate.

The choice of Weaver, once beaten as the Greenback candidate, was unfortunate. He had lost in a previous election but, nevertheless, the General proved to be a fair standard bearer. He was well educated, had practiced law for a time, and during the war had risen rapidly. Weaver had served several terms in Congress as a Greenbacker, having broken from the Republican party in 1877. He was not an outstanding figure, but was well balanced and a seasoned campaigner.

The success of the People's party in its first public contest in November, 1892, was heartening to its supporters. Weaver won over 1,000,000 popular votes and twenty-two electoral votes. The result was the best initial showing of any third party up until that time, except for the Republicans in 1856. Nevada, Colorado, Idaho, and Kansas were carried. Part of the electoral vote of Oregon and North Dakota was also won. In various states the People's party combined with one of the major parties and elected altogether ten Representatives and five Senators. Fifteen hundred state and county legislators were elected.

Continuing farm depression, deepened by the Panic of 1893, aided the " populist revolt." In the Congressional by-elections of 1894, the total vote for candidates of the People's party was forty per cent above the vote for Weaver in 1892. Seven Representatives and six Senators were elected. Leaders looked confidently toward the Presidential campaign of 1896. They felt certain that the rising tide would carry them to victory.

The program of the People's party was a culmination of demands by farmers and anti-monopolists during the generation which followed the War Between the States. It represented more than just agrarian sentiment, for during this period there had been considerable interaction between the farm movements and those of reform elements in the eastern cities. Many of the specific proposals taken up by the farm organizations originated in the East or in Europe. The ideas of men like Henry George, Edward Bellamy, and Henry D. Lloyd found wide acceptance across the nation, and many of the actual leaders of the populist movement had urban backgrounds.[11] Underlying the party's program was opposition to monopoly and special privilege, and the belief that wealth should belong to those who produce it. The platform adopted in 1892 gave first place, however, to the immediate economic needs of the farmers. Financial reform became the principal objective, as a direct means of raising prices and income. This program called for the establishment of a national paper currency, which would be issued directly to the people at a rate of interest not exceeding two per cent. Inflation by unlimited coinage of silver was also part of the program, and postal savings banks and a graduated income tax were proposed. In the important field of transportation and communication, the platform supported government ownership of railroads, telegraphs, and telephones. Land was to be reserved for native

[11] Chester McA. Destler, *American Radicalism, 1865–1901: Essays and Documents,* 1–31. New London: Connecticut College for Women, 1946. This study gives a full discussion of the ideological interaction.

settlers only, and tracts owned by aliens or by railroads in excess of actual needs were to be reclaimed by the federal government.

In addition to the official platform, which comprised the heart of populist demands, special resolutions were passed to appeal to groups other than farmers. These called for restriction of immigration, eight-hour laws, and abolition of private detective agencies. Generous pensions were supported for veterans of the War Between the States. Appeals were made to liberals and progressives everywhere by means of planks favoring the popular election of Senators and state laws providing for the initiative, referendum, and Australian secret ballot.

Ignatius Donnelly of Minnesota, one of the leaders of the farmers' greenback movement, was the author of the fiery preamble to the People's party platform. He was, in fact, a leader of every important agrarian movement from 1875 until his death in 1901. Forceful and aggressive, Donnelly was a real power in Minnesota politics, first as a Republican and later as an independent " Anti-monopoly " and " Farmers' " candidate. He stood until the end against fusion of the People's party with any other organization.

Such men as Ignatius Donnelly helped give the movement its peculiar nature. The People's party was a political organization and depended upon election victories and legislation to achieve its program. The campaign techniques of the party were unique, and they eventually assumed the nature of a religious revival and crusade. The people of the Middle-west were told that they represented the forces of Light and Goodness, struggling against Darkness and Evil. The issues—social, political, and economic—were painted in moral colors. Complex problems were over-simplified and interpreted as Right against Wrong, Freedom against Oppression.

Rallying the people for the Redemption Day in politics, leaders spoke to crowds everywhere in the Great Plains region—in schoolhouses, churches, and town halls. Picnics and outings of organized farm groups were turned into all-day exercises in the faith and platform of the People's party. Lecturers were in constant demand. State committees and local clubs were established to keep the campaign fires burning.

The permanent organization of the movement, however, did not have enough time to become fixed and hard. Growth was too rapid; elements were too fluid. The People's party was a great, surging wave and not a deep, steady current. When its initial energy was spent, the organization disintegrated. That was the story of 1896.

When the national convention was held on July 22, 1896, confusion supplanted the earlier optimism of party leaders. Distress was still widespread. The farmers were clamoring more loudly than ever. The issue of " silver " threatened to engulf the whole farmers' movement and the People's party with it. Producers of silver in the western states and all their supporters were determined to force the government to coin unlimited quantities of the metal at a fixed ratio to gold. Up until that time the United States was on a gold standard and accepted silver for coinage only in limited amounts, according to specific acts of Congress. Free coinage of silver would naturally have proved a boon to western mines. Well-organized " silver " groups worked strenuously for the fusion of all forces favoring that policy.

The People's party was already on record as approving unlimited coinage of both metals. It supported any proposal which would increase the supply of money, as a means of making money " easier " and of raising prices. The party, therefore, was considered by " silver " men as one of the main groups to be united in a drive against the " gold monopoly." And the majority of the party, many of whom were already silverites, were willing to make an alliance which was aimed toward that objective. Some of the leaders, however, rightly feared that the broader aims and foundations of the organization would be lost if it fell into the silver flood.

In spite of the fact that enthusiasm for silver drowned out other objectives, the People's party might at least have retained its identity if the Democrats had not declared for free coinage first. The Republican convention in 1896 supported a strict gold standard. Had the Democratic convention followed suit, the silver forces would have flocked to the banner of an independent People's party, which favored silver. But the Democrats, meeting on July 7, were won over by the silverites and the silver tongue of William Jennings Bryan.

The People's party, convening after the Democrats, on July 22, was helpless before the flood. Since one of the major parties had declared for free coinage, silverites everywhere urged all groups to fuse with the Democrats for the achievement of the great silver objective. The convention was forced to accept silver as the dominant issue and to endorse Bryan. The platform contained most of the earlier objectives, but all were subordinated to the glittering metal issue, which had the whole country hypnotized. Farmers merged with miners, workers, and other groups in the conviction that "free silver" would cure all the evils of mankind by overthrowing the "bondage of gold." The People's party struggled feebly to retain its identity. It kept its platform distinct from the Democrats; and while endorsing Bryan, it supported Tom E. Watson for Vice-president, instead of the Maine Democrat, Arthur M. Sewall. Watson, a sympathizer with the earlier farmers' alliance movement in Georgia, had become a leader of the rebel agrarian forces of the South.

The presidential campaign was the most exciting since 1860. The issue appeared simple—silver against gold—and moral values were inseparably attached. Emotions ran high; vituperation and slander poured from both sides. Propaganda through books, pamphlets, and cartoons rolled off the presses. Bryan, campaigning as the Democratic and People's candidate, traveled some 18,000 miles in his tour of twenty-nine states. He made nearly 600 speeches and his powerful oratory won many votes. William McKinley, the Republican candidate, spoke very little. He stayed at home during most of the campaign, greeting "pilgrims" from his front porch. But Mark Hanna, the power behind McKinley, was less reserved. The Republican National Committee Chairman tagged McKinley the "Advance Agent of Prosperity," raised millions of dollars for campaign work, and had the bulk of newspaper support. In the final days of the battle Hanna threw in his sharpest punches. Many large employers throughout the land, in co-operation with Hanna, let their workers know that they would retaliate with shut-downs and lay-offs if Bryan won.[12]

Collapse of the Agrarian Challenge

When the votes were cast in November, the Hanna forces triumphed. McKinley received 7,107,000 popular votes to 6,533,000 for Bryan. The electoral vote gave McKinley 271 against 176. The result showed a clear sectional division, with the eastern industrial states giving majorities to McKinley and the agricultural South and West favoring Bryan. The last great effort of agrarian and allied interests to win back political power from industry and finance had failed. The People's party, swallowed up in that effort, lay shattered.

After the defeat of 1896, the organization declined rapidly. Twenty-seven Congressmen were elected by the party in that year, but only ten were successful in 1898, and none in 1902. The remaining membership was split over the issue of merging with some other party or maintaining a separate identity; neither one of these remnants of a once-powerful party gained any successes. National conventions, weakly attended, were held in the presidential election years. In 1908 Tom Watson, who had been the Populist standard-bearer in 1904, became the last party candidate for President. But even the loyal few that named him confessed their political impotence. Watson received only 29,000 votes in the election. The last national meeting was held in 1912, when the breath of the People's party was so feeble that no endorsements or nominations were made.

The failure of the organization was due mainly to the fact that its program had been taken over by the major parties. The Democrats in 1896, and later, borrowed most of the objectives of the People's party. The " progressive " Republicans also absorbed many of their aims. Loss of power through loss of platform was accelerated by the plunge for free silver in 1896. Fusion with the Bryan forces was a gamble for the quick achievement of one aim, at the sacrifice of the broader program of an independent People's party. That strategy hastened the dissolu-

---

[12] Hacker, *op. cit.,* 317–318.

tion of the organization and its principles. But returning farm prosperity was the factor that checked the agrarian rebellion as a whole. The great upheaval, beginning in 1870 and lasting through 1896, was mainly a product of discontent due to distress. When good times returned, the farmers lost interest in reform.

In spite of its collapse, the People's party was not without some achievements. Its aims were realized later through other organizations, aided by the work of the party in awakening public consciousness. Nearly all its demands for political reform were answered in the " progressive " legislation of the 1900's. Monetary reform came in the Federal Reserve Act of 1913 and in subsequent measures giving easy credit to farmers. Railway regulation was developed to a point approaching government ownership. More than a generation later, broad agricultural reforms comprised a major part of the New Deal. The farmers' movement of the post-bellum period laid the groundwork for comprehensive changes in many fields of national life.

ILLUSTRATIVE DOCUMENTS

§6. *'Declaration of Purpose of the National Grange,' as adopted in the Seventh Session of the National Grange of the Patrons of Husbandry, St. Louis, Missouri, February 4, 1874.*

GENERAL OBJECTS. 1. United by the strong and faithful tie of agriculture, we mutually resolve to labor for the good of our Order, our country, and mankind.

2. We heartily endorse the motto: " In essentials, unity; in non-essentials, liberty; in all things, charity."

SPECIFIC OBJECTS. 3. We shall endeavor to advance our cause by laboring to accomplish the following objects:

To develop a better and higher manhood and womanhood among ourselves. To enhance the comfort and attractions of our homes, and strengthen our attachments to our pursuits. To foster mutual understanding and coöperation. To maintain inviolate our laws, and to emulate each other in labor to hasten the good time coming. To reduce our expenses, both individual and corporate. To buy less and produce more, in order to make our farms self-sustaining. To diversify our crops, and crop no more than we can cultivate.

. . . To systematize our work, and calculate intelligently on probabilities. To discountenance the credit system, the mortgage system, the fashion system, and every other system tending to prodigality and bankruptcy. . . .

BUSINESS RELATIONS. 4. For our business interests, we desire to bring producers and consumers, farmers and manufacturers into the most direct and friendly relations possible. Hence we must dispense with a surplus of middlemen, not that we are unfriendly to them, but we do not need them. Their surplus and their exactions diminish our profits.

We wage no aggressive warfare against any other interests whatever. On the contrary, all our acts and all our efforts, so far as business is concerned, are not only for the benefit of the producer and consumer, but also for all other interests that tend to bring these two parties into speedy and economical contact. . . .

We shall, therefore, advocate for every state the increase in every practicable way, of all facilities for transporting cheaply to the seaboard, or between home producers and consumers, all the productions of our country. We adopt it as our fixed policy to " open out the channels in nature's great arteries that the life-blood of commerce may flow freely." . . .

In our noble Order there is no communism, no agrarianism. . . .

THE GRANGE NOT PARTISAN. 5. We emphatically and sincerely assert the oft-repeated truth taught in our organic law that the Grange, National, State, or Subordinate, is not a political or party organization. No Grange, if true to its obligations, can discuss political or religious questions, nor call political conventions, nor nominate candidates, nor even discuss their merits in its meetings. . . .

We desire a proper equality, equity, and fairness; protection for the weak, restraint upon the strong; in short, justly distributed burdens and justly distributed power. These are American ideas, the very essence of American independence. . . .[13]

---

[13] J. R. Commons, *Documentary History of American Industrial Society,* X, 100–104.

§7. *People's Party Platform, adopted in national convention at Omaha, Nebraska, on July 4, 1892.*

The conditions which surround us best justify our coöperation: we meet in the midst of a nation brought to the verge of moral, political, and material ruin. Corruption dominates the ballot-box, the legislature, the Congress, and touches even the ermine of the bench. The people are demoralized; most of the States have been compelled to isolate the voters at the polling-places to prevent universal intimidation or bribery. The newspapers are largely subsidized or muzzled; public opinion silenced; business prostrated; our homes covered with mortgages; labor impoverished; and the land concentrating in the hands of the capitalists. The urban workmen are denied the right of organization for self-protection; imported pauperized labor beats down their wages; a hireling standing army, unrecognized by our laws, is established to shoot them down, and they are rapidly degenerating into European conditions. The fruits of the toil of millions are boldly stolen to build up colossal fortunes for a few, unprecedented in the history of mankind; and the possessors of these, in turn, despise the republic and endanger liberty. From the same prolific womb of governmental injustice we breed the two great classes of tramps and millionaires.

The national power to create money is appropriated to enrich bondholders; a vast public debt, payable in legal tender currency, has been funded into gold-bearing bonds, thereby adding millions to the burdens of the people. Silver, which has been accepted as coin since the dawn of history, has been demonetized to add to the purchasing power of gold by decreasing the value of all forms of property as well as human labor; and the supply of currency is purposely abridged to fatten usurers, bankrupt enterprise, and enslave industry. A vast conspiracy against mankind has been organized on two continents, and it is rapidly taking possession of the world. If not met and overthrown at once, it forebodes terrible social convulsions, the destruction of civilization, or the establishment of an absolute despotism.

We have witnessed for more than a quarter of a century the struggles of the two great political parties for power and plunder, which grievous wrongs have been inflicted upon the suffering people. We charge that the controlling influences dominating both these parties have permitted the existing dreadful condition to develop without serious effort to prevent or restrain them. Neither do they now promise us any substantial reform. They have agreed together to ignore in the campaign every issue but one. They propose to drown the outcries of a plundered people with the uproar of a sham battle over the tariff, so that capitalists, corporations, national banks, rings, trusts, watered stock, the demonetization of silver, and the oppressions of the usurers may all be lost sight of. They propose to sacrifice our homes, lives, and children on the altar of mammon; to destroy the multitude in order to secure corruption funds from the millionaires. . . .

We pledge ourselves, if given power, we will labor to correct these evils by wise and reasonable legislation, in accordance with the terms of our platform. We believe that the powers of government—in other words, of the people—should be expanded (as in the case of the postal service) as rapidly and as far as the good sense of an intelligent people and the teachings of experience shall justify, to the end that oppression, injustice, and poverty shall eventually cease in the land. . . .

We declare, therefore,—

First. That the union of the labor forces in the United States this day consummated shall be permanent and perpetual; may its spirit enter all hearts for the salvation of the republic and the uplifting of mankind!

Second. Wealth belongs to him that creates it, and every dollar taken from industry without an equivalent is robbery. " If any will not work, neither shall he eat." The interests of rural and civic labor are the same; their enemies are identical.

Third. We believe that the time has come when the railroad corporations will either own the people or the people must own the railroads; and, should the government enter upon the work of owning and managing all railroads, we should favor an amendment to the Constitution by which all persons engaged in the government service shall be placed under a civil service regulation of the most rigid character, so as to prevent the increase of the power of the national administration by the use of such additional government employees. . . .[14]

---

[14] *The Populist Compendium,* Auburn, Indiana, 1894, 76–79. Pamphlet in Library of Congress.

CHAPTER FOUR

The Progressive Movement

AMERICAN workers and farmers felt the impact of national economic change almost immediately after the War Between the States, but many years passed before the people as a whole became conscious of the need for reform. The structure of business enterprise after 1865 developed in sharp contrast with the simple, individualistic ways that had prevailed in earlier days. Far-reaching adjustments had to be made for protection of the general public.

The labor and radical movements described in previous chapters were largely the results of changes affecting wages, hours, job security, and general conditions faced by workers in a corporate, machine age. The agrarian upheaval was primarily a reaction from changes affecting world markets, farm prices, credit, and farm purchasing power. Before 1890 there was no movement stirring the people in response to the broader changes which affected Americans generally as consumers and citizens. Until then few realized that the fundamental pattern of society was being swiftly transformed—that the best interests of the nation demanded quick and effective reform of thinking, policy, and action.

The Nature of Progressivism and Its Supporting Forces

The progressive movement, which began in the 1890's and lasted until America's entry into World War I, was largely a culmination of the reform stirrings already described. It was at the same time a continuation of forces that developed early in the nation's history. Progressivism contained the traditional frontier advocacy of popular rights and equality.[1] It was closely associated with the persistent humanitarian spirit in America.[2] But it differed from all earlier " purifying " efforts, in that they were confined to local or particular abuses, such as the high tariff or the " spoils system " in politics. The progressive movement, on the other hand, was " remorselessly inquisitive and unscrupulously thorough " in its campaign for reform.[3] It questioned the whole economic, social, and political system of the United States and moved to repair it from the roots up.

This powerful effort, which produced sweeping changes of attitudes and relationships in business and politics, was supported by the great majority of the people. Yet there was never a united feeling in support of any integrated program. Here was a social reform movement with no set leadership, no single platform, no disciplined organization, and no planned means of action. In spite of this contrast with the efforts of well-organized interest groups previously considered, the progressive movement accomplished more than all the others put together. It succeeded because it did not seek advantage for any one class or group. It represented a national spirit and aimed toward making a wholesome adjustment for all.

Although many elements, including the organized workers and farmers, joined in this " ground swell " of reform, the crucial support came from the urban middle class. This ever-changing, shapeless element in American society is hard to define. Nevertheless, it holds the balance of power in this democracy. By combining with any one of the three other major economic groups—labor, farmer, or capitalist—the urban middle class can defeat the opposition.

Who belongs to the middle class? The term has many different meanings to many different people, and is used in this study only for want of a better expression. As related to the

---

[1] Harold U. Faulkner, *Quest for Social Justice,* xvi. New York: The Macmillan Company, 1931.

[2] Herbert Croly, *Progressive Democracy,* New York, 1914, 1. This book, by one of the leading ideological developers, contains the spirit of a contemporary in the progressive movement.

[3] *Ibid.,* 8–9.

reform movements here discussed, the middle class consists of small businessmen, low-salaried executives and clerks, and those wage-earners who do not consider themselves in a class sense as Labor. In addition, there are the professional groups—lawyers, physicians, teachers, engineers, artists, writers, and entertainers— most of whom call themselves middle class. The growing body of citizens past employment age is also included. Finally, there are the civil and military members of national, state, and local governments, numbering several millions.

Although in the last analysis the term refers to a state of mind or attitude, rather than a specific economic status, the urban middle class generally excludes organized labor and farmers; the very poor and the very rich, regardless of occupation, are likewise excluded. The complex remainder, living in thousands of American cities, both large and small, provided the main force behind " progressive " reforms.

Rise and Course of the Progressive Movement

Reaction against economic and political dominance by Big Business was the immediate background of the progressive movement. For several decades after the close of the War Between the States, Americans still believed that their nation was essentially one of small enterprise and free competition. Toward the close of the century the truth suddenly appeared to them; realization that their mental picture of the country was no longer accurate came as an unpleasant shock. The people were frightened to discover huge industrial monsters, which had mushroomed to maturity before being recognized. In 1901 the United States Steel Corporation appeared as the nation's first billion dollar concern. In 1904 John Moody showed what had been going on by listing 318 industrial trusts, representing the merger of some 5300 independent plants and a combined capitalization of over $7,000,000,000.[4]

Americans soon learned that the trusts, or monopolistic business combinations, not only fixed prices but also controlled

---

[4] Faulkner, *op. cit.*, 28, quoting John Moody, *The Truth about the Trusts,* New York, 1904, 486.

the government. The influence of money in politics was pointed out to an astounded public by hundreds of enterprising journalists. Flagrant graft and corruption, especially in state and local affairs, were exposed. Legislatures in several states were revealed as practically at the command of railroad or industrial interests. Supple politicians gave franchises, land grants, and favors for a price. Even the courts yielded to pressure. All this led to indignant demands for more direct popular control over office-holders. The disillusionment was sorrowful and sobering. " To many thoughtful men in the opening years of the twentieth century it seemed that America in making her fortune was in peril of losing her soul." [5]

Faced with the task of putting their national house in order, aroused citizens demanded action. But they hardly knew where to start or what methods to use. Unable to grasp the whole problem at once, the people could not develop a broad, unified program; so they had to wait for specific proposals to appear. Reformers in various fields came forward, pointed out certain evils, and asked support for remedial action. The course of the progressive movement followed closely the plans and fortunes of these public leaders.

Robert M. La Follette of Wisconsin was one of the pioneers of true progressivism. He was one of the first men to discover what was going on in America toward the close of the nineteenth century, and he realized the difficult, technical problems involved in business and political reform. La Follette first gained national attention in the 1890's when he left Congress and became deeply interested in the affairs of his own state. In Wisconsin he fought against control of the Republican party " machine " by the railroad interests, and aroused the voters to break that form of minority domination. After persistent and bitter campaigning, La Follette, as an " insurgent " Republican, was elected Governor in 1900. During six years of power in Wisconsin, he installed the principal progressive political reforms, which aimed to sever the union between corporations and " bosses." Provision for direct party primary elections and prevention of corrupt practices

---

[5] Faulkner, *op. cit.*, xv–xviii.

helped to bring government " back to the people " in La Follette's state. Wisconsin became a model and a pioneer in the far-reaching reform upheaval.

La Follette plunged into national affairs after entering the United States Senate in 1906. Since effective business reforms had to be national in scope, he came to believe that the federal government must be the principal instrument of action. During the early years of his term in the Senate he fought practically alone against the railroads and corporate trusts, but after 1909 La Follette was joined by a growing number of " insurgent " dissenters from the " Old Guard " Republican leadership.

While La Follette studied and pondered the intricate problems of reform, another man took the progressive spotlight after 1900. That man was Theodore Roosevelt. He was looked upon by La Follette and many other contemporary reformers as a pseudo-progressive.[6] Roosevelt had a strong feeling for reform, but he did not fully comprehend the technical nature of the problem. To him reform was mainly a moral problem: If evil men and practices could be rooted out of the corporate system, all would be well. In fact, that was the general popular attitude during the early reform period, and Roosevelt, as a keen politician, reflected it. Later, he became more critical of the basic elements of *laissez-faire* economics and favored greater intervention by government. His chief limitation, from the point of view of effective reform, was his lack of a carefully worked out, constructive program.

When Roosevelt succeeded to the Presidency in 1901, upon the death of William McKinley, he was expected to press quickly for reform measures. During his first term, however, the " trust-buster " proceeded cautiously in order to win the confidence of the Republican party organization and to establish himself firmly in the public eye. He succeeded very well in both respects and, at the same time, prevailed upon Congress to enact some limited reforms. Roosevelt's decisive election in 1904 over the Democrat, Alton B. Parker of New York, placed him in a powerful position of leadership, supported by overwhelming Republican

---

[6] Robert M. La Follette, *Autobiography*, 672–674. Madison, Wisconsin: *La Follette's Magazine*, 1913.

majorities in both houses of Congress. Yet in spite of strong pronouncements in favor of sweeping changes and against the vested interests, his reform achievements were not great. Although he brought about some desired changes, especially in the field of conservation of resources, Roosevelt worked intimately with the " stand-pat " party leaders in Congress. This seeming paradox may have reflected a recognition by Roosevelt that more drastic reforms were not politically feasible at the time. It should be remembered that fate thrust him into office during the high tide of conservative power; by exerting his leadership Roosevelt achieved moderate reforms, but a more extreme policy would doubtless have resulted in a stalemate with Congress.

Although Roosevelt was not a thorough-going progressive in the eyes of some of his contemporaries, he personified progressivism in the eyes of the common man. His intuitive dramatic sense doubtless accounted for this fact. From 1901 to 1913 the whole movement seemed to revolve around him. He said the things that millions were wanting to hear, and he said them with a vigor and conviction that were stimulating. Perhaps because he was not too far beyond the feeling and thinking of the majority, Roosevelt was the most effective individual in awakening public consciousness and crystallizing the demand for further reform.

When Roosevelt stepped out of the White House in 1909 and turned the office over to William H. Taft, there was a lull in reform progress. Taft, a conservative in thought and temperament, failed to supply leadership or enthusiasm for the adjustments which had to be made in national life. His administration enforced the laws against monopoly with greater energy than either Roosevelt's or Wilson's,[7] but Taft lacked the driving leadership necessary to compel broader legislation from Congress. Although sociable and fond of the public, he was neither inspiring nor dramatic. Even if he had felt a zeal for reform he would have had difficulty in producing it.

During Taft's term of office the progressives were developing

---

[7] Louis M. Hacker and Benjamin B. Kendrick, *The United States Since 1865*, 400–401, 469–470. New York: F. S. Crofts & Co., 1939. This work is the main source used for the succession of events in the progressive period.

strength in Congress. Their efforts were not to show major success until later, but much of the drive was generated between 1909 and 1913. La Follette had been staging a lone fight against the Senate conservatives from 1906 until 1909, but in the latter year several of his Republican colleagues turned insurgent with him. That was the year of the great fight on the Payne-Aldrich tariff. The attempt to push through a high duty measure, with the back-stage help of special interests, was held up in the Senate. A determined band of insurgent Republicans, in combination with the Democrats, strove to prevent the evil of excessive tariff rates. In the end the " Old Guard " won out, but the issue served to complete the breach between the conservative and the progressive Republicans.

Leading the fight against the Payne-Aldrich Bill was Albert J. Beveridge of Indiana. He was one of a group of mid-western Republican Senators that formed the nucleus of the progressive movement in Congress. Representing farmers of the Mississippi Valley region, this group had a particular interest in opposing high duties on manufactured goods. It was natural that the tariff issue should become the immediate cause of their revolt. Beveridge, whose rise to power resembled an Horatio Alger story, was alert, energetic, and a great orator. Joseph L. Bristow of Kansas joined the Senate with Beveridge and fought at his side on progressive measures. Although a poor speaker and ungainly in appearance, Bristow was a defiant, courageous antagonist. His uncompromising character was balanced by that of Moses E. Clapp of Minnesota; this tall, quiet Senator was the conciliator and peacemaker for the insurgents. The oldest of the group was Albert B. Cummins of Iowa. He was well known for his persuasive powers. Jonathan P. Dolliver, also of Iowa, had all-around charm and power. Dolliver rebelled against the " Old Guard " mainly on the question of railroad regulation. Another outstanding progressive in the Senate—a youthful, studious individualist—was William E. Borah of Idaho.

This able group fought only a delaying action against the majority conservatives in the Senate. But it soon appeared that the insurgent movement within the Republican ranks was gaining strength in many sections of the country. In the Congressional elections of 1910, insurgent Republicans gained control of their party in Wisconsin, Michigan, Indiana, and nearly every state west of the Mississippi. In the same year, reaction against the conservative Republican leadership was further shown by Democratic gains in the North and Middle-west. The Democrats elected several new governors and won control of the House of Representatives.

The return of Theodore Roosevelt from his African and European adventures rekindled the progressive fires. In his absence there had been no real focus for the movement. For a while the former President held aloof from politics, but he soon became restless. On August 31, 1910, Roosevelt indicated that he was still very much alive and interested in the issues of the day. At Osawatomie, Kansas, he issued his creed of the " New Nationalism," which attacked large aggregations of capital and called for extensive reforms. In January of the next year the insurgent Republicans, hoping to capture the national party organization in 1912, formed the National Progressive Republican League. Roosevelt, after being " urged " by many political leaders to seek the Republican nomination for the presidency, accepted the endorsement of the Progressive Republican League on February 24, 1912.

The majority of the Republican rank and file doubtless favored Roosevelt and progressivism, as was shown in the November election. The conservative Republicans, however, with Taft as their candidate, controlled a majority of the delegates to the National Convention, which met on June 20, 1912. Contesting delegations supporting Roosevelt were refused seats by the convention bosses. A conservative platform was adopted, and Taft was renominated on the first ballot.

In angry disappointment the progressive Republicans stamped away from the convention and determined to " take a walk " as a body. They met on August 5th to form an independent Progressive party, and in a wildly cheering session nominated Theodore Roosevelt by acclamation. Hiram Johnson of California was put up for the vice presidency, and a broad reform platform endorsed. The failure of the Republican conservatives to permit democratic procedures in their convention had forced a crack-up of the party organization and led to victory for the Democrats. At the same time the bolt of the insurgents gave unchallenged control of the national Republican organization to the Old Guard—a control which remained unbroken for more than a generation.

Meeting on June 25th, the Democratic convention adopted a liberal platform, similar to that later written by the Progressives. Woodrow Wilson, a successful reformer from New Jersey, was chosen the nominee for President. Party workers, exuberant over the Republican breach, went into the campaign confident of winning.

In the November contest Wilson won because of the split between Roosevelt and Taft. He received some 6,290,000 votes, less than Bryan's total in 1896, but it was enough to defeat either of his opponents. Roosevelt received 4,120,000, and Taft 3,480,000. In the electoral vote Wilson dominated, with 435 against 88 for Roosevelt. The Democrats also won full control of both houses of Congress.

After 1912 the progressive movement followed mainly the course of Woodrow Wilson and his party. The Progressive party rapidly declined. In the Congressional elections of 1914, Progressive candidates received less than half the vote cast for Roosevelt in 1912. With Roosevelt himself growing cool toward the new party, it was plain that it had no chance of success against the two major political organizations.

Wilson, in carrying on the program of progressive reform, lacked a comprehensive, detailed plan. He had the reformist feeling and a marvelous ability to frame his notions in grand language. But he was a better orator than practical planner. In this respect Wilson was not different from his contemporaries. Americans have yet to provide definitive answers to the riddles of modern social living.

So far as answers were known, Woodrow Wilson worked vigorously to apply them. As Governor of New Jersey he had championed regulation of the trusts, measures against corrupt practices, and other generally accepted progressive reforms. He carried into the White House a determination to carry on the same program in national affairs. Wilson achieved the principal progressive aims before the country's zeal for reform gave out. America's entry into the World War in 1917 choked progressivism for sixteen years.

Progressive Aims and Purposes

The major objectives of the progressive movement have been suggested in the survey of its general course. Leaders from La Follette to Wilson emphasized the need for a new approach to national problems and the exercise of greater intelligence, devotion, and honesty. They demanded of business a larger sense of responsibility toward workers and the general welfare. The progressive movement was described as a kind of " newer individualism," or a " higher conservatism," that aimed to preserve the individual through governmental regulation of those who abused power.[8] Wilson described his version of it as the " New Freedom." It was a kind of mean between *laissez-faire* and socialism—a program for modified business competition, with government lending a helping hand to the under-privileged. Progressives wanted to supplant the conservative slogan of " Live and let live " with " Live and *help* live." [9]

Specific aims of the movement can be found in the programs of particular reformers. Since there was never a national organization or platform embracing all of the progressive effort, it is necessary to look in many places to find the whole sweep of objectives. No group of progressives, furthermore, would have supported all the aims of all the others.

Theodore Roosevelt summed up the earlier reformist demands in certain of his messages to Congress. On December 3, 1901, he called for extension of the regulatory powers of the Interstate Commerce Commission, more control over trusts and corporations, conservation of national resources, reciprocal tariffs, and extension of the civil service. These generalities were supplemented in 1907 by suggestions that Congress license all interstate enterprises, outlaw interstate holding companies, and protect the investing public.

[8] Edward R. Lewis, *A History of American Political Thought,* 364–367. New York: The Macmillan Company, 1937.
[9] Croly, *Progressive Democracy,* 426–427.

The National Progressive Republican League, formed on January 21, 1911, set forth the principal aims of the movement as they stood at that time; their Declaration of Principles supported most of the economic controls proposed earlier by Roosevelt. The League wanted greater control over railroad rates and service, further laws regulating business combinations, conservation of all resources, revision of the tariff in the interest of consumers, and reconstruction of banking and monetary legislation. In the political field the League demanded direct election of United States Senators, direct party primary elections, corrupt practices acts, and the initiative, referendum, and recall.

When the Progressive party was established in 1912, with Roosevelt as its nominee, progressive aims in the platform were mingled with purely political appeals to all voters. The Bull Moose party called for a sounder basis in railroad rate regulation, rigorous supervision of corporations, conservation of resources, and all means of direct popular legislation. In addition, it appealed to organized labor with a plank for anti-injunction laws. It went years beyond its time in demanding women's suffrage, social welfare laws for the protection of women and children, and social insurance against sickness, unemployment, and old age.

Woodrow Wilson, who defeated the Progressive party, carried many of its objectives into power. He did not, however, accept the emerging philosophy of the Progressives. Theodore Roosevelt's " New Nationalism " of 1912 outlined a complete reorganization of the economic and political system, with a substitution of social policy for individualism as the guiding force in national life. Wilson's " New Freedom," on the other hand, accepted the system of *laissez-faire* as essentially sound. He wanted free enterprisers to remain the dominant force. Government was to act not as a positive, primary force, but only as a check against abuses in private business. Wilson was confident that if monopolistic and unfair practices were prohibited by government, free enterprise would flourish and give well-being to all. Summing up this attitude, which reflected the viewpoint of middle-class businessmen, Wilson stated:

Business we have got to untrammel, abolishing . . . all forms of unjust handicaps against the little man. . . . We have got to set the energy and the initiative of this great people absolutely free. . . .[10]

He believed that if initiative were so freed, economic individualism would "run itself" and answer adequately the needs of modern society. This pre-war Democratic doctrine was later echoed by leading Republicans, notably Herbert Hoover,[11] while his successor, Democratic President Franklin D. Roosevelt, abandoned it for the philosophy of governmental responsibility for social welfare.

Specifically, Wilson aimed toward downward revision of the tariff, more effective anti-trust legislation, and banking and currency reform. With these major objectives in view, he put vigorous pressure on Congress to translate them into fact.

Since fundamental economic adjustment had to be made on a national basis, progressive leaders of the states emphasized objectives of a different nature. Congress alone could act against nation-wide corporate business interests. The states, as the principal political subdivisions of the country, could move against corrupt control of government. In many states the progressives endeavored to return political control to the people. Their aims included laws against lobbying, stricter supervision of the granting of franchises, creation of regulatory public utility commissions, direct party primaries, extension of civil service for state employees, and the initiative, referendum, and recall. Many of the large cities, where political fraud was at its worst, became centers of progressive agitation. Reformers demanded more independence of cities from legislatures, training schools for firemen and policemen, city planning, and public ownership of utilities.

Techniques of Action

Legislation was the principal method used to achieve reform objectives. Leaders favoring certain proposals sought public

---

[10] Wilson, *op. cit.*, 292.

[11] See, for example, *The Challenge to Liberty*, New York: Charles Scribner's Sons, 1934.

support and, if elected, tried to write such proposals into law. Political parties were often won over and their organizations used as implements for progressive ideas. The necessary popular backing, however, was developed largely by the writings of reformist philosophers and journalists. Literary propaganda was an instrument of first importance in the achievement of goals.

Much of what was written in the period would have fallen upon deaf ears had it not been for earlier and contemporary radical writings. Although the socialist movement failed to gain any large voting support, its press had considerable influence. Americans, while not generally convinced by socialist doctrine, were awakened to facts and evils that they otherwise would not have known. In 1887 Edward Bellamy's *Looking Backward,* showing an attractive picture of a socialist commonwealth, was published; its wide popular acceptance was indicated in the sale of over 500,000 copies. Henry D. Lloyd's *Wealth against Commonwealth,* published in 1894, was significant primarily for its effect on other writers and thinkers of the progressive generation. Many of the social philosophers and journalists of the period, as well as the political reformers, were influenced by this book. Lloyd, through his writings and speeches, helped to spread non-Marxian socialist ideas among workers, farmers, and the middle class. These ideas, compounded with traditional humanitarianism and the anti-monopoly sentiments represented by populism, formed the basic ingredients of progressive doctrine.[12]

With Americans feeling uneasy about the soundness of their institutions, progressive writers found ready response to their criticisms and proposals. A number of outstanding social thinkers, signaling the start of long careers, made their names during this period. Herbert Croly, Walter Lippmann, Ben Lindsey, Jane Addams, Louis Brandeis, and Felix Frankfurter were some of the youthful pioneers in progressive literary efforts.

Another company of writers, however, proved more effective in reaching the masses. Journalists for enterprising popular magazines soon discovered the fact that stories of fraud and corruption

[12] Chester McA. Destler, *American Radicalism, 1865–1901: Essays and Documents,* 160. New London: Connecticut College for Women, 1946.

made attractive reading for the public. Some of these authors became genuinely interested in reform, and others contributed to the "literature of exposure" just because it was profitable journalism. In either case the people were given strong doses of reform propaganda. Magazine writers became so productive of these stories of business and political scandal that President Theodore Roosevelt in 1907 reprimanded them as "muckrakers."

One of the high-grade journalists of this era was Ida M. Tarbell, who told an amazed America about the Standard Oil giant. Another outstanding writer was Lincoln Steffens, who specialized in exposing city corruption and later became a radical. David Graham Phillips exposed the business connections of many august Senators. Thomas W. Lawson described the vagaries of "high finance," and Samuel H. Adams opened up the field of fraud in medical practice and advertising.

Principal Achievements in National Affairs

The progressive movement stands above all previous reform efforts from the point of view of accomplishments. It has already been pointed out that this is true because progressivism was a general movement, supported by the overwhelming majority of the people. Admittedly many of the reforms achieved did not end abuses or bring the results expected. They certainly did not solve the social problems of America for all time, but that would be too much to expect. However, the reformers were able to put into effect most of the known remedies for what they were worth. In this respect the movement may be viewed as one of the most successful models in the history of social reform.

Progressive action occurred on many fronts, and it is difficult to summarize the principal achievements. Results in national, state, and city affairs were all part of a single effort in spirit, but they came out of separate situations. Since the most vital successes were gained in the national field, these will be reviewed first.

The primary purpose of the reformers in Congress was to overhaul certain features of the economic system. Effective railroad regulation was a leading objective, and steady accomplishments were made in that direction. In response to President Theodore Roosevelt's request for extension of the powers of the Interstate Commerce Commission, Congress passed the Elkins Act of February 19, 1903. This defined more clearly what constituted discrimination toward shippers and stipulated the penalties. Rebates by railroads to favored customers were specifically barred. On June 29, 1906, the authority of the Interstate Commerce Commission, by approval of the Hepburn Act, was again enlarged to include rate-fixing for interstate pipe lines and express companies. The Mann-Elkins Act of June 18, 1910, brought telegraphs, telephones, wireless, and cables under regulation. Finally, on March 1, 1913, the important Physical Valuation Act was signed by President Taft as one of his last official deeds. This law permitted the Interstate Commerce Commission to study and set the valuation on railroad properties, so that rates could be fixed on the principle of producing a fair return on investment. Objective valuation was the indispensable basis for scientific rate-making.

Much of the progressive effort was directed against business monopoly and combination. The foundation stone of this action was the Sherman Anti-trust Act, signed on July 2, 1890. It made illegal every contract, combination, or conspiracy in restraint of interstate commerce. It also prohibited monopoly of any part of interstate trade and imposed fines and imprisonment for violations. This law was Roosevelt's club in his "trust-busting" adventures. During his administrations the Department of Justice brought a number of actions against the outstanding business combinations; the oil, tobacco, and beef trusts were attacked in prolonged litigation. President Taft continued the most rigid execution of the Sherman Act. The number of proceedings during his administration was about double that under Roosevelt, and the principal targets were United States Steel, American Sugar, International Harvester, General Electric, and National Cash Register companies. Several dissolutions were forced, but in most of these cases the same powerful interests managed to maintain their control in some other way. Furthermore, the effectiveness of the Sherman Act was largely nullified by a Supreme Court decision on May 15,

1911.[13]   In ordering the dissolution of the Standard Oil Company of New Jersey, Chief Justice White declared in the majority opinion that the prohibition of restraint of trade referred only to " unreasonable " restraint.   Up until that time the majority of the Court had held that *any* proven conspiracy in interstate commerce, unreasonable or otherwise, was illegal.   This new principle made interpretation of the Sherman Act so elastic that enforcement efforts became almost futile.   Effective action against monopolistic practices called for remedial legislation of a specific, concrete nature.

In spite of the obvious inadequacy of the Sherman Act, it was a long time before the needed action was taken by Congress. During the Roosevelt and Taft administrations, every move to strengthen anti-trust legislation was smothered in the conservative Senate.   But Wilson was able to do better.   After 1912, his Democrats were in control of both houses and they knew that their continuance in power depended upon their ability to produce results.   After careful consideration by Congress, an amendment of the Sherman law, called the Clayton Anti-trust Act, was signed by the President on October 15, 1914.   It appeared to be an effective, constructive measure and specified the specific business practices which were to be outlawed if tending toward monopoly.   These included price discriminations and exclusive selling contracts.   Large corporations were prohibited from reducing competition through inter-company stock ownership or interlocking directorates.

In addition to anti-trust legislation, the progressives established other approaches to the problem of business regulation.   On February 14, 1903, a federal Department of Commerce and Labor was created by Congress.   The Bureau of Corporations, part of the new department, investigated large industrial combinations.   On September 26, 1914, President Wilson signed the Federal Trade Commission Act, which became an integral part of the system of business regulation.   It abolished the old Bureau of Corporations and set up an independent bi-partisan commission of five, appointed by the President and Senate.   This

---

[13] United States *vs.* Standard Oil Co. of N. J., 221 U. S. 1.

body was empowered to examine commercial practices and to require reports from private firms. It could hold hearings and investigations into alleged violations of the anti-trust laws. The Federal Trade Commission could issue "cease and desist" orders to corporations found guilty of illegal practices; such orders were subject to appeal to the federal circuit courts on questions of interpretation of the laws.

Conservation of natural resources remaining in government control was one of the most solid achievements of the progressive movement. The problem of preventing waste of basic materials arose after the Homestead Act opened the public lands to general entry in May, 1862. Timber, oil, coal, and natural gas in vast areas were rapidly exhausted. In 1891 Congress authorized the President to withhold timber lands, but Grover Cleveland was the only Chief Executive before 1900 who made large use of that power. Other preliminary steps were taken by creation of the Forestry Bureau in the Department of Agriculture and the Geological Survey in the Department of Interior. These agencies began to make an inventory of national resources.

Theodore Roosevelt was an enthusiastic conservationist, and his accomplishments in this field were probably his main contribution to the nation's welfare. Under his prodding, Congress passed the Newlands Act of June 17, 1902. This measure authorized the government to build irrigation projects on federal lands. In the years that followed, Congress brought millions of arid acres under cultivation. Roosevelt, through his Secretary of the Interior, closed from public entry approximately 148,000,000 acres of forest lands, 80,000,000 acres of coal lands, 5,000,000 acres of phosphate lands, and 1,500,000 acres of waterpower sites. He did this by executive order, with no legislative authorization.[14] Roosevelt further stimulated conservation on private, state, and federal lands by important White House conferences on the problem, and he appointed a National Conservation Commission to enlighten the public.

Tariff revision was a continuous objective of the reformers, but results came slowly. Vested interests, profiting from the high

---

[14] Hacker, *op. cit.*, 411.

" protective " rates of the Dingley tariff of 1897, fought with all their economic and political power against reduction in duties. When a new tariff had to be drawn up in 1909, conflict broke into the open between these interests, which were represented by the " Old Guard " Republicans in Congress, and the " insurgent " or " progressive " legislators. In the end the protectionists triumphed with the passage of the Payne-Aldrich measure. Some rates were lowered on items where American producers had no real competition, but the principle of high duties was maintained.

One of Wilson's chief pledges was the lowering of the tariff. With the conservatives removed from control of Congress in 1913, he urged speedy legislation to answer the will of the people. His first important achievement and one of the outstanding gains of the progressives was the passage of the Underwood tariff on October 3, 1913. It brought hundreds of reductions of specific rates and placed wool and sugar on the free list. The average duty rate of thirty-five per cent in the Payne-Aldrich Act was lowered to about twenty-five per cent. This new law marked a definite break from the principle of high protection. It aimed at moderate duties which would favor American producers without cutting off foreign competition altogether. An income tax was incorporated in the law as a supplementary revenue measure; this long-standing progressive demand was realized after the Sixteenth Amendment, declared in force on February 25, 1913, made it legally possible.

Another vital progressive aim became law under Wilson. For years, farmers, as well as businessmen, had complained about the banking and monetary situation. The system of currency issue by the national banks did not provide sufficient flexibility to meet the fluctuations of commerce. Reserves were too widely scattered to support banks when special demands for currency arose. It was further charged that a great " money trust " dominated finance and business in the country.

Following extensive Congressional investigation, the President called for monetary legislation which would provide for a more elastic currency, mobilization of bank reserves, and decentralized public control of the banking system. After careful consideration

Congress replied with the Federal Reserve Act of December 23, 1913. It satisfied Wilson's request for greater elasticity of the currency by provision for federal reserve notes, issued on the security of commercial or agricultural paper. It provided for mobilization of reserves by establishing twelve regional bankers' banks, which served as currency reservoirs. This regional system offered decentralization instead of domination by a single bank. Unified public control was effected through a co-ordinating Federal Reserve Board, chosen by the President and Senate.

Farmers received some help from the Act through its general and special provisions. Adequate provisions for long-term farm financing, however, came three years later. On July 17, 1916, Wilson signed the Federal Farm Loan Act. It established a structure similar to the Federal Reserve System, but specifically for the purpose of placing farm finance on a sound basis. Twelve regional Federal Land Banks were created. They were empowered to make easy loans to farmers over long periods and to raise money for such purposes by selling their own bonds.

A truly great first step in the direction of consumer protection was also won by the reformers. After exposures were made of the unsanitary conditions in the meat industry, the Meat Inspection Act was passed on June 30, 1906. This act provided for official examination of all meat carried in interstate commerce. On the same day another pioneer law was approved—the Pure Food and Drugs Act, designed to check distribution of injurious commodities.

The major concern of the progressive thinkers in the field of national legislation was over economic matters. Some important moves were also made to purify politics. In 1907, for example, a law was passed by Congress prohibiting campaign contributions by industrial corporations in national elections. After a long fight, progressives in the House of Representatives succeeded in stripping the Speaker of his autocratic powers. And, in line with the effort to " give the government back to the people," Congress proposed a Constitutional amendment for the direct election of Senators. On May 31, 1913, the Seventeenth Amendment was declared in force.

State and Municipal Reforms

Although effective attack upon major economic problems had to be made by the national government, many states pioneered in the field of workers' protective legislation. One of the outstanding accomplishments of the progressives was the passage of workmen's accident compensation laws. Such laws were common long before in most European countries, but it required some time before Americans realized that changed factory conditions demanded them here. Maryland passed the first law in 1902, but New York provided the first one having broad application in 1910. By 1920 all the states and territories except five had protective legislation of this kind.

Woman and child workers were guarded in several states. During the progressive period a series of state laws was enacted which established maximum work-hours for both women and children. Compulsory school laws were strengthened. An attempt by Massachusetts in 1912 to establish minimum wages for women was later declared unconstitutional by the Supreme Court.

Maximum hours for men in certain types of occupations were fixed by law in a number of states. This important health legislation had no connection with the limitation of working hours for men as a whole. It was still generally felt that male laborers in regular employments needed no such protection. Even these restricted laws were at first nullified by the courts, but in 1917 the Supreme Court clearly approved the constitutionality of limited protective legislation as a valid exercise of state " police power." [15]

Beginnings were made in the broad field of social security. After 1911, Missouri and Illinois led the way by providing financial grants to needy mothers with dependent children. This was a break from the traditional almshouse system. In the years that followed, nearly all states passed laws of this type. The first old age pension was enacted in Arizona in 1914. It was at first declared unconstitutional, but persistent attempts

---

[15] Bunting *vs.* Oregon, 243 U. S. 426.

followed and many states succeeded in establishing sound plans, which were approved in judicial tests.

The principal progressive achievements in the states were in the political field. It has already been noted that Governor La Follette of Wisconsin brought most of the significant reforms to his state in the early 1900's; provision for direct primaries there was quickly followed by similar action in most other states. These laws usually were accompanied by corrupt practices acts. A number of states followed Wisconsin's lead in adopting presidential preference primaries for the instruction of party delegates to national nominating conventions. Farther west, Wisconsin's achievement was rivaled by that of Oregon. As early as 1891 Oregon adopted the secret Australian ballot and in 1899 enacted a voters' registration law. It established the initiative and referendum procedures in 1902, and many states soon followed this example.

To most Americans at the turn of the century, the large cities seemed the main centers of political corruption. "Muckrakers" like Lincoln Steffens exposed to millions of readers the graft and fraud in the nation's cities. Crusading local reformers campaigned to "turn the rascals out" and bring good government by electing good men to public office. The problem, however, was far more difficult than the reformers or the people knew. It was a problem that could not be solved once and for all.

The progressives did what they could to improve the situation. In 1894 the National Municipal League was formed as a means of organized attack on corruption in city government. It studied conditions, produced model charters, and outlined a complete program of reform objectives. In many of the leading cities, research bureaus were established, and a scientific approach to the problem was instituted when colleges and universities began to offer courses in municipal government and public administration.

There were many examples of personal achievements in municipal reform, but most of these were transitory. One of the most colorful figures was Samuel "Golden Rule" Jones. A smiling, pleasant gentleman, Jones was a successful manufacturer who conducted operations on the " Golden Rule " basis. Following his humanitarian ambitions, he ran for the office of Mayor of Toledo and was elected in 1897. During three terms as an Independent, Jones introduced many reforms. Because of his abhorrence of force and coercion, he took clubs away from Toledo patrolmen. He established an eight-hour day for municipal employees, introduced free kindergartens, public playgrounds, and free concerts.

Tom L. Johnson of the nearby city of Cleveland was doing many of the same things for the people. Johnson had made a fortune in manufacturing steel, and at the height of his industrial career he suddenly turned to the ideas of reform. Elected to Congress in 1890 and 1892, he found he could accomplish little there. In 1901 he was made Mayor of Cleveland and served for eight years as the best city executive of the period. His intelligence, combined with strong personal charm, helped him to gain his objectives. Johnson lowered street-railway fares and brought the lines under city control. He pioneered in city planning efforts and achieved a general clean-up of municipal affairs. Newton D. Baker, later Mayor of Cleveland, followed the pattern laid down by Tom Johnson.

Most of the reformers in city politics became disillusioned sooner or later. They discovered that when the people tired of the tension of reform the old party machines generally regained control. They found that their carefully planned devices, like the direct primary, the initiative, and the referendum, could be used by special interests. Instead of paying bribes to the old machine bosses, wealthy interest groups could spend money for propaganda to turn the voters in their favor. But it cannot be doubted that political reforms of the progressives represented some solid gains. They at least provided the means whereby an intelligent and duty-conscious electorate could control government if it wanted to. Mechanical changes alone will not insure successful democracy. That can be guaranteed only by continual vigilance of the people. The progressives gave citizens their primary tools of control. More important, they forced upon politicians a greater responsiveness to the public will.

ILLUSTRATIVE DOCUMENTS

§8. ' *Robert M. La Follette on the Growth of Monopoly in the United States.*' *Speech delivered at the Annual Banquet of the Periodical Publishers' Association, Philadelphia, February 2, 1912.*

The great issue before the American people today is the control of their own government. In the midst of political struggle, it is not easy to see the historical relations of the present Progressive movement. But it represents a conflict as old as the history of man—the fight to maintain human liberty, the rights of all the people.

A mighty power has been builded up in this country in recent years, so strong, yet so insidious and far-reaching in its influence, that men are gravely inquiring whether its iron grip on government and business can ever be broken. Again and again it has proved strong enough to nominate the candidates of both political parties. It rules in the organization of legislative bodies, state and national, and of the committees which frame legislation. Its influence is felt in cabinets and in the policies of administrations, and is clearly seen in the appointment of prosecuting officers and the selection of judges upon the Bench.

In business it has crippled or destroyed competition. It has stifled individual initiative. It has fixed limitations in the field of production. It makes prices and imposes its burdens upon the consuming public at will.

In transportation, after a prolonged struggle for government control, it is, with only slight check upon its great power, still master of the highways of commerce.

In finance its power is unlimited. In large affairs it gives or withholds credit, and from time to time contracts or inflates the volume of the money required for the transaction of the business of the country, regardless of everything excepting its own profits.

It has acquired vast areas of the public domain, and is rapidly monopolizing the natural resources—timber, iron, coal, oil.

And this THING has grown up in a country where, under the Constitution and the law, the citizen is sovereign!

The related events which led to this centralized control are essential to a clear understanding of the real danger—the magnitude of this danger now menacing the very existence of every independent concern remaining in the field of business enterprise.

The First Period—The Individual and the Partnership.—For nearly a century after Jefferson declared for a government of " equal rights for all, and special privileges for none," the business of the country was conducted by individuals and partnerships. During this first period business methods were simple, its proportions modest, and there was little call for larger capital than could be readily furnished by the individual or, in the most extreme cases, a partnership of fair size.

From the beginning, when men bartered their products in exchange, down through all the ages, the business of the world had been conducted under the natural laws of trade—demand, supply, competition. Like all natural laws, they were fair and impartial; they favored neither the producer nor the consumer. They had ruled the market and made the prices when the individual and the partnership conducted substantially all commercial enterprises during the first period of our business life.

But as the country developed, as the population poured over the Alleghenies, occupied the Mississippi Valley, pushed on to the Rocky Mountains and down the western slope to California, discovering the boundless wealth of our natural resources—the fields and forests, the mountains of iron and coal and precious metals, there was a pressing call on every hand for larger capital beyond the power of any individual or any partnership to supply. We had outgrown the simple methods; there was a demand for a new business device strong enough to unlock the treasure house of the new world.

The Second Period—The Private Corporation.—The modern corporation was invented to meet that demand, and general statutes for incorporation were soon upon the statute books of every state. Their adoption marked the beginning of the second period of our business life. It was the best machine ever invented for the purpose; simple in organization, effective in operation.

A hundred, a thousand, any number of men could associate their capital, and employing the representative principle upon which our country was based, vote for and elect a president, a general manager, a board of directors, a body of men, no larger than an ordinary partnership, and clothe them with power to conduct the business to the success of which the aggregate capital was contributed.

Men no longer stood baffled by the magnitude of any undertaking, but promptly enlisted an army of contributors, large or small, massed together the required capital and under the direction of the officers and directors of the corporation, a small executive body, seized upon these waiting opportunities, and this second period marked a material development, surpassing anything in the world's history. It was not the era of greatest individual fortune building, but it was the period of greatest general prosperity. And why?

The natural laws of trade—demand, supply and competition—still ruled the market and made the prices in the second period of our business life. The private corporation, in a large measure, supplanted the individual and the partnership in mining, manufacturing and large commercial enterprises, but each corporation competed with every other in the same line of business. Production was larger, development more rapid, but, under the free play of competition, the resulting prosperity was fairly distributed between the producer and the consumer, the seller and the buyer, because profits and prices were reasonable.

Big capital behind the private corporations drove business at a pace and upon a scale never before witnessed. Competition was at once the spur to the highest efficiency and the check against waste and abuse of power.

In this period of our industrial and commercial progress, America amazed and alarmed our business rivals of the old world. We were soon foremost among the nations of the earth in agriculture, in mines and mining, in manufactures and in commerce as well.

The American market became the greatest thing in all the material world. Its control became the one thing coveted.

The Third Period—The Combination of Corporations.—The evil hour was come upon us. Daring, unscrupulous men plotted in violation of the common law, the criminal statutes and against public right to become masters of that market and take what toll they pleased. To do this thing it was necessary to set aside, abrogate, nullify the natural laws of trade that had ruled in business for centuries. Production was to be limited, competition stifled and prices arbitrarily fixed by selfish decree. And thus we entered upon the third period of our business and commercial life—the period of a combination of the corporations under a single control in each line of business. It was not an evolution; it was a revolution.

And yet certain economists set it down in the literature of the day that the Supreme Ruler of the universe reserved in His great

plan a divinely appointed place and time for a Rockefeller, a
Morgan, a Carnegie, a Baer, to evolve this new law, which should
enable them to appropriate the wealth of the country and Mexican-
ize its business and its people.

The combination became supreme in each important line, controlling the markets for the raw material and the finished product,
largely dictating the price of everything we sell and the price of
everything we buy—beef, sugar, woolens, cottons, coal, oil, copper,
zinc, iron, steel, agricultural implements, hardware, gas, electric
light, food supplies.

Monopoly acquired dominion everywhere.

It brought with it the inevitable results of monopoly—extortionate
prices, inferior products. We soon found shoddy in everything we
wear, and adulteration in everything we eat.

Did these masters of business stop there? By no means! " Increase of appetite had grown by what it fed on." The floodgates
of fictitious capitalization were thrown wide open. These organizations of combinations overcapitalized for a double purpose. The
issue of bonds and stocks in excess of investment covered up the
exaction of their immense profits, and likewise offered an unlimited
field for promotion and speculation.

The establishment of this third period was the beginning of
rapidly advancing prices, increasing the cost of living upon people
of average earning power until the burden is greater than they can
bear.

The Fourth Period—The Combination of Combinations.—The
strife for more money, more power—more power, more money—
swept everything before it.

It remained only to bring together into a community of interest
or ownership the great combinations which controlled, each in its
own field—in short, to combine these combinations.

One needs but to study the directory of directories of the great
business concerns of the country to determine the extent to which
this combination of combinations has been successfully accomplished, thus carrying us over into the fourth period of our industrial
and commercial life—the period of complete industrial and commercial servitude in which we now unhappily find ourselves. And
this supreme control of the business of the country is the triumph
of men who have at every step defied public opinion, the common
law and criminal statutes.

This condition is intolerable. It is hostile to every principle of democracy. If maintained it is the end of democracy. We may preserve the form of our representative government and lose the soul, the spirit of our free institutions.[16]

§9. *'Platform of the Progressive Party,' adopted in national convention at Chicago, Illinois, on August 7, 1912.*

The conscience of the people in a time of grave national problems has called into being a new party, born of the nation's awakened sense of justice.

We of the Progressive Party here dedicate ourselves to the fulfillment of the duty laid upon us by our fathers to maintain that government of the people, by the people, and for the people, whose foundations they laid. . . .

This country belongs to the people who inhabit it. Its resources, its business, its institutions, and its laws should be utilized, maintained, or altered in whatever manner will best promote the general interest. It is time to set the public welfare in the first place.

Political parties exist to secure responsible government and to execute the will of the people. From these great tasks both the old parties have turned aside. Instead of instruments to promote the general welfare, they have become tools of corrupt interests which use them impartially to serve their selfish purposes. Behind the ostensible government sits enthroned an invisible government owning no allegiance and alleging no responsibility to the people. To destroy this invisible government, to dissolve the unholy alliance between corrupt business and corrupt politics, is the first task of the statesmanship of the day.

The deliberate betrayal of its trust by the Republican Party, the fatal incapacity of the Democratic Party to deal with the new issues of the new time, have compelled the people to forge a new instrument of government through which to give effect to their will in laws and institutions. Unhampered by tradition, uncorrupted by power, undismayed by the magnitude of the task, the new party offers itself as the instrument of the people to sweep away old abuses, to build a new and nobler commonwealth. . . .

The Progressive Party, committed to the principle of government by a self-controlled democracy expressing its will through repre-

---

[16] Robert M. La Follette, *Autobiography*, 762–769. Madison, Wisconsin: *La Follette's Magazine*, 1913.

sentatives of the people, pledges itself to secure such alterations in the fundamental law of the several states and of the United States as shall insure the representative character of the government. . . .

The Progressive Party, believing that a free people should have the power from time to time to amend their fundamental law so as to adapt it progressively to the changing needs of the people, pledges itself to provide a more easy and expeditious method of amending the Federal Constitution.

Up to the limit of the Constitution and later by amendment of the Constitution, if it was found necessary, we advocate bringing under effective national jurisdiction those problems which have expanded beyond reach of the individual states.

It is grotesque as it is intolerable that the several states should by unequal laws in matter of common concern become competing commercial agencies, barter the lives of their children, the health of their women, and the safety and well-being of their working people for the profit of their financial interests. . . .

We demand that the test of true prosperity shall be the benefits conferred thereby on all the citizens, not confined to individuals or classes, and that the test of corporate efficiency shall be the ability better to serve the public; that those who profit by control of business shall justify that profit and control by sharing with the public the fruits thereof.

We therefore demand a strong national regulation of interstate corporations. The corporation is an essential part of modern business. The concentration of modern business in some degree is both inevitable and necessary for national and international business efficiency. But the existing concentration of vast wealth under a corporate system, unguarded and uncontrolled by the nation, has placed in the hands of a few men enormous, secret, irresponsible power over the daily life of the citizen—a power insufferable in a free government and certain of abuse. . . .[17]

§10. *'Woodrow Wilson on Monopoly,' in excerpts from his campaign speeches of 1912.*

I take my stand absolutely, where every progressive ought to take his stand, on the proposition that private monopoly is indefensible and intolerable. And there I will fight my battle. And I know

---

[17] *Platform of the Progressive Party,* Chicago, 1912, 3–6. Pamphlet in Library of Congress.

how to fight it. Everybody who has even read the newspapers knows the means by which these men built up their power and created these monopolies. Any decently-equipped lawyer can suggest to you statutes by which the whole business can be stopped. What these gentlemen do not want is this: they do not want to be compelled to meet all comers on equal terms. I am perfectly willing that they should beat any competitor by fair means; but I know the foul means they have adopted, and I know that they can be stopped by law. If they think that coming into the market upon the basis of mere efficiency, upon the mere basis of knowing how to manufacture goods better than anybody else and to sell them cheaper than anybody else, they can carry the immense amount of water that they have put into their enterprises in order to buy up rivals, then they are perfectly welcome to try it. But there must be no squeezing out of the beginner, no crippling his credit; no discrimination against retailers who buy from a rival; no threats against concerns who sell supplies to a rival; no holding back of raw material from him; no secret arrangements against him. All the fair competition you choose, but no unfair competition of any kind. And then when unfair competition is eliminated, let us see these gentlemen carry their tanks of water on their backs. All that I ask and all I shall fight for is that they shall come into the field against merit and brains everywhere. If they can beat other American brains, then they have got the best brains.

But if you want to know how far brains go, as things now are, suppose you try to match your better wares against these gentlemen, and see them undersell you before your market is any bigger than the locality and make it absolutely impossible for you to get a fast foothold. If you want to know how brains count, originate some invention which will improve the kind of machinery they are using, and then see if you can borrow enough money to manufacture it. You may be offered something for your patent by the corporation,— which will perhaps lock it up in a safe and go on using the old machinery; but you will not be allowed to manufacture. I know men who have tried it, and they could not get the money, because the great money lenders of this country are in the arrangement with the great manufacturers of this country, and they do not propose to see their control of the market interfered with by outsiders. And who are outsiders? Why, all the rest of the people of the United States are outsiders.[18]

---

[18] Woodrow Wilson, *The New Freedom*, New York, 1913, 172–174.

PART TWO
SINCE 1917

CHAPTER FIVE

Labor Divides Ranks

T HE WORLD WAR of 1914–1918 profoundly altered the economic, social, and political order of Western civilization. Institutions everywhere were touched directly or indirectly by the conflict and the " peace " which followed. In the difficult post-war period, the people of all countries strove to build a workable system on the ruins of the past.

The Effect of World War I on Labor

American workers felt the full impact of these world-wide forces and the first economic effect was a boon to organized labor. By 1916 the demand of the Allies for American goods had prompted business expansion. Employment increased and union membership rose, and the restriction of immigration reduced competition for jobs. Employers, earning high profits, yielded more easily to labor demands in order to keep production at a high level, and the conservative policy of the A.F. of L. also inspired general employer-confidence. Therefore, organized workers won more gains during the war period than they could ordinarily have made in decades. An early example of these gains was the passage by Congress of the Adamson Act on September 3, 1916, which established an eight-hour maximum work-day on all interstate railways.

America's entry into the war on April 6, 1917, accentuated the developments favorable to labor. Samuel Gompers at once pledged the full co-operation of the A.F. of L. with the government's war effort. He was given important positions on the

Council of Defense, which was formed to mobilize production, and on the War Labor Board, organized to promote industrial peace. An implicit bargain was made between organized workers and employers, with the aid and blessing of government. Business, favored by profitable orders and suspension of the anti-trust laws, wanted steady production. In order to secure work uninterrupted by disputes, it offered and made large concessions to labor. Union gains and prestige reached unprecedented heights. Nearly 2,000,000 new workers joined A.F. of L. unions from 1917 to 1920, almost doubling their total membership.[1]

Soon after the end of hostilities, organized labor experienced serious reverses. The "honeymoon" with business was over. In 1919, soaring prices sharply cut the workers' purchasing power, and when the unions resorted to strikes as a means of raising wages, they precipitated a bitter and widespread industrial conflict. A vigorous anti-union drive led by the National Association of Manufacturers gained the support of a public frightened by the Red Scare. The succeeding economic slump of 1921 brought extensive unemployment, and many strikes were lost. By 1923 the A.F. of L. membership had fallen more than 1,000,000 from the 1920 peak.

The "New Unionism"

The fact was that labor faced a new economic situation. The artificial war-time labor scarcity had passed, and a different industrial picture was taking shape. Business policies of the pre-war era were as out-moded as the horse and buggy. The Roaring Twenties opened up a period of "scientific" enterprise, with emphasis on efficiency, technological improvement, elimination of waste, reduction of labor turn-over, and higher productivity. Lowering of costs, the ultimate aim, was to be achieved mainly through more co-operative relations with workers. By offering good wages and conditions, employers hoped to prevent unionism and strikes, and specialists were hired to carry these

[1] Carroll R. Daugherty, *Labor Problems in American Industry*, 444–446. Boston: Houghton Mifflin Company, 1933. This work is the main source used for the effects of the war on labor.

plans into effect. The old-time employer was overshadowed by personnel managers, technicians, and industrial engineers.

The policy of "welfare capitalism" threw the old union leaders into confusion. It offered voluntary improvements by employers—fair wages and hours, job security, benefit plans, and profit sharing—which could be had through company unions, instead of independent labor organizations. Aided by good times, "welfare capitalism" provided good standards for millions of workers. Union membership consequently dropped sharply, and adjustment in union policy appeared necessary to save the labor movement.

The "New Unionism" was an adaptation to the changed situation confronting organized workers. No effective attack was possible on the employer policy of "welfare capitalism." During the 1920's capitalism was triumphant, economically and spiritually. The biggest boom in American history was in full swing. Real wages were rising. If the unions were to survive, they had to embrace the system and work with it. That is what many of the leading organizations did; in return for recognition they offered full co-operation with the new plans laid down by business. Instead of standing as militant, class-conscious groups, the unions caught the spirit of the times and tried to "sell" themselves to employers as labor service agencies.

An outstanding example of this new type of union-management co-operation was the plan put in operation on the Baltimore and Ohio lines. Daniel Willard, president of the railroad, took personal interest in the idea. He offered to work with the union, granting recognition, increased employment, and better conditions in return for co-operation in achieving efficiency. The International Association of Machinists was the chief union involved, and it accepted Willard's proposition in 1922. Help and advice from workers on questions of labor management were stressed. Joint local committees representing the unions and management worked on problems in each railroad shop. The resulting efficiency caused a number of other lines to follow the example of the Baltimore and Ohio.

Especially prominent in these experimental efforts were the unions in the clothing industry. The largest of these was the

International Ladies' Garment Workers' Union. This organization and others in the same business made agreements with employers for co-operation in labor management. The Garment Workers', however, was no mere service agency for manufacturers. Unlike many of the unions of the period that embraced the existing order and abandoned reform, the Garment Workers' was at heart socialistic. Prevailing conditions of insecurity in the clothing industry convinced most workers that capitalism needed overhauling. They were willing, however, to bide their time and accept immediate objectives as a start toward the larger goal. They felt that co-operating with managers would serve to train workers for eventual control of production. Education of labor was considered a necessary step before " emancipation."

The Amalgamated Clothing Workers' Union, composed of producers of men's wear, shared this viewpoint. In 1925 this union made a notable agreement with the Hart, Schaffner, and Marx Company, which provided that the Amalgamated should relieve the management of shop discipline. Improved efficiency resulted, and the arrangement was hailed as a remarkable venture in employer-employee relations. The union, with a strong financial basis built on accumulated dues, even offered the company commercial advice and the aid of its own banks.

Independent Labor Politics

While a number of labor organizations were experimenting with the " New Unionism," others turned toward independent political action. This was not a new idea; earlier labor attempts in politics have been described in a previous chapter. In view of the failures of the past it seemed strange to many observers that the workers would again support an independent campaign. Furthermore, the American Federation of Labor, at the height of its power when the war ended, traditionally opposed political action.

The disillusionment of labor in the post-war years was the primary cause of this move toward politics. The " new day " for workers, to be attained through direct economic bargaining, had not really come at all. In trying to face squarely the new industrial conditions of the post-war era, many of the unions felt that political action was necessary, because the power of government as an opposing or helpful force was increasingly recognized. Some leaders were beginning to see the ultimate need of government regulation of certain industries as the only means of producing stability of employment.

Representatives of many unions, some of them under socialist influence, met in Chicago on November 22, 1919. This group, mainly from the Middle-west, founded the American Labor party. In the following year a national convention of the party nominated candidates for the election of 1920: Parley Christenson of Utah, a liberal, was named for the presidency; Max Hayes, an old socialist and trade unionist, was named for the vice presidency. Although only a few farmers attended the convention, the delegates decided to attempt a union of all "producer" forces and changed the party name to Farmer-Labor. Restricted in support almost entirely to the Mississippi Valley and parts of the West, the Farmer-Labor ticket polled a total of 300,000 votes. In Washington and North Dakota it ran second.

Another convention, held in June, 1922, moved to broaden the movement to include as many co-operating groups as possible. Invitations were sent out to labor, farm, and progressive groups for a joint conference to be held on July 3, 1923. This attempt to build a strong organization before the election of 1924 was wrecked by the Communists, who succeeded in gaining control of the July convention. Chagrined at seeing their plans converted to radical ends, the labor groups that had originated the Farmer-Labor party repudiated it.

The move toward political action was meanwhile expressing itself in other developments. Since the railroads and railroad labor had come largely under government control as a result of successive acts of Congress, the railroad unions began to see advantages in having more influence over government. They became interested in the creation of some kind of organization which would serve as a means of political action. Other important unions, notably in the clothing and mining industries, joined with the railroad workers in this idea.

After sending invitations to numerous groups, these unions met with farm and progressive groups in Chicago on February 20, 1922. It was a significant convention in that it represented large elements of workers, farmers, and liberals. Many of the delegates were hopeful that a real farmer-labor party might ultimately result. But for the time being they took the name of the Conference for Progressive Political Action.

The objectives of the Conference were a curious expression of the aims of the trade-unionist, socialist, farm, and progressive elements which combined in the movement. In December, 1922, a special convention adopted a broad legislative program. Among other things it demanded restriction of the use of injunctions against labor; repeal of the Esch-Cummins Act, which governed railroad labor relations; federal regulation of the coal industry and child labor; amnesty for political prisoners; and maintenance of civil liberties. Increased income and inheritance taxes were favored, as well as the direct election of the President and Vice President of the United States.[2]

In preparation for political activity, the association adopted a special kind of organization. Conferences were set up in each Congressional district to determine local strategy. A national co-ordinating committee of fifteen became the chief permanent agency. All the groups affiliated with the Conference were represented on this committee.

As to the methods of achieving political power, there was a difference of opinion: Socialists in the organization supported independent action, but the majority decided, in 1922, to proceed cautiously. District conferences were instructed to use discretion, according to local circumstances. If the prospects for success were good, they were to support an independent candidate on a Socialist or Farmer-Labor ticket. Otherwise, support was to be offered the major party which appeared closest to the Conference platform.

Failure of the Republicans and Democrats to propose positive economic reforms led the Conference to move toward inde-

---

[2] Selig Perlman and P. Taft, *History of Labor in the United States, 1896–1932*, 533. New York: The Macmillan Company, 1935. This book gives a good account of the Conference and of the whole post-war labor movement.

pendent action in the national election of 1924. In convention on July 4th, they nominated Robert M. La Follette of Wisconsin and Burton K. Wheeler of Montana, a nominal Democrat. La Follette accepted the nomination but refused to start a national third-party organization. He and Wheeler ran as independents under various party designations. They had the support of the powerful labor, farm, and liberal elements belonging to the Conference for Progressive Political Action, as well as endorsements by the Socialist party and the American Federation of Labor.

Although lacking organized party machinery, except in a few states, La Follette and Wheeler gained large support at the polls. Nearly 5,000,000 votes were cast for them. This vote clearly showed that labor was interested in independent politics, but the resulting optimistic predictions failed to materialize. The La Follette votes came almost entirely from urban centers, and obviously could not be increased sufficiently to beat either of the major parties. Organized labor alone cannot succeed with an independent candidate in a national election. Since the Conference for Progressive Political Action gained no large response from major groups outside of labor, it could not win. Facing the situation realistically, a meeting of leaders liquidated the organization in February, 1925.

Decline and Revival of the A.F. of L.

The triumph of practical, craft unionism as the dominating principle in labor organization has already been outlined. During the early 1900's the American Federation of Labor, under Samuel Gompers, rose to a position of unquestioned power; America's entry into World War I had the effect of bolstering the organization still further. In 1920 the Federation claimed over 4,000,000 members and more than $1,000,000,000 in accumulated dues. At the same time it commanded general public respect for its co-operative attitude during the war.

In the twelve years following, however, the membership was cut practically in half. The sudden decline of the Federation, which was almost uninterrupted until 1933, was due to a number of factors. The influence of new industrial conditions and "welfare capitalism" has already been pointed out; when employers offered good wages and conditions, workers had little desire to join unions and pay dues. Organization of satisfied, loyal employees proved difficult. The "New Unionism," furthermore, had slight dramatic or militant appeal. Class-conscious workers were not emotionally fired by the idea of capitalist-labor collaboration for greater industrial efficiency and profits.

The basic structure of the A.F. of L., which was built upon narrow craft unions, was not well adapted to labor developments in the 1920's. Mechanization in industry was destroying skilled jobs and increasing the number of unskilled. The growing millions of unskilled workers were not eligible to join craft unions and were therefore outside the Federation structure. Some industrial unions, including workers of all skills, were affiliated with the Federation. But the craft union idea was dominant, and this idea was no longer applicable to the main body of American workers. Normal growth of the organization was checked by the fact that it gave insufficient attention to the expanding ranks of unskilled labor.

If its structure was outmoded, the same could be said about A.F. of L. policy. It stood traditionally for "voluntarism," or direct action by workers without aid or interference from government. This position was an outgrowth of labor experience in the generation before World War I. Legislative help in the past had usually proved illusory; politicians often failed to abide by their splendid promises. The Federation came to feel that it could trust only itself and therefore opposed any move toward State paternalism, which might weaken the workers' reliance upon themselves. This policy might have fitted the pre-war situation, but it was inadequate in the 1920's. Many of labor's basic problems after the war could be solved only through government. The stabilization of certain industries, effective limitation on working hours and wages, unemployment relief, and general economic security were possible only by means of government regulation. These were the principal needs of workers in the new industrial situation. A labor organization which deliberately shunned the means of meeting those needs was not likely to have a strong appeal.

These shortcomings of the Federation were the essential causes of its decline, but other forces continued to pound the organization from the outside. " Open shop " movements were launched by employers to break the unions, and the courts issued injunctions freely against labor during industrial disputes. Some employers made use of " Yellow-Dog " contracts, as they were branded by labor, under which workers pledged not to join any union as a condition of employment.

Although its position in the labor world declined during the 1920's, no rival appeared to challenge the A.F. of L. It persisted as the most powerful workers' organization in the country. After the death of Samuel Gompers, William Green became the recognized leader. He was made president on December 19, 1924, and was thereafter the principal spokesman of Federation policies. Green was born in Coshocton, Ohio, in 1873. The son of a Welsh miner, Green entered his father's trade and joined the United Mine Workers. A flair for politics sent him to the Ohio Senate in 1913 as a Democrat, but his career developed in the field of unionism. Rising in influence in the United Mine Workers, he was appointed eighth vice president of the A.F. of L. in 1914. Deaths of other officers moved Green up to third vice president by 1924, and in that year he was chosen president. His principal support in the Federation was the United Mine Workers, which was controlled by Green's long-time friend, John L. Lewis.

The new president tried to follow in the footsteps of Gompers. He was slow to move from traditional attitudes even although many conditions were changing. His conservative and exclusive policy endeared him to the old craft unions, which feared competition from the rising numbers of unskilled workers. Green possessed suitable political qualities—he was an old-fashioned spell-binder, a " family man," a Sunday school teacher, and a teetotaler.

Fundamental aims of the A.F. of L. have already been described. Realistic demands for better living standards continued to dominate in the period following World War I. As a

part of the " New Unionism," the Federation also encouraged
" uplift " measures for workers. It placed new stress upon
development of union benefit and insurance plans, pensions and
homes for aged members, labor banks, and workers' education.
It persevered in opposing social legislation by government, fearing
that such assistance would detract from the services of unions to
their members. Workmen's accident compensation laws were
supported and old age pensions passively approved, but compulsory state unemployment insurance was rejected until the
Federation convention of 1932.

Techniques of the Federation were adapted to the new economic situation after 1920. The leadership still believed in
direct union action as the primary means of gaining objectives,
but the type of action was modified. Instead of emphasizing the
use of militant strikes and similar tactics against employers, the
Federation encouraged " co-operation " and the gaining of
good will from business and the public. This change in method
was forced by the fact that employers were in command of the
situation. " Welfare capitalism " weakened the striking power
of labor. Mechanization decreased the dependence of industry
upon skilled workers, and the courts proved effective bulwarks
for employers during labor disputes. The unions could not fight
back successfully, so they tried to " sell " themselves as service
agencies through promises of co-operation and greater efficiency.
The trade agreement with employers remained the chief technique for solidifying labor gains, but the approach was new and
in keeping with the triumphant spirit of business.

Although there was a shift in some groups of the A.F. of L.
toward government action as a means of achieving labor goals,
the majority stood fast against partisan political activity. Lobbying by national, state, and local officers remained an important
device, and the traditional method of supporting " friends of
labor " and opposing its " enemies," regardless of party, was also
supported. But independent political action was disavowed.

A temporary deviation from this policy occurred in the presidential campaign of 1924. The Conference for Progressive
Political Action, composed mainly of labor unions, had nominated La Follette and Wheeler as independent candidates. In

this experiment the Federation Executive Council decided to break precedent and endorse the Progressives. The Council tried to make it clear that this action did not constitute independent political action by the Federation—that it was merely an endorsement. This claim was technically true, but the move was in fact a flirtation with independent labor politics, which many Federation leaders hoped would succeed. The failure of La Follette in 1924 dampened the prospects of victory by that method, and the A.F. of L. was not again lured into support of any third-party effort.

The steady fall in strength of the Federation reached bottom in the winter of 1932–1933. The deepest depression and largest unemployment in American history threatened to undermine the whole organization. But the summer of 1933 brought a stimulant to the Federation that lifted it up and started it upon a new and militant expansion. Passage of the National Industrial Recovery Act of June 16, 1933, with its famous section 7a, guaranteeing labor the right of collective bargaining, paved the way for a large-scale organizing campaign. By the end of the 1930's the A.F. of L. regained most of the members lost in the previous decade. The force which revived it, however, set other labor elements in motion. A newly born, fearfully growing giant soon appeared to challenge the leadership of the Federation.

Industrial Unionism: Formation of the Congress of Industrial Organizations

Although A.F. of L. organizers were greatly aided by the labor provisions of the National Industrial Recovery Act, they did not make a serious attempt to unionize unskilled workers. The craft unions which dominated the Federation were afraid that they would lose control of the organization if its membership became swamped by the unskilled. They were interested primarily in maintaining the highest possible wages and conditions for craftsmen. They did not want to be part of an organization that was concerned primarily with improving the situation of unskilled workers.

The neglect of the industrial masses was disappointing to many labor leaders. After World War I many of them saw that craft unions were no longer suitable to the majority of workers and hoped for the larger development of industrial unions, which included all types of workers in each industry. Earlier examples were unions like the Amalgamated Clothing Workers and the United Mine Workers. During the 1920's almost all the newly formed unions were of the industrial type, and there was a strong movement toward amalgamation of narrow craft unions. The basic industries, however, remained unorganized in 1933. Unskilled workers in steel, automobiles, textiles, food, and agriculture were outside any labor organization.

A minority in the A.F. of L. favored industrial unionism and tried to convince the rest of the members that the time was ripe to send organizers into the important industries. The conservative majority, however, persistently soft-pedaled demands for that kind of action. At last a number of the industrial unionists affiliated with the Federation decided to take the initiative themselves. Meeting in Washington, D. C., on November 9, 1935, representatives of seven large unions established the Committee for Industrial Organization. The immediate purpose was the organization of workers in key industries. John L. Lewis of the United Mine Workers was the leading force in the creation of the C.I.O., and he was named chairman. Charles P. Howard of the Printers' Union was made secretary.

Lewis has been the most publicized man in recent labor history. His bulking figure, large head, and bushy brows have helped mark him as a colorful figure, and his stubborn defiance has repeatedly made him the object of private and public wrath. Born in Iowa of Welsh parents in 1880, Lewis became a coal miner. As a member of the United Mine Workers, he grew interested in its affairs and served in official capacities for many years. In 1920 he was made president of the union, and during the 1920's he and the United Mine Workers ran into serious troubles. There were many costly disputes and strikes, but the miners failed to improve their conditions because the coal industry itself suffered from instability. As the union membership declined and general depression descended after 1930, Lewis, with his $12,000 a year salary, became increasingly unpopular. Then came the National Industrial Recovery Act of 1933, which gave fresh impetus to labor organization. Lewis launched a vigorous campaign, and the attainment of a new high in membership of the United Mine Workers restored his prestige. He became the unquestioned leader of industrial unionism and in 1935 led the revolt against the conservative leadership in the A.F. of L.

After the formation of the C.I.O., the Executive Council of the Federation repeatedly reprimanded its organizers for acting contrary to the expressed wishes of the Federation Convention. On August 4, 1936, the friction culminated in suspension by the Executive Council of the unions involved. Subsequent refusal of these unions to disband the C.I.O. led to their final expulsion from the A.F. of L.

The founders of the Committee for Industrial Organization were not dismayed. They had hoped to establish their proposed new industrial unions as affiliates of the A.F. of L., but they were willing to organize them independently if necessary. With money supplied by the United Mine Workers and other strong unions, the C.I.O. sent trained organizers into important labor fields. In December, 1936, Lewis and his group won their first major triumph. After months of agitation, C.I.O. organizers in General Motors plants won thousands of converts to their newly formed United Automobile Workers union. After a forty-day strike the U.A.W. won recognition from General Motors as the bargaining agent for workers in all its plants, under the National Labor Relations Act of 1935. This union soon became a dominant force in the industry and a powerful affiliate of the C.I.O.

Another outstanding victory was won in March, 1937. Without resorting to a strike, representatives of the Steel Workers' Organizing Committee were recognized as bargaining agents for employees of the United States Steel Corporation; the company also agreed to raise wages ten per cent and establish a forty-hour week. Leaders of the S.W.O.C. believed that after gaining this agreement from " Big Steel," they would readily win recognition from the smaller companies. But the leaders were mistaken. " Little Steel " employers put up a bitter fight. Led by Tom Girdler of the Republic Steel Company, they battled prolonged and bloody strikes to a standstill.

In spite of set-backs in the summer of 1937, industrial union organizers were making progress in many important areas. Effective campaigns were under way among shipping, textile, and rubber workers. Beginnings were made in the public utilities, meat packing, furniture, and aluminum industries. It could not be doubted that the C.I.O. had become a major force in American labor. In recognition of the trend of the movement, Lewis and his followers decided to give it a more permanent organization and name. On November 14, 1938, the official title was changed to Congress of Industrial Organizations, indicating that the temporary Committee was transformed into a permanent central body. Affiliated with the Congress in 1938 were thirty-two national unions, nine national organizing committees, and twenty-three state industrial councils, 115 city industrial councils, and 130 local industrial unions. By 1940 the total membership in affiliated unions was approaching the 4,000,000 mark.

The aims of the C.I.O. were broader than those of the A.F. of L. The Federation had virtually ceased to be a reform movement, although it gave strong support to the N.I.R.A. and other New Deal measures which strengthened unions. The A.F. of L. desired chiefly to maintain the interests of skilled labor through collaboration with employers. The Congress, on the other hand, established as a first objective the organization of all workers into industrial unions. Its leaders desired to alter the existing basis of labor bargaining. They believed that representation by individual crafts was not suitable when employers were organized in broad industrial associations. They favored industrial unions for labor as a proper balance to employer organization. Collective bargaining on that basis was expected to achieve better conditions for all workers.

Government intervention in positive form was also supported by the C.I.O. It called for governmental control of production and prices in unstable industrial fields, as a means of regularizing and insuring employment. This attitude came largely as an outgrowth of the experience of the United Mine Workers. Lewis, as president, became convinced that coal miners could never win security so long as the mining industry suffered under severe competition and instability. The essential problem could not be solved by strikes, but only by co-ordination of producers. Lewis looked to government as the only sound means of performing that function.

Aside from favoring regulation, the Congress wanted broad social legislation. This stand was in contrast with the Federation, which traditionally opposed State paternalism. The C.I.O. proposed laws to establish minimum wages and maximum hours, limitation of women's and children's labor, unemployment and health insurance, and old age security. It also supported increased taxes on incomes and inheritances, stronger guarantees of civil liberties, and legal protection of labor's right to strike, picket, and boycott.

The kind of organization established in 1938 broadly resembled that of the rival A.F. of L. The Congress was a central body having a large number of affiliated groups. The chief constituent elements were the national or international industrial unions, which were autonomous in their own affairs. Also affiliated were local industrial unions, organizing committees, and state and city industrial union councils. The power of issuing charters, organizing new areas, and co-ordinating industrial union action, was vested in the central body. Exercise of that authority was in the hands of a National Convention and a permanent executive board. The latter agency was composed of the president of the C.I.O., two vice presidents, the secretary, and a representative from each national or international union and organizing committee.

The broad reform appeal of the movement was accompanied by militant tactics. The " soft," business-like methods of the A.F. of L. were condemned by leaders in the Congress. All of the economic weapons of labor—the strike, picket, and boycott— were to be marshalled by strong industrial unions. The C.I.O. rejected the general labor policy of the 1920's which accepted the commanding position of employers. It felt that the Depression had taken the starch out of triumphant capitalism, and that labor's newly organized millions, with the blessing of a sympathetic national government, could fight on equal terms with employers. Strikes for union recognition reached great proportions by 1937, and the C.I.O. shocked an already frightened public by introducing a new weapon—the "sit-down" strike. Although this tactic was never formally recognized by the Congress, it was unofficially condoned. This clearly illegal method was widely used by striking unions until public opposition reached a prohibitive point. Although it proved effective in some disputes, the "sit-down" at last boomeranged in a wave of popular reaction against the C.I.O.

Because of its belief in the need for government action, the C.I.O. emphasized politics as a method of achieving its program. It did not belittle the importance and necessity of direct economic action, but it desired to supplement that action with political influence. In one sense the C.I.O. can be considered a continuation of the drive for governmental power that has been persistently at work in the American labor movement. In 1936 a special political arm of the organization was formed. This was called Labor's Non-partisan League. It was to act as a coordinating and assisting agency for political efforts of labor in all parts of the country.

The general C.I.O. strategy was one of co-operation with liberal and progressive elements, through endorsement of either of the major parties. In 1936 one of its main affiliates, the United Mine Workers, contributed $500,000 to the Democratic campaign fund.[3] But there was a strong feeling for militant, independent tactics. In New York State the American Labor party was supported against the major parties. John L. Lewis, breaking from his previous endorsement of Franklin Roosevelt, proposed Burton K. Wheeler as the C.I.O. choice for the Democratic nomination in 1940. Failing to convert the Democrats to his will, Lewis angrily threatened to launch a third-party effort. This bluff was ignored by both major parties, but Lewis planned another means of demonstrating his power. He desired to show that his influence was great enough to swing the balance in a national election and thereby to serve notice on both parties that he could be the arbiter of national labor policy. Confident of his strength, he made a dramatic, sermon-like declaration for

[3] Herbert Harris, *American Labor,* 408–409. New Haven: Yale University Press, 1939.

the Republican candidate, Wendell L. Willkie. His self-estimate proved exaggerated. Most of the C.I.O. rank and file ignored his exhortation and voted for Roosevelt. The prestige of Lewis and his supporters consequently declined, and, in keeping with a prior pledge, Lewis resigned as president of the C.I.O. when Roosevelt was re-elected. He was succeeded by the second-in-command, Philip Murray.

In its short years of growth before America's entry into World War II, industrial unionism made a powerful showing. In addition to organizing millions of unskilled workers, the C.I.O. improved wages, hours, and conditions in many fields. It gave, above all, a new feeling of strength to the industrial masses and substituted for the limited, conservative policy of the A.F. of L. a vigorous program of broad labor reform. But the moves initiated by the C.I.O. were only a half-step toward a comprehensive and integrated workers' organization. The immediate result of independent industrial organization was a deep cleavage in the ranks and leadership of labor. Friction and conflict, costly to workers and the public alike, were serious consequences of the dual labor movement.

Labor During World War II

Pearl Harbor opened a new era in the history of the labor movement, which paralleled in most respects the experiences of World War I. The new period had its beginnings as early as 1940, when America undertook to become the arsenal of democracy. Large foreign orders for weapons, supplemented by government contracts for defense and lend-lease purposes, gave powerful stimulus to industry. After the nation became engaged in open war against the enemy, expenditures for materiel could be measured only in billions. The period, 1940–1945, was one of abnormal production, profits, and employment. The peak of wartime employment in manufacturing was reached in 1943, when the number on factory payrolls was seventy-five per cent higher than in 1939. The all-out effort for victory and profit placed labor at a premium, and the period, like that of World War I, was favorable to the growth and prosperity of unions.

Total membership in labor organizations increased from over

10,000,000 in 1941 to more than 14,000,000 on VJ-Day; the latter figure represented about thirty per cent of the number of workers subject to organization. Unions affiliated with the A.F. of L. claimed 7,000,000 members in 1945, while those of the C.I.O. claimed 6,000,000. The unions outside the major federations, having some 1,700,000 members, included the independent railroad brotherhoods, the United Mine Workers (seeking reaffiliation with the A.F. of L.), and numerous smaller groups.

The improved position of the unions during the war gave them not only additional members, but more favorable contract provisions. By 1945, the unions had negotiated agreements which covered an estimated sixty-five per cent of all workers in manufacturing and thirty-five per cent of all workers in non-manufacturing employment. A considerable proportion of these contracts provided for the closed or union shop, maintenance-of-membership, dues check-off, and other features strongly desired by union leaders. Important progress was also made toward broader establishment of job classifications, with pay rates or ranges for specific jobs.

Wages went up as a result of the competition for manpower. Average hourly pay in manufacturing rose more than sixty per cent from 1939 to 1944; because of longer hours and over-time rates, average weekly earnings were doubled during the same period. The cost of living also went up, however, and this factor made the gain in purchasing power considerably less than the gain in dollars. The Department of Labor's consumer price index advanced twenty-five per cent from 1939 to 1944; labor leaders alleged that the real increase in living cost was closer to fifty per cent when the deterioration in quality of goods and forced buying of higher grades were considered. It was also true that, because of longer hours, the average employee in 1944 was putting in the equivalent of an additional day's work each week, as compared with his hours in 1939. All workers, furthermore, did not share equally in the wage increases, and some groups remained at a disadvantage. But the evidence clearly shows that organized labor, as a whole, enjoyed a substantial gain in purchasing power during the war years.

The relative stabilization of wages and prices which was achieved did not result from natural economic forces. Soon after the declaration of war President Roosevelt moved swiftly to establish effective stabilization agencies. Within the month a National War Labor Board was created to act as a kind of supreme court for the settlement of labor-management disputes. The Office of Price Administration was established in January, 1942, and was authorized by Congress to fix ceilings on rents and prices. The underlying aim of these two agencies and of a multitude of related wartime offices was to assure a steady flow of production. The cost of living had to be controlled in order to prevent a spiral of price increases, wage demands, and strikes. The unions wanted wages to go up with each rise in the cost of living. The War Labor Board, in disposing of unsolved disputes which threatened to stop production, at first agreed to wage hikes if the employers were willing to pay them. It soon became obvious, however, that such a policy would open the door to unchecked inflation, and in April, 1942, the President ordered the Board to follow a policy of wage stabilization. All wage disputes in war industries were henceforth subject to review by the Board, which opposed any increases of an inflationary nature.

Details of the wage-price stabilization formula were announced in July, 1942, when the Board passed upon wage demands of workers in the smaller steel plants. The Board permitted increases up to fifteen per cent (based on the increase in cost of living from January, 1941, to May, 1942), but stated that further adjustments would not be allowed. The " Little Steel " formula was strengthened and clarified by subsequent executive orders forbidding any further wage increases, except those necessary to correct gross inequities or substandard living conditions. The Board continued to grant a fifteen per cent increase over rates prevailing in January, 1941, in cases where the boost had not already been obtained.

Organized labor bitterly criticized the " Little Steel " formula, because it blocked additional increases in most wage rates regardless of mounting living costs. Union leaders, nevertheless, generally continued their support of the Administration and all-out war production. Pearl Harbor had cinched this support, which was gradually solidified during the " aid to democracies " phase of the United States defense preparation. Philip Murray, Lewis' successor as president of the C.I.O., had supported the arms program during 1941 while opposing drastic curtailment of consumption industries. He was one of those who believed, before the Japanese attack, that intelligent planning would permit production of consumers' goods and sufficient quantities of arms at the same time. " Strikes as usual " had been tolerated during most of 1941; the number of strikes had been considerably above the average of the preceding five years. Several of those strikes, in aviation and lumber, were inspired by Communists during the period of the Russian-German Pact.

Immediately after Pearl Harbor, President Roosevelt called a meeting of management and labor leaders in Washington. The most important result of that conference was the recommended establishment of a national war labor board, which was created soon afterwards. In addition to reaching agreement on a number of minor issues, the conference also pledged unanimously to oppose strikes and lock-outs for the duration of the war. John L. Lewis, who had issued a personal statement of support of the Administration's war effort, following the Japanese attack, was the dominant figure at the labor-management meeting. Although he had been critical of the President and his foreign policy since his disavowal of Roosevelt in 1940, it now appeared that Lewis was moving toward a reconciliation with the President. When he failed to receive a prominent place in government councils, however, Lewis withdrew in the direction of his earlier hostility. He subsequently demonstrated that his concern for the national war effort was subordinate to his interest in his union and personal power. Murray and Green, on the other hand, gave strong representations of their support of the President. In April, 1942, they took part in a unity rally at Pittsburgh; it was their first appearance together since the schism of 1935. Both leaders repeated their promises to oppose strikes and pledged unreserved support of the Administration and the war.

Since organized labor was split into two major camps, it was difficult to give unified representation to labor in the important wartime administrative agencies. President Roosevelt faced the delicate task of giving proper voice to the workers' organizations, without offending either major group. In the earlier months of the defense program he succeeded fairly well. Labor was represented by Sidney Hillman on the Advisory Commission of the Council of National Defense, established in May, 1940, as the first important defense agency. Hillman had a long and distinguished record of leadership in the Amalgamated Clothing Workers' Union (C.I.O.) and was widely respected in labor circles. When the Office of Production Management was created in January, 1941, Hillman was appointed by the President as associate director with the industrialist William S. Knudsen. In subsequent reorganizations of the controlling wartime boards, Hillman continued to represent labor. Broader participation by other union leaders was provided in December, 1942, when the presidents of the A.F. of L., C.I.O., and each of the independent railroad brotherhoods were appointed to serve on the Management-Labor Policy Committee, a consulting body for the powerful War Manpower Commission. The National War Labor Board consisted of one representative of labor, one of management, and one of the public; there were countless other examples of direct participation and co-operation by labor leaders in the direction of war production.

As the war progressed, however, the relative influence of labor in high government councils declined. The Administration, turning further and further from social reform objectives to the all-absorbing aim of winning the war, gave decreasing attention to the voice of labor. New Dealers and labor spokesmen near the President were quietly crowded out by the captains of industry. The industrialists and financiers, called into service because of their skill in production and administration, naturally brought with them the management point of view. Labor watched this trend with growing annoyance; at the same time it saw prices and profits moving upwards while wages remained frozen by the Little Steel formula. The mounting discontent of the workers was aggravated by delays of the W.L.B. in deciding wage disputes, and a wave of unauthorized strikes began in the latter part of 1942. Green and Murray, honoring their prior pledges, condemned these actions, as did most of the responsible union officials. But millions of man-hours were lost as workers in various industries fretfully stayed off their jobs. Union apologists argued that the loss was a tiny percentage of the total man-hours worked, but strikes of any proportion, while a shooting war was in progress, aroused public dismay and anger.

The most serious and defiant walk-out during the war years was taken by the United Mine Workers. Lewis was infuriated by the stabilization order and by the adamant position of the W.L.B. in resisting demands for further wage increases. Green and Murray shared his opposition to the Little Steel formula, but Lewis alone, knowing that war production depended upon coal, struck boldly to break the anti-inflation line. In the spring of 1943, the miners asked the operators for a pay increase of two dollars per day, " double-time " on Sundays, and a guaranteed fifty-two-hour work-week, in addition to larger vacation allowances and " fringe demands." When the operators refused and the dispute went to the War Labor Board, the miners left the pits. Lewis refused to appear at the scheduled hearings, flouted the authority of the Board, and attacked its members as well as the stabilization formula. Rather than yield to this challenge, the Board continued its consideration of the case and placed the problem of the strike in the hands of the President. For Roosevelt there was no alternative to upholding the Board, which was the keystone of the stabilization program. On May 1, he ordered Harold L. Ickes, Secretary of the Interior, to take over the mines in the name of the government; on the following day he appealed to the miners by radio to return to work. They went back to the pits, but only because Lewis, a few minutes before the President went on the air, ordered them to do so for a truce period. The W.L.B. handed down its decision on June 18, rejecting the daily pay increase but approving most of the other demands. After another protest strike the men returned to work, with Ickes in control of the mines. Public tension was relaxed, and in August, President Roosevelt ordered a longer work-week for the miners, which meant more hours at over-time pay. This provision, augmenting the take-home pay of the workers, appeased the miners and increased the output of coal. Lewis had won a partial victory in breaking the anti-inflation line, but Roosevelt had upheld the authority of the W.L.B. and prevented a break-down of war production.

Lewis' willingness to jeopardize the national war effort in order to advance his union was duplicated in other instances of labor irresponsibility. Although the great majority of workers remained loyally on the job, regardless of grievances, those who did strike contributed to the rising groundswell of anti-labor sentiment. While changes, significant for the future, were developing in the public attitude toward unions, important developments were also taking place in the labor movement itself.

Even before the outbreak of war, the A.F. of L. was moving toward a somewhat broader collection of objectives. William Green declared in 1939 that the movement must adapt itself to changing conditions and came out strongly for all kinds of government-sponsored social insurance. This declaration was a far stride from the position of the A.F. of L. before 1932, when it opposed all such plans as undesirable state paternalism. During the war Green gave full support, and although he fought the wage freeze and the Smith-Connally anti-strike law of 1943, he yielded to public policy and kept his " no-strike " pledge. The A.F. of L. unions continued their business-like, limited relations with employers. While Green favored the formation of labor-management councils to increase wartime production efficiency, he assured industrial leaders that the A.F. of L. recognized a clear line of demarcation between the functions of unions and management. Green reiterated his acceptance of the enterprise system as it existed and opposed participation by labor in the actual management of an employer's property. The Federation convention of 1944 gave strong endorsement to consumers' co-operatives, and created a special department, whose function was to educate union members about co-operatives and to stimulate the formation of such associations. This stimulus to general consumer co-operation represented a departure from traditional A.F. of L. policy, which had formerly indorsed co-operatives of union members only.

On other issues, the A.F. of L. in 1944 proposed to fight the restrictive labor laws enacted in twelve states, as well as the federal Smith-Connally statute. While opposing the poll tax and supporting the principle of a Fair Employment Practices Committee, the Federation objected to permanent legislation barring racial discrimination in employment. It argued that such a law would force the cancellation of many union contracts which contained restrictive clauses. In the field of world-wide labor organization, the A.F. of L. refused the general invitation of the British Trades Union Congress to plan for a new international federation. The A.F. of L. wished to revitalize the pre-war International Federation of Trade Unions, to which it belonged. The I.F.T.U. was open to only one labor organization from each country where a " free " labor movement was recognized; the A.F. of L. declined to participate in discussions of a broader federation, which would involve representation of totalitarian countries.

Although the A.F. of L. unions during the war moved toward a larger acceptance of governmental intervention in economic and social affairs, they continued to place chief dependence upon direct action for the achievement of their aims. This was especially true in matters concerning pay and job conditions. Toward the end of the war, labor as a whole became increasingly dissatisfied with government stabilization policies and the action of official boards; conservative unionists were confirmed in their conviction that they made greater gains by dealing directly with the employers. The traditional policy of political neutrality was maintained by the A.F. of L. during the war, but in the 1944 campaign Green urged the unions to form local political committees for the purpose of getting out the vote. Federation neutrality, furthermore, was not binding upon the constituent unions or their members. Daniel Tobin, president of the Teamsters' Union, served as head of the labor division of the Democratic National Campaign Committee.

The C.I.O. continued to be the mighty rival of the A.F. of L. in the labor movement. After the resignation of its president, John L. Lewis, the organization came under new management. When Philip Murray became president in November, 1940, it was thought that Lewis might possibly remain the silent power in the C.I.O. Murray and Lewis had worked together for years as an effective team; Lewis had sponsored his younger colleague for many high offices in the United Mine Workers and the C.I.O. But a break in their friendship was anticipated when Lewis quit the presidency, and the issues which later arose between the men developed into an irreparable schism. One of the principal issues was support of the Administration during the war. Murray loyally backed the Roosevelt policies while Lewis continued his criticism of the President. Lewis was also affronted by Murray's collaboration with Sidney Hillman, labor's principal representative in governmental councils. Lewis and Hillman had been at odds for many years. Personal feeling between Murray and Lewis came to a head after left-wing members of the C.I.O. sharply criticized the anti-Administration views of their former chief. When Lewis bitterly counterattacked these critics, Murray found himself in the position of having to defend his own people. He thereby stood in direct opposition to his one-time colleague and leader. In order to demonstrate the finality of the break between them, Lewis in 1942 moved to have Murray expelled from his position in the United Mine Workers; at about the same time Lewis led his powerful union out of the C.I.O.

Philip Murray had come up through labor's ranks the hard way. As a boy he helped his father in a Scottish colliery; in 1902 he came to America and started work in the mines of Westmoreland County, Pennsylvania. This was the territory of District 5–U.M.W., and Murray rose steadily in influence within the district. In 1916, he became the district's president, and four years later he was made a vice president of the U.M.W. by John L. Lewis. During the difficult 1920's when the U.M.W. was fighting for survival, Murray became Lewis' right-hand man. He developed extraordinary skill as a negotiator and a remarkable ability to grasp statistical facts in relationship to individual workers and the economy as a whole. During the C.I.O. organizing campaign of 1936–1937, his primary union interest shifted from mining to steel; he became president of the Steelworkers in 1942. Murray has been described as a " radical conservative," because he was prepared to employ " radical " tactics such as a national steel strike in order to achieve ends which were essentially conservative. But he is not a " pure and simple " trade unionist. Murray supports government intervention for protection of the workers and regional and national planning as a means of providing full production. He is personally mild, patient, and reasonable.

Phil Murray's philosophy of unionism closely approximated the objectives indorsed by the C.I.O. during the war. Helping to win the struggle with the Axis was listed as the first of these objectives, but after that came expansion of the ideas which had given birth to the C.I.O. The organization, as stated in its constitution, continued to sponsor broad and effective unionization of all workers of the country, without regard to race, color, creed, or nationality. Protective social legislation, which only gradually won the indorsement of the A.F. of L., continued to be a prime objective of the C.I.O. During the war the C.I.O. proposed greater participation by labor in the direction of the nation's economy. As early as April, 1942, Murray suggested that the President establish a labor-management council in each basic war industry, with a government representative acting as chairman. The industry councils, whose chief purpose was to speed production through a pooling of skills and processes, were also seen by Murray as an aid to reconversion at war's end. The proposal was ultimately rejected, however, by Sidney Hillman, principal labor adviser to the President, who remembered the experience of similar councils under the N.R.A.

The C.I.O. pioneered in the demand for a worker's guaranteed annual wage. The Steelworkers in 1944 asked that this provision be made a part of the new contract with employers; it was argued that successful demonstration of the feasibility of the plan in the steel industry would show it to be practicable on a national scale. C.I.O. leaders contended that the annual wage would steady the nation's economy by stabilizing purchasing power, and at the same time would free labor from the insecurity of recurrent unemployment. The plan, rejected by the industry on the grounds of impracticability, has not been dropped from the back-log of C.I.O. aspirations.

While the A.F. of L. showed a newly awakened interest in co-operatives during the war, the experience of the C.I.O. gave rise to skepticism concerning their general value. The tendency within the C.I.O. was to restrict co-operatives to high-profit consumption fields. One of the sharpest differences between the two labor organizations was in regard to international affiliations. The C.I.O., excluded from the International Federation of Trade Unions, eagerly accepted the invitation of the British Trades Union Congress to join in planning for a broader international association. In December, 1944, Sidney Hillman, Emil Rieve, and R. J. Thomas were sent by the C.I.O. to London, where they joined in a preliminary conference with labor representatives of the other United Nations. From this meeting, boycotted by the A.F. of L., the World Trade Union Conference evolved in 1945.

Internal problems showed themselves to be more serious within the C.I.O. than the A.F. of L. The principal cause of the C.I.O. difficulties was Communist infiltration, which dated back to the early days of the organization. In 1935, having failed to gain influence in A.F. of L. unions, the Communists saw a chance to move in on the ground floor of the new unions being sponsored by the Committee for Industrial Organization. John Lewis, for his part, welcomed recruits of any brand and found the Communists especially useful as organizers. The left-wingers toiled laboriously and worked their way into positions of influence; then Lewis, who expected to keep them in their place, quit the C.I.O. in 1942. Phil Murray inherited an organization in which the Communists wielded power far beyond their numbers; he could not, even had he wished, get rid of the Communists and pro-Communists without wrecking the C.I.O. Key positions were held by leftists such as the shrewd Lee Pressman, general counsel of the organization; Len De Caux, editor of the C.I.O. *News;* Harry Bridges, president of the International Longshoremen; and a number of other leaders in the constituent unions. Communist influence declined during the awkward period of the Russian-German Pact, but after June, 1941, the pro-Communist members became zealous workers and opposed strikes of any kind which diminished the war effort and aid to Russia. They were never strong enough to dominate the C.I.O., but by aligning with one faction against another, they exerted substantial influence. The continual jockeying by leftist elements to improve their position and the efforts of anti-Communists to deprive them of control, fomented interminable disagreements and conflicts.

Although the organization was divided by fundamental ideological differences, the C.I.O. was united in its effort to support legislative demands by vigorous political action. Labor's Nonpartisan League, formed by the C.I.O. in 1936, was a precursor of the more effective organization achieved during the war period. In July, 1943, the C.I.O. Political Action Committee was created; it was destined to have a significant impact upon public opinion and party politics in the United States. The stated purpose of the C.I.O.-P.A.C. was to assure a continuation of the New Deal program and legislation favorable to labor and the public. The committee consisted of seven C.I.O. union executives, with Sidney Hillman as chairman. Under the committee some fourteen regional offices were established to coordinate the political activities of C.I.O. union locals. The action of the locals remained voluntary and autonomous, but suggestion from above proved effective.

The formation of the C.I.O.-P.A.C. in 1943 was aimed, of course, at the elections of 1944. By July 23, 1944, the organization had collected $630,000 from the contributions of individual union treasuries. After that date, when the major party conventions had chosen their national candidates, money was no longer received from unions, and the balance of such funds on hand was frozen until after the general election. These steps were taken to comply with the federal law barring contributions by unions during a general election campaign. . Additional income was derived after July from dollar contributions by individual union members. After the party conventions had acted, the C.I.O. also sponsored a broader-based organization, the National Citizens P.A.C., which was separate from the C.I.O.-P.A.C. This organization was open to all sympathetic individuals and included many writers, artists, and well-known liberal crusaders. The N.C.-P.A.C., independent of the C.I.O.-P.A.C., filled its own campaign chest by means of individual contributions, but co-ordination of effort was achieved through Hillman, who served as chairman of both organizations. The general public, bemused by this political mirror game, was further perplexed by the existence of hundreds of local P.A.C.'s, connected with individual unions or the N.C.-P.A.C.

The principal activity of all the P.A.C.'s, large and small, was to arouse political interest and get out the vote. In order to assist volunteers in this work, the C.I.O.-P.A.C. issued bulletins of instructions, speakers' manuals, and hundreds of pamphlets supplying facts and interpretations on specific issues. Some of these, written by professionals, were excellent guides to practical politics. In this respect the C.I.O.-P.A.C. made the most ambitious attempt in history to train, by extension as it were, an army of effective precinct workers. As might have been expected, this aim could not be even partially achieved in so short a time. But the P.A.C. did not depend upon precinct work alone. It conducted nation-wide radio programs; issued clip-sheets and cartoons to union and other newspapers; and distributed millions of campaign posters and buttons.

The effectiveness of C.I.O. political action in 1944 is difficult to judge. Its leaders were sorely disappointed when they failed to nominate Henry Wallace as Roosevelt's running mate in the Democratic national convention. They blamed that failure on the weak organization of the liberal elements in the party and on Roosevelt's famous "second letter," which indicated his willingness to accept someone other than Wallace. The P.A.C. leaders claimed credit for exerting the strongest progressive force at the Chicago convention. They concluded that their pressure had at least succeeded in forcing the convention to nominate a liberal substitute for Wallace, rather than a conservative like James F. Byrnes or, possibly, Harry F. Byrd. After swallowing their regrets, the P.A.C. leaders plunged wholeheartedly into the campaign for Roosevelt and Truman, and for liberal Congressional candidates. The results of the election appeared to justify the faith of the founders of the movement. The national C.I.O. convention in November, 1944, took on the air of a political victory celebration and gave an impressive ovation to Sidney Hillman. The delegates felt that P.A.C. had perhaps elected a President and had certainly defeated a number of Congressmen. By unanimous action the convention voted to continue the C.I.O.-P.A.C., and directed it to emphasize long-range political education. Some $350,000, which had been frozen in the P.A.C. treasury during the general election campaign, was made available to finance the program.

Although virtually all the candidates whom it supported in 1944 were Democrats, after the election the C.I.O. officially reaffirmed the traditional non-partisan policy of organized labor. It favored vigorous political action, but free from any permanent party affiliation. Some C.I.O. unions, as well as some of the A.F. of L., had sponsored the American Labor party in New York State. Many of the sponsors withdrew in 1944, however, on the grounds that the Communists had gained control of the new party. Although the alliance may indeed have been temporary, it appeared during the war years that the C.I.O. had an interest and an investment in the Democratic party.

The C.I.O. went further than the A.F. of L. not only in the field of political action, but in worker education as well. The primary purpose of the educational program was to give members an understanding of unionism. It was believed that such an understanding was basic to the maintenance of a sound movement, especially in the period of reconversion and readjustment. The educational courses, conducted chiefly through local unions, also embraced broader economic problems and issues of international scope. Although the program was conceived chiefly as a means of furthering union aims, it may become still more significant as an instrument of adult education in civic responsibility.

When America entered World War II the labor movement was divided into two major camps, and, as the war progressed, a further division was threatened. John Lewis, who helped to precipitate the major split of 1935, hoped to form a third organization which would rival the other two. After he left the presidency of the C.I.O. in 1940, Lewis did not intend to retire or withdraw to the confines of the United Mine Workers; he moved with patience and deliberation toward the building of a new labor empire. In this new bid for power Lewis aimed to recover his former position as the leading spokesman of labor, drive a wedge into labor's support of the Administration, and develop a farmer-labor organization which he might deliver to the Republicans in 1944. Thus could Lewis achieve what he had failed to do in the campaign of 1940.

Soon after Pearl Harbor the fates smiled briefly upon Lewis, and it appeared that the war had intervened to present him with a short-cut to power. During the course of the labor-management conference in December, Lewis stood out as the primary figure; in January, with the war as a pretext, he joined William L. Hucheson of the A.F. of L. in a call for unity of the rival labor organizations. He did this without consulting Murray or other C.I.O. leaders; it was a thinly veiled attempt to place himself in the key rôle. Shrewd observers in the labor movement realized that in a merger of the C.I.O. and A.F. of L. Lewis would hold the balance of power. The C.I.O. executive board quickly repudiated the Lewis-Hucheson proposal, and the Administration, fearing the political effects of a Lewis-dominated labor combine, also moved to crush the idea. President Roosevelt proposed and the C.I.O. approved, as an alternative to the merger, creation of a joint committee of labor to advise the government. The committee was to consist of three representatives of the A.F. of L. and three from the C.I.O. Both Lewis and Hucheson were quietly excluded from membership by the Administration.

Seeing his attempted master stroke collapse, Lewis began to build again from the grass roots. The spearhead in his new adventure was to be District 50 of the U.M.W. Established in 1936 as a catch-all organization for workers in the coke, chemical, and allied industries, District 50 had about 50,000 members before America's entry into the war. Shortly thereafter Lewis launched his organizing campaign, and by March, 1942, the membership of District 50 had risen to 100,000. But the new venture was not restricted to workers of the coke and chemical industry, who numbered about 1,000,000; District 50 was opened to some 3,000,000 dairy farmers and 2,000,000 utility workers. Successful organization of these workers and producers, joined with the U.M.W., would have placed in Lewis' hands a power which could challenge both the A.F. of L. and C.I.O. The bid for the dairy farmers, furthermore, was a possible lead to the formation of a still greater economic and political power—a farmer-labor alliance.

Lewis, following the successful methods of the original C.I.O. drive, established separate organizing committees in each subdivision of District 50. Campaigns were begun almost at once in twelve states, and the organizers paid no respect to the existence of established unions in many of the industrial fields. The raiding of C.I.O. jurisdictions was, in fact, one of the principal operations. The existence of a state of war proved no deterrent either; on the contrary, District 50 organizers hoped to exploit the mounting resentment of workers toward wage stabilization and other wartime controls. Lewis hoped for a duplication of his spectacular successes in organizing the C.I.O. unions. But, in spite of an impressive start, the early success was short-lived. The U.M.W. seceded from the C.I.O. in 1942 and Lewis, unable to reach a new and distant shore, began steering back to the A.F. of L. within a year. Failing to build another virgin kingdom, he turned to reconquer the old.

It came as a surprise to some observers when the A.F. of L. executive council revealed in August, 1943, that the U.M.W. had applied for re-affiliation. Lewis was known to have little sympathy with many of the leaders who ousted his union in 1936. Other observers knew equally well that the opportunistic Lewis could not stand still. He aimed to broaden his influence before the 1944 elections; with the District 50 campaign on the wane, he tried the only other door which might remain unlocked. Lewis doubtless hoped that by returning to the A.F. of L. in 1943 he would be in a position a year later to swing a substantial labor vote against the Administration. The effort to re-enter the Federation proved premature, although Lewis had strong support from Hucheson and other Republican leaders in the A.F. of L. Daniel Tobin, the Democratic labor adviser of the President, counterbalanced Hucheson; it was apparently Green, not yet prepared to retire before Lewis, who kept the door locked awhile longer. But overtures continued between the U.M.W. and the A.F. of L. Agreements were reached over questions of jurisdiction, especially those concerning District 50, and by the end of the war it appeared certain that the return to the fold would be approved. The Federation, in its competition with the C.I.O., could hardly afford to turn down the rich and powerful U.M.W.

Division weakened the voice of organized labor during the war and contributed in some degree to loss of productive effort. In view of this, the general public as well as many union men indulged a quiet hope for the achievement of labor " unity." But true unity could hardly have been attained in face of the fundamental differences and rivalries. The numerous unity " feelers " sent out during the war were not prompted primarily by a conscientious desire to help the war effort. Rather, the war was used as a pretext for a union of forces which would further the power of a given group or individual.

The Lewis-Hucheson proposal of January, 1942, was the first of several schemes of this nature. Serious talks between A.F. of L. and C.I.O. leaders in August, 1942, showed that genuine agreement was a long way off; organic unity was favored by either group only if attainable on its own terms. Theoretical differences relating to the form of unions, craft or industrial, were no longer important. The chief barriers to unity were the vested interests of the organization leaders, ideological differences, and political disagreements. The influence of the Administration, furthermore, was not directed toward unity at any price. The President spoke of unity in general terms and would have welcomed greater harmony in the labor movement, but he kept a critical eye on the various unity maneuvers. Roosevelt stood ready to exert his influence against any move which aimed to consolidate labor under Republican leadership and thereby undermine the foundation of Democratic voting strength. It was clear by the end of the war, in view of unreconciled internal issues and the general political situation, that organic unity of labor was not likely to be achieved.

Though organized labor failed to compromise its differences during World War II, the emergence of new leaders gave promise for the future. As the older labor chiefs approached the age of threescore and ten, younger men were preparing to take their places. Youthful, dynamic leaders like Walter Reuther of the United Automobile Workers, John Green of the Shipyard

Workers, and James Carey of the Electrical Workers, represented the rising generation of leaders. They seemed better prepared to solve the labor-management problems of their day than were most of the old-time spell-binders. Their approach was more scientific and statistical, less personal and intuitive. They brought a more businesslike approach to unionism, which had indeed become a big business of its own. This approach did not mean that they had adopted the viewpoint of the employers, but it did mean that they looked upon labor-management relations as predominantly a technical problem. The new leadership saw the need, accordingly, for expert advisers; they hired trained economists, public relations men, and lawyers, in order to gain information and counsel. Some unions initiated the practice of sending representatives to graduate schools, where they studied not only such matters as labor economics, but business administration as well. The wartime experience gave impetus to these significant trends. The older labor chiefs tend to hold the prejudices and predilections of a bygone period of industrial strife; it may be hoped that the rising leaders, of both labor and management, will depend more on facts and reason in a developing era of industrial co-operation.

The Aftermath of the War

After VJ-Day it was by no means clear to labor that a better day was about to dawn. Long before the cessation of hostilities, union leaders were frankly apprehensive concerning the post-war period. They well remembered the reaction against labor following World War I; they feared a repetition of economic inflation and crisis, succeeded by vigorous anti-union campaigns. Labor spokesmen were not alone in predicting serious difficulties during reconversion and afterwards. John W. Snyder, Director of War Mobilization and Reconversion, predicted in October, 1945, that unemployment would reach eight million by the following spring. Deflation, as a consequence of huge curtailments in war orders, was viewed by many responsible economists as the immediate danger. But the return to peacetime production was accomplished without any serious difficulty. In spite of material shortages and the delays involved in re-tooling,

he change-over proceeded at an astounding pace. In anticipa-
ion of Germany's defeat, production of implements of war was
harply reduced in the early months of 1945; by the end of the
ear, spurred on by the surrender of Japan, civilian production
ad already surpassed the level of 1941. Immediately after
J-Day, total employment fell off considerably, but by Novem-
er, 1945, the number of workers was mounting steadily. The
otal number seeking jobs at no time reached the three million
nark, and a year after VJ-Day it amounted to approximately
wo million. This figure was an almost irreducible minimum
or a national labor force of sixty million; it would have been
ubstantially larger, of course, had it included the men and
vomen still in uniform, those in schools and colleges, and those
n apprentice-training under the Veterans' Administration.

The surprising speed of reconversion had not been anticipated
y labor and government experts. As a move against the feared
eflation, and as compensation for the general reduction of
ver-time hours in industry, the major unions commenced a
ound of demands for pay-rate increases. The Truman adminis-
ration gave support to this move in the belief that the main-
enance of purchasing power was a sound guarantee against a
usiness recession. In the spring of 1946, the wage-price stabili-
ation formula was modified to allow some wage increases and
orresponding price rises where necessary. These developments
vere immediately favorable to the unions which won wage
oosts. In the autumn of 1946, before the collapse of the O.P.A.
rice line, the members of these unions could purchase more with
heir weekly incomes than they could before the war. Lewis'
oal miners enjoyed the most impressive relative advance; their
veekly check bought sixty per cent more goods than in 1939.

The buying power of labor's dollars, and of consumers gen-
rally, began to dwindle after President Truman abandoned the
O.P.A. and wage stabilization late in 1946. The drive against
ontrols, successfully maneuvered through Congress in the early
ummer, had resulted in a breakdown of the effort to hold the
ine. Presented with an impossible O.P.A. law, with meat and
ther important items already loosened from control, Truman
ad no alternative to dropping the stabilization program. In

doing so, he appealed for restraint on the part of businessmen and farmers; but as Truman knew only too well, such appeals were futile in face of the inflationary tide which had been released. Many labor leaders, irked by the wartime wage freeze, received the President's de-control action with approval. They felt secure in their power to gain future wage increases if the price level should wash away their gains.

The inflation feared by workers during the war years quickly became a reality. By the spring of 1947, conservative estimates placed the cost of living at more than fifty per cent above the level of 1939. The price rise was oppressive to people on small fixed incomes and wiped out the recent advance in wage rates won by many unions. Another round of wage demands and strikes was bound to come. John Lewis seized the opportunity to show the way to the other union leaders. Although the mines remained under government operation, through Julius Krug, Secretary of the Interior, Lewis informed the Administration in December, 1946, that the existing work contract was void. Lewis argued that the previous contract with the coal operators permitted him to take such action after due notice, and that the government had agreed to continue in effect the provisions of that contract. The government contended that it had agreed only to the conditions of the old contract, not to any right of termination by the union while the United States remained in control. Both parties had legal cases.

Attorney General Tom Clark sought an injunction against the U.M.W.; the order was accordingly issued by a federal district court, but defied by Lewis. While the Truman administration stood fast against this bold challenge to public authority, and refused to make any " deal " with Lewis to resolve the crisis, the federal court laid down a thumping fine for contempt of its injunction. Lewis, realizing he had no further cards to play, meekly submitted. He directed the miners to return to work, pending appeal of the injunction to the Supreme Court. His last hopes in this adventure were dashed in March, 1947, when the high court upheld the injunction although reducing the fine. Lewis this time had been beaten. The treasury of the U.M.W.

and, more important, Lewis' prestige as a strategist, were considerably diminished.

But defeat was only part of the game for John L. Lewis. Bowing to superior force while the mines remained in government hands, the U.M.W. leader looked to the day when the seizure power would expire. By terms of the wartime federal law, the government had to return the mines to the operators after June 30, 1947. Lewis waited patiently while other union chiefs won minor gains during the second major round of wage demands following the close of the war. Then, after June 30, the miners quit the pits while Lewis pressed the operators for the biggest wage stakes yet. After a brief strike the operators capitulated, largely because of the desire of the steel men, who owned some of the mines, to prevent an interruption of steel production. The resulting increase in the cost of coal pushed upward all prices dependent upon coal, and thereby aggravated the threat of inflation to the whole economy. But settling of the strike averted an immediate breakdown of production; and Lewis, pushing to the limit the strategic importance of coal, was able to resume his position as labor's most successful go-getter.

Although the struggles of organized labor to keep ahead of the price spiral had little to do with social reform, they provided the back-drop for labor's action on other fronts. Immediate wage and hour demands continued to be important aims of the unions, but these did not preclude the development of broader objectives during the post-war period. Both the A.F. of L. and C.I.O. recognized the need for reform in the field of international relations; they supported American participation in the emerging organizations for world-wide political, economic, and social cooperation. The C.I.O., reflecting in part the influence of its pro-Russian element, placed special emphasis on the maintenance of Big Three unity, but by the summer of 1947 the wartime alliance had already disintegrated. The A.F. of L., in its 1946 convention, assumed a strong anti-Communist position. Both major labor groups favored public control of atomic energy, subject to international regulation.

On the home front, too, the A.F. of L. and C.I.O. were in agreement on most goals. They gave united support to the

" Full Employment " bills of 1945 and 1946. These bills proposed that the President submit to Congress annually a national production and employment budget. The budget would estimate the number of jobs necessary in the coming year to achieve full employment, the amount of investment required to produce those jobs, and the amount of investment actually expected. If the anticipated investment was less than that required for full employment, the federal government was then to take corrective action. Congress could provide special incentives to private investors, increase public expenditures, or combine both methods. Sponsors of the legislation believed that appropriate adjustments in banking, currency, taxation, and other government policies would prove effective in keeping investment at the level required for full production and employment. Although Congress was not to be bound by the President's budget or his recommendations, the proposal represented a far step in the direction of government planning and regulation at the highest level. Labor leaders felt that the legislation offered the best available guarantee against mass unemployment. With strong backing by union leaders, a modified bill became law in 1946. President Truman delivered to Congress the first production and employment estimate in January, 1947, but the Eightieth Congress paid scant attention to his recommendations.

Extension of the social security system was endorsed by both the A.F. of L. and C.I.O. The principal focus for this support was the Wagner-Murray-Dingell bill to establish pre-paid health insurance as part of the federal security program. This bill, opposed by a majority of the medical profession and by conservatives generally, never got out of the Senate committee, but the idea still commands labor backing. The unions joined also in support of an effective national housing program, specifically, the Wagner-Ellender-Taft bill, which outlined a long-range plan of construction involving public as well as private enterprise. This proposal also failed to see the light of the Senate floor.

Reversing its earlier stand, the A.F. of L. in 1946 officially favored creation of a permanent Fair Employment Practices Commission. This proposal, intended to prevent racial discrimination in hiring, was repeatedly blocked in Congress by threat of a southern filibuster; like the perennial anti-lynching bill, the proposal will come up again and again, but its passage is improbable. The idea of the F.E.P.C. has always been championed by the C.I.O. In other fields of reform, too, the C.I.O. has moved somewhat faster and more vigorously than its older rival. It has placed greater emphasis on economic planning at all levels, expansion of federal aid to education and conservation, and radical tax reform to give relief to low-income groups. Particular unions of the C.I.O. have developed objectives of their own. Walter Reuther of the U.A.W., for instance, has proposed greater participation by labor in the councils of management, a guaranteed "annual wage," and a complete system of social security within the union, financed by the auto industry.

In the period after World War II there was no important change in the techniques used by labor in seeking to attain their objectives. In addition to direct action through conventional strikes, boycotts, and picketing, the unions employed the standard tactics of pressure groups. The official views of labor were made known through public statements of their national leaders. The radio became increasingly important as a medium of propaganda; in October, 1945, the American Broadcasting Company signed a contract with the C.I.O. for a series of paid broadcasts. This contract marked a significant precedent and was made possible by a revision of the code of the National Association of Broadcasters, which had previously forbidden the sale of network time for the regular presentation of controversial issues.

Other mass media were also utilized by labor organizations to present their views to the nation; the C.I.O. showed greater initiative than the A.F. of L. in the broad field of public relations. The effective work of Len De Caux, director of these activities for the C.I.O., was recognized by the independent American Public Relations Association. This organization of experts in 1946 presented its annual award to the C.I.O. for "outstanding public relations accomplishments" during the preceding year. De Caux used not only the radio, but the daily press, union publications, pamphlets, motion pictures, and even comic-book techniques in order to spread the gospel of the C.I.O.

In the narrower field of lobbying, representatives of the A.F.

of L., C.I.O., and the independent railroad brotherhoods carried on in the usual fashion. They appeared before legislative committees, encouraged the rank and file to write or wire their political representatives, made special attempts to persuade key party leaders, and kept score cards on the voting records of the legislators. In general, the C.I.O. tactics were the boldest and most obnoxious to legislators. Backed by their Political Action Committees, the C.I.O. lobbyists could exert vital pressure upon representatives from industrial areas. When important measures were pending, the lobbyists frequently encouraged delegations from home to make direct calls at the legislators' offices.

The C.I.O. continued to place greater faith in direct political action than did the A.F. of L. The Federation convention of 1946 exhorted its membership to " all out political action in the coming election." But its political organization was not comparable with that of the C.I.O.-P.A.C., and the effectiveness of Labor's League for Political Education, created by the A.F. of L. in 1947, was not impressive. A poll, conducted by *Fortune* magazine in November, 1946, revealed the differences in attitudes within the rank and file of the two major labor groups. Thirty-one per cent of the C.I.O. members polled favored keeping out of politics altogether, while forty-three per cent of the A.F. of L. members favored abstaining. Sentiment for starting a third party was substantial after the disappointing performance, from labor's standpoint, of the conservative bipartisan bloc which controlled the Seventy-ninth Congress. Twenty per cent of the A.F. of L. members advocated a third party, and twenty-nine per cent of the C.I.O. concurred.

After the apparent successes of 1944, the C.I.O.-P.A.C. entered the campaigns of 1946 with confidence. Philip Murray and other C.I.O. leaders declared that labor was in politics to stay; Murray reiterated his opposition to a third party because of its proved futility and stated that the P.A.C. would work through the traditional two-party system. In some areas the P.A.C. supported Republican candidates; issues, not parties, were important. The P.A.C. leaders hoped, however, to prevent the Republicans from winning control of either house of Congress, because they opposed the policies of the national G.O.P.

The November elections proved a stunning blow to the P.A.C. The Republicans, swept into office by a wave of reaction against war-time restrictions and union excesses, won undisputed control of Senate and House. So dismayed were the Democrats that some of their own leaders called upon President Truman to resign. The C.I.O. made a frank assessment of its defeat. The setback to labor and reform hopes was even greater than represented by the Republican majorities, because many of the Democrats elected were conservatives. Numerous factors were responsible for the outcome of the 1946 campaign; one reason was the ineffective organization work by the Democratic party and the political action groups. The P.A.C. was certainly not so strong as in 1944. The absence of Franklin Roosevelt as a symbol and the death of Sidney Hillman several months before the election contributed to the weaker showing. But the C.I.O. did not abandon its political work; it sought rather to intensify it. The C.I.O. campaign of 1948, together with a strong drive by the A.F. of L., contributed mightily to Democratic victory that year. Labor's political comeback was sudden and impressive.

Outlook for the Labor Movement

The future prospects for the labor movement as a whole depend upon the general economic situation. The recurrence of large-scale unemployment would prove a serious setback to union membership. Early in 1947, predictions were made freely that membership losses would occur during the year, because most economists were expecting an early recession. But the recession did not develop and, instead, employment rose steadily. Leaders of both the A.F. of L. and C.I.O. claimed gains in the membership of their constituent unions during 1947, and the total number of organized workers reached an all-time high, near the fifteen million mark.

Serious dangers lie ahead, however. The recession has not occurred, but as the inflationary boom continues, a more devastating collapse is threatened. Many of the difficulties anticipated at the end of the war, such as resettlement of the industrial population and the re-absorption of veterans, have already been overcome. The principal worry of labor leaders remains the

163

possibility of a major economic crash. Such an event would not only reduce union income, but, by increasing the competition for members would intensify jurisdictional strife. Other matters causing concern to organized labor are the possible effects of restrictive labor laws, and a decline in worker sentiment toward representation by unions. The latter trend has been revealed in recent elections supervised by the National Labor Relations Board. In order to strengthen their position against possible future setbacks, both the A.F. of L. and C.I.O. launched determined organization drives in the southern states late in 1946. The "Solid South" has been traditionally unfriendly to labor organizers, and progress of the recent campaigns has been slow. One of the major aims of the effort is to prevent damaging competition by unorganized southern workers with northern labor in time of depression. A secondary objective is to drive a wedge into the conservative political control of the South.

In face of the difficulties which lie ahead, union leaders need to display wise statesmanship. Their general policies during the year 1947 were cautious and moderate. Responsible chiefs in the A.F. of L. and C.I.O. tried to avoid serious strikes; they wished to protect their treasuries and regain public confidence. During the round of wage demands begun in the spring of 1947, the unions showed extraordinary willingness to compromise. Employers were not called upon to follow a general pattern for pay increases. Instead, the union leaders studied the earning position of individual industries and companies, and adjusted their demands accordingly. In the 1947 negotiations there was greater emphasis upon "fringe" demands, rather than boosts in hourly pay rates; these demands involved paid vacations, welfare funds, and retirement plans. The unions hoped to gain long-range benefits without contributing unduly to the inflationary trend. The number of major strikes in 1947, as a result of the conciliatory policies of both labor and management, was far smaller than had been feared. The attitude of moderation continued to prevail through the year 1948.

The basic aspirations of labor for the future have not been altered by the prospect of uncertainties ahead. One of the most deeply rooted of these objectives is the attainment of a greater voice in the direction of industry. Organized labor regards itself as a full-fledged partner in the production process, and wants to be recognized as more than just a silent partner. This desire for " industrial democracy " is more strongly expressed in the C.I.O. philosophy than in the A.F. of L., but it is common throughout the whole union movement.

There seems to be little likelihood that organic unity will soon be achieved among labor organizations; a second withdrawal of John Lewis and his United Mine Workers from the A.F. of L. has added once again to the division. During 1947, overtures and counter-overtures were exchanged frequently between the heads of the A.F. of L. and C.I.O. But the obstacles to unity that existed during the war have not been removed. The general attitude of the older federation was simply to invite the C.I.O. to return to the fold, leaving basic issues to be settled later. Philip Murray, while urging close co-operation between the two groups, steadfastly opposed the merger without a prior settlement of issues. He argued that the sacrifice of fundamental principles was too high a price for achieving organic unity. Merger of the principal union groups would have increased the organizational strength of labor, but it did not necessarily follow that such a combine would be good for the labor movement. So long as important differences exist between the two groups, it is perhaps fortunate that they remain distinct. The separation has the virtue of allowing open competition of ideas and methods, rather than smothering minority expressions in order to maintain a façade of unity. An harmonious union of forces is a generally desirable goal in human affairs, but an unhappy marriage of antagonisms is a dubious venture.

Although fair competition between the A.F. of L. and C.I.O. would exert a wholesome influence, it is possible that the rivalry may degenerate into a bitter struggle for survival. Such an outcome is the principal danger of the division; it is a risk that Philip Murray has accepted. After John Lewis rejoined the A.F. of L. early in 1946, he was expected to lead a broad attack against the C.I.O. His aim, and that of the other leaders in the Federation, was to bring all the workers under unified control by one means or another. If voluntary merger, under threat of attack, would not be agreed to by the C.I.O., then efforts would go on to undermine the rival organization. The principal techniques of the A.F. of L. were to exploit the charge that C.I.O. unions were Communist controlled and to attempt to win over any disaffected right-wing leaders. In a radio address in September, 1946, William Green sounded the keynote of the campaign. He predicted that " disintegration " of the C.I.O. would continue in the coming months and that its affiliates would soon break away and come " knocking at our door." Green promised to forgive and forget their " wanderings " in the name of labor unity—which could be obtained, he declared, only under the banner of the A.F. of L. In such an all-out struggle, the odds for success would favor the older federation. It has more members, more money, and greater internal cohesion. The more conservative policies of the A.F. of L., furthermore, are in consonance with the prevailing trend of national sentiment. The C.I.O. was a peculiar symbol of the era of reform which found broad expression in the New Deal. The passing of the New Deal, followed by the conservative reaction after the war, favored the A.F. of L. Although its rival held prominence during the days of reform, the A.F. of L. may now prove able to recapture its former position of dominance.

But the C.I.O. cannot be counted out. Its leaders have demonstrated extraordinary courage and enterprise. The chief vulnerability of the C.I.O. is the internal split between the right wing and the left wing; if the leadership holds the organization together, the C.I.O. can weather the storm. The total number of Communists in C.I.O. unions is extremely small, but, with their sympathizers, they have succeeded in entrenching themselves in positions of influence. The anti-Communists have been working quietly and steadily to remove them from such positions. The progress within individual unions has been slow; in the middle of 1947 it was reliably estimated that fourteen unions, having one-quarter of the total membership of C.I.O. unions, were still Communist-dominated. But steady progress has been achieved in minimizing Communist influence, especially in the regional and national councils of the C.I.O. Murray has employed every legitimate device to oust Communist sympathizers from power and remove the Red tinge from his organization. In all this he has proceeded cautiously, in order to avoid wrecking the movement and playing into the hands of his enemies. Given time and public understanding, the C.I.O. can eradicate Communist influence and avoid a major breach in its ranks.

The predicted all-out struggle between the A.F. of L. and the C.I.O. did not materialize in 1947, because both organizations were compelled to turn their attention to a serious threat against the whole union movement. The rising tide of public feeling against the unions and their leaders was at least as serious as the division between the major labor groups. This groundswell in sentiment was caused, in part, by specific abuses, mounting fear by non-labor groups of the growing power of labor, employer propaganda, and widespread ignorance of the facts of modern industrial life. But the irresponsible attitudes and actions of a few unions during the war did more than anything else to crystallize public opinion. John Lewis became the embodiment of labor selfishness in the eyes of the man-on-the-street. Even while granting the justice of the miners' grievances, the average man could not condone a strike against the government at a moment when the fate of all groups was seriously menaced. While the overwhelming majority of union workers and leaders served loyally during the war, a small number planted seeds of resentment in the public mind—seeds which could develop into demands for correction and punishment of all labor.

Opinion polls during and after World War II measured the growing feeling against unions. Some of the specific complaints by the public were justified; others were based on half-truths or distortion. One of the chief criticisms was that unions treated the workers unfairly by coercing them and charging exorbitant dues. The other major charge was that unions were unmindful of the public interest and used their power, when they chose, to paralyze the economy. The most dramatic substantiation of this charge was the strike called by the railroad brotherhoods in June, 1946, when the demands of all but two of the unions had been met and the remaining issues were inconsequential by comparison with the threatened collapse of production and distribution.

The public pressure for regulation of unions, though largely unorganized, approached the nature of a social reform movement. Indeed, there was need for reform of certain labor practices. Some effective method of protecting the nation from strikes in vital industries was necessary; the waste and futility of jurisdictional strikes cried out for action; and the time had come for a guaranteed bill of rights for union members in relation to their organizations and leaders. But many of the regulations proposed were not aimed at true reform. They were veiled attempts to turn back the clock and return the nation to a bygone age of crude industrial strife. When the Republican Congress assembled in 1947, it regarded labor regulation as its primary mandate from the people. Various anti-union measures had been pressed in previous sessions of Congress, but until 1947 they were checked by Presidential vetoes. The new Congress had the votes to override the President.

The Taft-Hartley law, which emerged just before the close of the first session of the Eightieth Congress, provided a sweeping overhaul of unions and labor-management relations. Upsetting many of the established practices under the National Labor Relations Act of 1935, it left innumerable questions to the lawyers for interpretation. Some of its features were generally acceptable, but the law was unfortunate in that it attempted too much too fast, and consequently incorporated many unwise provisions. Its chief immediate effect was to antagonize labor, which called for a " finish fight " against the statute. The law provided for " cooling off " periods when strikes threaten in key industries, abolition of the closed shop, statutory liability of unions for breaches of contract by their members, and outlawry of jurisdictional strikes and " featherbedding." [4] There were hundreds of other provisions, governing such matters as relations of workers to their unions, labor-management relationships, and union political activity. One of the most controversial sections required that union officers swear a " non-Communist " oath in order to qualify their organization for protective benefits of the National Labor Relations Board. Refusal to make such an oath was the immediate cause of John Lewis' resignation as an A.F.

---

[4] This is a term used to designate all practices whereby a union may force an employer to hire more people than he actually needs or wants.

of L. vice president and the subsequent withdrawal of the U.M.W. from the Federation. The full effect of the Taft-Hartley law had not been determined by the courts before the Eighty-first Congress undertook its repeal. The ultimate outcome of Congressional action will probably be a moderate reform of union practices; but it is unlikely that a serious reduction of union power or alteration of union-management relations will result.

ILLUSTRATIVE DOCUMENTS

§11. *'Platform of the Conference for Progressive Political Action,'* adopted at Cleveland, Ohio, on July 4, 1924.

For 148 years the American people have been seeking to establish a government for the service of all and to prevent the establishment of a government for the mastery of the few. Free men of every generation must combat renewed efforts of organized force and greed to destroy liberty. Every generation must wage a new war for freedom against new forces that seek through new devices to enslave mankind.

Under our representative democracy the people protect their liberties through their public agents.

The test of public officials and public policies alike must be: Will they serve, or will they exploit, the common need?

The reactionary continues to put his faith in mastery for the solution of all problems. He seeks to have what he calls the " strong men and best minds " rule and impose their decision upon the masses of the weaker brethren.

The progressive, on the contrary, contends for less autocracy and more democracy in government, and for less power of privilege and greater obligation of service.

Under the principle of ruthless individualism and competition, that government is deemed best which offers to the few the greatest chance for individual gain.

Under the progressive principle of co-operation, that government is deemed best which offers to the many the highest level of average happiness and well-being.

It is our faith that we all go up or down together—that class gains are temporary delusions and that eternal laws of compensation make every man his brother's keeper.

In that faith we present our program of public service:

The use of the power of the Federal Government to crush private monopoly, not to foster it.

Unqualified enforcement of the constitutional guarantees of freedom of speech, press and assemblage.

Public ownership of the Nation's water power and creation of a public superpower system. Strict public control and permanent conservation of all national resources, including coal, iron and other ores, oil and timber lands, in the interest of the people. Promotion of public works in times of business depression.

Retention of surtaxes on swollen incomes; restoration of the tax on excess profits, on stock dividends, profits undistributed to evade taxes; rapidly progressive taxes on large estates and inheritances and repeal of excessive tariff duties, especially on trust-controlled necessities of life, and of nuisance taxes on consumption, to relieve the people of the present unjust burden of taxation and compel those who profited by the war to pay their share of the war's costs and to provide the funds for adjusted compensation solemnly pledged to the veterans of the World War.

Reconstruction of the Federal Reserve and Federal Farm Loan System to provide for direct public control of the Nation's money and credit, to make it available on fair terms to all, and National and State Legislatures to permit and promote co-operative banking.

Adequate laws to guarantee to farmers and industrial workers the right to organize and bargain collectively, through representatives of their own choosing, for the maintenance or improvement of their standards of life. . . .

We denounce the mercenary system of foreign policy under recent administrations in the interests of financial imperialists, oil monopolists and international bankers, which has at times degraded our State Department from its high service as a strong and kindly intermediary of defenseless governments to a trading outpost for those interests and concession seekers engaged in the exploitation of weaker nations, as contrary to the will of the American people, destructive of domestic development and provocative of war. We favor an active foreign policy to bring about a revision of the Versailles Treaty in accordance with the terms of the Armistice, and to promote firm treaty agreements with all nations to outlaw wars, abolish conscription, drastically reduce land, air and naval armaments, and guarantee public referendums on peace and war. . . .[5]

---

[5] Edward Stanwood, *History of the Presidency*, rev. ed., II, 450–452. Boston: Houghton Mifflin Company, 1928.

§12. *'William Green on Labor Unity,' in letter of reply to President Roosevelt's appeal for labor peace, written on November 18, 1940.*

To the President of the United States,
The White House,
Washington, D. C.:

Please accept the profound thanks of all those in attendance at our convention for your most inspiring message. Be assured the full support of the membership of the American Federation of Labor in the execution of the government's defense plans and policies.

You can rely upon us to give freely of our skill, training, service and labor to America in order to safeguard and protect our common heritage of freedom, liberty and democracy and in the realization of the common objectives set forth in the first paragraph of your appealing communication wherein you state: " Labor will lend its aid in planning for full efficiency of industrial production, in planning for selection, training and placement of new workers, in planning for full labor and social legislation, in maintaining sound and uninterrupted work in the defense industries and in promoting sound employer-worker relationships at a time like this when the steady flow of production may be our greatest need.

" Sacrifice may be necessary in the future for everyone. Responsible action and self-discipline, physical and moral fitness are now required of all of us as our part in the defense of our country and democracy."

We deeply appreciate the suggestion you make that " an unselfish, a farsighted, and patriotic effort be made to bring about a just and honorable peace within the now divided labor movement." Fortunately, we can officially make answer to your suggestion in a most definite and sincere way.

The executive council included in its report to the sixtieth annual convention of the American Federation of Labor the following recommendation:

" The executive council is firmly of the opinion that labor in America can be solidified and united through affiliation with the American Federation of Labor. In order to accomplish this purpose and realize this objective the executive council reports to the sixtieth annual convention of the American Federation of Labor that it has endeavored to re-establish unity within the labor movement through conferences with representatives of the C.I.O. and has endeavored to bring about a settlement of existing differences during the past year. The committee representing the American Federation of Labor stands ready and willing to meet with a committee representing the C.I.O. for the purpose of negotiating a settlement, anywhere, any time, any place."

Your suggestion, therefore, that when men of honor and good intentions sit down together they can work out a solution which will restore the much-needed harmony either by unity or by a sensible working arrangement is coincidental with this recommendation of the executive council to the convention now in session. . . .

WILLIAM GREEN,
President, American Federation of Labor.[6]

§13. *'John L. Lewis on Labor Unity,' in parts of a speech to the convention of the Congress of Industrial Organizations, on November 19, 1940, in Atlantic City, New Jersey.*

. . . When we are organized in sufficient number and the strength of our organization in comparison with the A.F of L. becomes more obvious, then you can hasten the day when labor can be united. . . .

And they say peace. Peace. Ain't it wonderful? . . .

No plan or plan of peace will be acceptable to the A.F. of L. that will bring in an organization of four million. Why? Because that would disturb the balance of power. Under these circumstances there would no longer be a guarantee that the federation's executive council would be returned. And that's why any honorable plan that looks to peace will fail as long as these gentlemen have the veto power. . . .[7]

§14. *Philip Murray on Labor Unity, in a report on A.F. of L.-C.I.O. unity conferences, May 16, 1947.*

. . . If fundamental principles must be sacrificed as the price for achieving organic unity, then the price is too high. Organic unity on this unprincipled basis could have been achieved several years ago, and the millions of members of the C.I.O. in mass production industries would have remained unorganized.

---

[6] Reprinted by permission of *The New York Times*, November 20, 1940, 17.

[7] Reprinted by permission of *The New York Times*, November 20, 1940, 16.

A labor movement wedded to antiquated concepts and values, no matter how snugly it might fill its shell of organic unity, will not meet the needs of American labor in 1947. . . .[8]

§15. *Sidney Hillman's Explanation of the P.A.C., as stated in the New Republic, August 21, 1944.*

So many statements concerning the C.I.O. Political Action Committee and the National Citizens' Political Action Committee have recently appeared in print—some correct and some incorrect, some friendly and some hostile—that it may not be amiss to set down some of the fundamental facts about these two organizations.

The C.I.O.-P.A.C. was organized in July, 1943, by the Congress of Industrial Organizations for the primary purpose of arousing the working men and women of America to a sense of their own responsibility as citizens of this nation and, in a broader sense, as citizens of a free world. What really started the C.I.O.-P.A.C. happened the year before the organization came into being. The congressional elections held in November, 1942, gave clear evidence that a powerful reactionary trend had set in, which, if it continued through 1944, might well reverse all the progress of recent years and render this nation incapable of making its indispensable contribution toward the eventual establishment of lasting peace. One could not help but recall the congressional elections of 1918, in which Woodrow Wilson lost control of both Houses of Congress, and with it a large measure of his prestige. One could not help but remember the dire consequences both at home and abroad.

Whereas Woodrow Wilson actually lost majority control to the Republican opposition in 1918, the 1942 elections left President Roosevelt with a reduced but still substantial Democratic majority in the Senate and a bare majority in the House. But this distinction was illusory. Actually, through the Unholy Alliance of obstructionist Republicans and reactionary Democrats, a coalition had come into power which was determined not merely to block any further progressive legislation, but to undermine where possible the whole structure of New Deal reform.

Did this mean that the American people had changed its mind? Did the dramatic change in Congress reflect a conservative trend on the part of a majority of the population? We thought not. We

---

[8] Reprinted by permission of *The Washington Post,* May 17, 1947.

thought not, because an analysis of the vote cast in the 1942 election clearly showed what had happened. Only a little more than 28,-000,000 American citizens had cast their ballots in these elections, as against 49,800,000 in 1940. Almost 22,000,000 Americans who had voted in the presidential year had failed to go to the polls two years later. The percentage of those who failed to vote was highest among the normally progressive groups of the population and lowest among those population groups which are normally conservative. The inference was clear. The forces of reaction were organized for political action; the progressive forces were not organized.

That is why the C.I.O.-P.A.C. was born one year later. . . .

First of all, the C.I.O.-P.A.C. put on a nationwide drive to register the vote; it embarked upon an educational campaign among the workers to show them why they had a duty as citizens to exercise their franchise; why this year it was more than ever important for them to do so; and how they could help to organize themselves and other progressives outside of the labor movement for effective political action. This campaign was carried on in the labor press, by means of pamphlets distributed in large quantities, and—when it was possible to obtain time—over the radio.

Second, the C.I.O.-P.A.C. endeavored to mobilize the progressive vote in certain important primary elections throughout the nation, in order to help unseat outstanding reactionary incumbents seeking renomination and to assist outstanding progressive candidates to obtain their party's nomination. Such activity is permissible under the law, since the Smith-Connally Act does not apply to primary contests. The C.I.O.-P.A.C. was active in the primary contests for nomination in both parties. It does not claim to have brought about the nomination or the defeat of a single candidate. It does claim to have contributed important support to the already existing progressive forces in many states—perhaps decisive support in a few instances. By and large, these efforts were more successful in the Democratic primaries than in those of the Republican Party. This is undoubtedly due to the fact that in the Democratic primaries the C.I.O.-P.A.C. was working with the prevailing trend, which has already taken a considerable toll of outstanding reactionaries and isolationists, whereas in the Republican primaries it was working against the pronounced nationalist and reactionary trend which fully manifested itself in the repudiation of Willkie and in the recapture of the Republican leadership by Herbert Hoover and the Old Guard. . . .

That is the job the C.I.O.-P.A.C. set out to do among the industrial workers; and that is the job which the N.C.-P.A.C. has now undertaken to do among the population as a whole. . . .

The response we have had so far to the membership drive in the National Citizens' Political Action Committee is most encouraging. Already it is clear that, so far at least as this election is concerned, farmers, publishers, educators, writers and progressives from every part of the country and from every occupation are ready and eager to unite with the industrial workers in order to reëlect the President and to elect a Congress which will responsibly and loyally support progressive policies at home and abroad.

The N.C.-P.A.C. is committed to Roosevelt and Truman against Dewey and Bricker. Beyond that it has no partisan commitments whatsoever. It will support for election to Congress those men and women who, irrespective of party affiliation, seem best qualified to represent this nation in the critical times which lie ahead. It will support those candidates who have shown that they believe in the principles set forth in President Roosevelt's Economic Bill of Rights, who have shown that they understand that our domestic problems and our foreign problems are opposite sides of the same coin, and that neither can be solved at the expense of the other. It will support those candidates who, in the words of Thomas Jefferson, " have confidence in the people, cherish them and consider them the wise repository of the public interest." It will oppose those candidates who openly repudiate these ideals, or who render lip-service to them in order to conceal their opposition. . . .

This [PAC] " ideology " is neither a mystery nor a closely guarded secret. It is clearly stated in the P.A.C. program, which was adopted last May and which was officially presented to the resolutions committees of both the Republican and Democratic Parties. This program is both a statement of principles and a concrete plan of action. It rests upon the belief that we can and must find a way to utilize the vast spiritual and material resources of this nation that every American who is reasonably industrious and prudent may enjoy at least the minimum elements of a good life—that is, adequate housing, food, clothing, medical care, education, recreation and an opportunity for advancement. It rests upon the belief that too many Americans have died and are dying in foreign lands in defense of democracy for us any longer to permit democracy to be betrayed here at home by social or economic barriers erected against anyone by reason of his race, religion or national origin.

There are people—and they are by no means all Republicans—who do not agree with these principles, and who do not wish to see the progressive forces unite for the purpose of putting them into effect. Some of them have told us that we are unwise to organize for political action, because by doing so we might stimulate the forces of reaction to take similiar action. The forces of reaction have taken this action long ago. They are entrenched and fortified on every rise of ground on the economic contour map of the world. They are fighting grimly behind their Maginot Lines to perpetuate their privileged position.

But the united progressive forces of the world are on the march and will not be denied. They are fighting not for special privilege, but for equality of opportunity for all men everywhere, of every race, of every nationality and of every religious faith.

The fight for human dignity and freedom will not end when we shall have achieved victory at the polls on November 7, any more than it will end when we shall have achieved military victory over Germany and Japan. All that we shall have gained by these victories is survival—survival to fight for freedom, to vote for freedom and to work for freedom—until finally freedom shall have been gained for all men who inhabit this earth.[9]

[9] Sidney Hillman, "The Truth about the PAC," *New Republic*, 111 (Aug. 21, 1944), 209–211. Reprinted by permission of *New Republic*.

CHAPTER SIX

Radical Efforts Since World War I

THE far-reaching influence of both world wars upon the labor movement has been described. Still greater were the effects on radical efforts. American entrance into the first great war split the main radical party of the country and broke its hopes of becoming a real power. The triumph of Bolshevism in Russia, an outgrowth of that war, resulted in a world-wide revolutionary movement—with a branch office in the United States.

Decline of the Socialist Party

The American Socialist party, founded on July 29, 1901, made impressive gains in the years before the war. By 1912 it boasted of a large paid-in membership and a national voting strength of nearly 1,000,000. Although an extremist minority clamored for militant, revolutionary tactics, the socialist majority adhered to a moderate, " gradualist " program. Thousands of native Americans were attracted to the movement, and there was reason to believe that it would become a powerful force.

All this was changed by World War I. Outbreak of hostilities in Europe at once opened a breach in the ranks of socialists everywhere. Marxian doctrine strongly opposed " imperialist " war, which was regarded as a senseless struggle of workers against workers. Socialist leaders in all nations before 1914 vowed to make war impossible by refusing to fight. But, when the crisis struck, socialists were overcome by nationalistic feeling and yielded to the pressure of their governments.

In the United States, however, party members stood fast

against participation in the war. They had more time to think and plan than did the socialists of Europe; they were relatively smaller in numbers and were not caught in the pressure of immediate conflict. During the early years of the war the Socialist party in America agitated for strict neutrality. Support for this line of action was strengthened by the presence of many Germans in the party, but the Socialist position rested squarely upon doctrinal opposition to " imperialist " wars.

When America stood on the brink of the conflict in the spring of 1917, the socialist position was put under heavy stress. While the United States remained a non-belligerent, the attitude of groups within the country was not taken too seriously by the government and the public. The prospect of war, however, changed that situation. After Congress declared war on April 6th, the Socialist party was faced with an immediate decision.

The majority held true to their earlier statements and passed a declaration opposing American participation. In spite of minority dissent, the resolution was overwhelmingly approved by a referendum vote of the Socialist membership. The declaration outlined a specific course of action by workers, calling for continuous opposition by means of petitions and demonstrations. It called also for opposition to all legislation for military or industrial conscription, resistance to all limitations on civil liberties, and persistent propaganda against militarism and imperialism. The declaration also demanded that the government restrict food exports to the Allies in order to protect home consumers.[1]

A number of leaders who put patriotism first left the party in protest against that stand. This was especially true of the trade union members, whose labor organizations came out for full co-operation in the war effort. Direct losses in membership, however, were small compared with the weakening of strength caused by popular reaction and government prosecution.

As nationalistic fervor rose, feeling against the socialists increased. Many Americans who had been sympathetic with party aims began to believe that the organization was unpatriotic

---

[1] Nathan Fine, *Labor and Farmer Parties in the United States, 1828–1928,* 314–315. New York: Rand School of Social Science. This book is the main source used for the effect of World War I on the Socialist party.

and foreign-controlled. Backed by public indignation, the federal government struck out against the obstructionist socialists. On June 15, 1917, President Wilson signed the Espionage Act, which imposed severe penalties on anyone interfering with conscription or making false statements intended to retard the success of the military forces. These provisions made illegal most of the publications of the Socialist party, which called for opposition to the " draft." The *American Socialist,* principal organ of the party, was almost immediately barred, and nearly all other socialist papers were stopped. Continual raids by government agents were made on party offices; records were seized and many leaders imprisoned. Numerous school teachers of socialistic leanings were dismissed by local authorities. Socialist meetings, where permitted, were closely watched. The United States government, engaged in a death-struggle abroad, was unwilling to tolerate interference at home.

Organization activities of the Socialist party were paralyzed by the government's action. The hands of the authorities were further strengthened by an amendment to the Espionage Act of May 16, 1918. This amendment, popularly called the Sedition Act, prohibited the utterance of practically any statement opposing the existing form of government or war aims and methods. Since it covered almost every form of dissent, it gave legal grounds for complete throttling of socialist opposition. Victor Berger defied the law on June 16, 1918, by speaking at Canton, Ohio, against continued American participation in the war. He was arrested, tried, and sentenced to ten years' imprisonment.

The Armistice by no means ended the attack on the socialists. Emotions had been deeply stirred, and the people did not forget the party's attempted interference with the war effort. In February of 1919 all the national officers were indicted and tried for violation of federal laws. The accused, including the party's recognized standard-bearer, Eugene Debs, were sentenced to twenty years' imprisonment. In 1921, however, with war feeling cooled, the Supreme Court reversed the original verdict. It charged that the trial judge, Kenesaw M. Landis, had been prejudiced in handling the case.

Further difficulties were in store for the unhappy socialists in

1919. From the early days of organization the party had brought newly arrived immigrants into the movement by means of "language federations." The Finnish Federation, established in 1907, was the first of these. By 1915 there were fourteen federations, each containing members of a particular tongue. They had a special status of almost complete autonomy within the party. Although the numbers in "language federations" comprised less than one-sixth of the total socialist membership before the war, they increased in proportion during the conflict. While many of the native Americans dropped out of the party on account of its attitude toward the war, the "language federations" steadily grew. In 1919 they represented over half the membership, and several of them were extremely left-wing in viewpoint. Fearing loss of control of the organization, the moderate Executive Committee expelled the Hungarian, Lettish, Lithuanian, Polish, Russian, South Slavic, and Ukrainian federations in May, 1919. This move saved the party from the extremists, but deprived it of about one-third of its members.

The rising star of communism in the United States after 1919 drew away the remaining revolutionaries in the Socialist party. The minority "impossibilist" wing of the Socialist party was thereby broken off, leaving only the war-battered "evolutionary" remains. From that time forward the Marxist movement in the United States was split in two main columns.

In spite of the mutilation resulting from the effects of World War I, the Socialists did not give up. They held to their traditional objective of government ownership of basic industries. An incredible vote of confidence was given to candidate Eugene Debs although he was still in jail. He received nearly 1,000,000 votes for President in the 1920 election. But the socialists could not regain the stride of expansion which was broken by the war upheaval. The general prosperity of the 1920's and the victories of "welfare capitalism" weakened the socialist try for a comeback. New competition was also encountered from the communists on the left and farmer-labor-liberal groups on the right. Norman Thomas won the largest recent socialist vote in the year when American capitalism was faltering. He received nearly 900,000 votes for President in 1932. But Thomas' support fell to less than 200,000 in 1936 and to 120,000 in 1940. It became obvious that the Socialist party had no chance of major success in the United States, but it continued to be the largest radical group in national politics.

Norman Thomas, who was the Socialist candidate for President after 1924, was one of the chief sustaining forces in the party. Born in 1884, the son of a Presbyterian minister, Thomas studied to become a preacher and was ordained in 1911. His humanitarian evangelism led him into social fields, and he at last was converted to the principles of socialism. An ardent pacifist, he joined the party in 1917 when it came out against American participation in the war. A Princeton graduate, scholar, and orator, Norman Thomas proved to be a great asset to the organization. As a capable journalist he carried socialist principles into numerous liberal periodicals and books. In personal appearance and character he had natural attributes of leadership. Although often adhering rigidly to doctrinal attitudes in face of a dynamic world situation, Thomas worked in a broad way for uplifting of the masses.

With such a leader the Socialist party remained strictly an American organization. Its internal structure was basically the same as in earlier days. Co-operation with foreign socialist groups, however, was developed. In May, 1923, a convention at Hamburg, Germany, united the world forces of socialism. The main groups represented were parts of the old "Second International," which had collapsed in 1914; it had been established originally in 1889 as the successor of Karl Marx' "First International." The International Working Union of Socialist parties, which had vainly attempted to re-unite the communist "Third International" with the socialist movement, also joined in. The resulting merger was called the Labor and Socialist International. The American Socialist party joined that association, which had a unified program but no discipline over its affiliates.

The methods of the Socialist party continued the same in the years between two world wars. Aims were to be achieved through education and democratic processes. Strong economic organization of workers was regarded as indispensable to their welfare, but violence was condemned. The socialists hoped to gain political power by peaceful means and to erect the socialist commonwealth in an orderly fashion. They desired to avert blood-shed, civil war, and dictatorship during the transition period. This hope was ridiculed by a rival group which unfurled its red banner at the close of World War I.

Organization of the Third International

From the beginning there was a sharp difference of opinion among the followers of Karl Marx. One group, the "evolutionaries," or "reformists," looked to the gradual accomplishment of socialism through legal and peaceful means. The other group, the "revolutionaries," or "impossibilists," believed that establishment of the new order could come only through sudden and complete overthrow of capitalism. In all countries the socialist organizations reflected that division of thought. In the United States it appeared in the old Socialist Labor party and in its successor, the modern Socialist party. The "evolutionaries" generally were in the majority and controlled the movement.

In 1914 socialist parties throughout the world were split on the issue of backing their respective governments in the spreading conflict. In belligerent countries the majority "evolutionaries," in line with their spirit of co-operation with other classes, supported the national war efforts. The "revolutionaries," however, refused to participate in "imperialist" war and quit the regular socialist organizations.

In Russia the "revolutionaries" constituted the Bolsheviki, or majority, element in the Marxist movement. When they seized control in the 1917 Red Revolution, they became the leading force among all left-wing socialists. Dissenting extremist groups in many nations began to look to Moscow for organization of a unified world-wide movement.

They were not disappointed. After numerous preliminaries, a meeting was held in Moscow from March 2 to 6, 1919. The Bolsheviki, who had taken on the name of Communist party, met with tried and true "revolutionaries" of various countries to form the Communist Third International, distinguishing it from the Socialist Second International. Popularly known in abbreviated form as the Comintern, it aimed to foster a universal revolutionary movement by all extreme Marxist groups. It declared immediately its hatred for " reformist " socialist parties, as well as all other radical organizations which refused to accept the communist platform and tactics. International communism emerged as the culmination of a split in socialist thinking which had persisted since Marx' earliest utterances. Since communism in the United States was only a part of the world-wide movement, it is necessary to examine the basic characteristics of the Comintern.

The communist movement was composed only of proven proletarian workers. While socialists welcomed co-operation from " intellectuals " and other sympathizers, the communists tried to label and separate all but genuine " revolutionaries." This does not mean that they would not set up " front " organizations, in which communist and allied groups appeared to co-operate. But the real communist movement itself was kept pure. Persistent efforts were made to remove moderates from all posts in the organization. These efforts sometimes developed into purges.

The objective of the Comintern was world revolution on the Russian model. This meant temporary dictatorship of the proletariat in each country while collectivization of national life was being effected. The dictatorship, set up to guard against counter-revolution and capitalistic attacks, was ultimately to give way to a highly democratic system. But in spite of the promulgation of a liberal constitution, the ultimate goal has not been reached even in Russia, the communist homeland.

Communists declared themselves especially opposed to imperialism. They called for vigorous anti-colonialism in all countries having possessions. Freedom of colonial workers through revolution was an important goal, which would in turn bring nearer the predicted collapse of capitalism everywhere. The communists opposed " immediate demands " for workers. They hoped that the plight of labor would become so bad that complete overthrow of the existing order would appear as the only means of relief. They declared for world peace through the abolition of capitalism and its international conflict for markets.

The Communist International was one of the most highly centralized organizations in history. Affiliated groups in various countries were but sections, or branches, of the International. Each section had to be called the Communist party of the nation in which it was established. The objectives and methods of every branch were controlled by the Comintern in Moscow. Decisions of the international Executive Committee and Congress were binding on all affiliates, and the local party journals were obliged to print all official notices of the International. The sections in each country were ordered to organize themselves on the principle of " democratic centralization," which meant concentrated power in the leadership and absolute discipline in the rank and file.

Techniques for achieving objectives were to be worked out in Moscow and followed strictly by sections everywhere. All agents, all party publications, and all propaganda were to follow a unified " line." This line changed from time to time according to evolving world conditions. In the beginning it emphasized secret, illegal methods of action as the only ones possible in face of widespread restrictions and prohibitions. Ultimate conversion of the armed forces to communism was considered an indispensable technique; spreading propaganda within labor unions, co-operatives, and other workers' organizations was also stressed. Winning of farmers to the idea of collectivization was regarded as a supplementary means to the envisaged proletarian revolution. Outright seizure of the government and of the means of communication was to be the final step to power.

Early Communist Groups in the United States

Communism in the United States sprang from the " revolutionary " wing of the Socialist party and was concentrated in foreign groups. Friction between the majority " reformists " and dissenting elements reached such a point that in May, 1919, the party Executive Committee expelled seven extremist " language federations," as already noted. At the same time other " revolutionaries," mostly foreign-born, seceded from the party.

Each of these elements, after vain attempts at unity, tried to become the American section of the Communist International.

The seceded groups first met on August 30, 1919, and formed the Communist Labor party. It was less extreme than the organization later set up by the expelled " language federations." Its membership, however, reflecting the line from Moscow, was strictly proletarian. Only workers were eligible. All those receiving their principal income from rent, interest, or profit were barred. Its objectives were the same as communistic aims everywhere—abolition of capitalism and establishment of a collective system on the Russian model. Its organization, true to the principle of " democratic centralization," gave chief power to the secretary and the Executive Committee. The Communist Labor party hoped to achieve a dictatorship of the proletariat after preparing the workers for action by successive mass strikes. The foundation for these strikes was to be the building of a new, revolutionary trade union movement. " Dual " unions were to be established in major fields to draw members from the conservative A.F. of L. unions.

The expelled language federations met on September 1, 1919, to launch their own organization. These groups, dominated by the Russian and South Slavic federations, were wholly foreign and very extreme. They took the name of Communist party. Neither this party nor the Communist Labor party, however, was a party in the ordinary political sense. They were both illegal, revolutionary bands. Their names appeared on no election ballots. Indeed, they did not plan to work by voting methods at all. Revolutionary unionism and large-scale strikes were to be the means of action.

Federal, state, and local authorities made war upon all communist groups from 1919 to 1921. A. Mitchell Palmer, President Wilson's attorney general, gained national attention for his raids and prosecutions against illegal elements. The underground communist movement was further hindered by growing factional disputes. In the spring of 1920 Moscow took a hand in the situation. The Comintern ordered the merger of the Communist Labor party and the Communist party. On June 12, 1920, a secret unity convention was held. The merger was carried out, but the Russians in the Communist party and some others refused to unite and remained independent until 1923. The unity group was called the United Communist party. In a later public statement its leaders declared for mass action, intensive propaganda in the army and navy, and secret preparation for the eventual armed struggle. Members were instructed to join labor unions and attempt to win them over to communism.

Formation and Development of the Communist Party of America

Although the United Communist party represented the principal forces in the movement, a few independent groups remained. Since the International insisted on unity of effort in each country, an attempt was made to bring together all communist forces. A convention in New York City, meeting from December 23 to 26, 1921, united diverse elements into the Workers' party.

It was, however, only an " upper story " to the communist movement in the United States. The Workers' party appeared in the open in response to orders from Moscow, but it was controlled by an underground organization directly affiliated with the Comintern.[2] Leaders of the secret group joined the Workers' party and became its most active members. But they also continued their illegal efforts through the real communist body under the surface. It was not until April, 1923, that the underground was dissolved and the Workers' party was recognized as *the* Communist party in the United States. With the approval of Moscow it inherited the membership and assets of the secret organization. The " upper " and " lower " stories were thereby consolidated.[3] In 1928 the Workers' party threw off the mask and changed its name to the Communist party of the U. S. A.— a section of the Third International.

Membership in the Communist party grew slowly during the

[2] Selig Perlman and Philip Taft, *History of Labor in the United States*, 425–426. New York: The Macmillan Company, 1935.

[3] James Oneal, *American Communism*, 140–143. New York: Rand Book Store, 1927.

1920's. Since many of the party records were kept secret, it is impossible to find accurate figures. The main element in membership was undoubtedly foreign-born, although increasing numbers of native Americans joined the movement during the Depression. Support at the polls was greater than the number of actual members. The first Communist candidate for President, William Z. Foster, received some 30,000 votes in 1924. The break-down of capitalist prosperity swelled Foster's vote in 1932 to over 100,000. But apparently the peak of popular strength was passed in that year. Earl Browder received only 80,000 votes in the Presidential campaign of 1936, and less than 50,000 in 1940.

Objectives of the Communist party were not so extreme as those of the early Communist Labor party. The fundamental purposes were the same, but the immediate aims were different. It must be remembered, of course, that the Communist party in the United States was established as a branch of the Comintern. Its program, techniques, and line were ordered from Moscow. The objectives changed somewhat from earlier communist aims because world conditions altered the outlook for revolution.

During the period of world-wide social upheaval following the close of World War I, the Comintern called for preparation for civil war, propaganda in the armed forces, and other steps toward a sudden revolutionary stroke. But when " normalcy " set in during the 1920's, it appeared that there was no immediate likelihood of overthrow of the existing system. Consequently, the Third International shifted to more practical objectives, and realistic and immediate demands were set forth. This shift in aims, conceived in Moscow and carried out by the Communist party, was intended to appeal to the masses of workers. The communists hoped to pull the workers farther and farther in their direction—and then gain control of the whole labor movement.

William Z. Foster was the outstanding leader of the party in the 1920's. A railway carman by trade, he joined the Industrial Workers of the World in 1909. He was also a left-wing member of the Socialist party in Seattle. In 1911 Foster went to Europe as a correspondent for the I.W.W. press. Association with Leon

Jouhaux and other French radical leaders convinced him that the "dual union" policy of the I.W.W. was wrong. Returning to the United States, Foster attempted to convert the Industrial Workers into a propaganda agency for working within the A.F. of L. However, during World War I he gave up syndicalism for straight unionism. When the post-war reaction came down upon labor, the shifting Mr. Foster plunged again into radicalism—this time into the Communist movement. He became the leader of the Worker's party, later called Communist, and was its presidential candidate in three consecutive campaigns. In the middle of the 1930's, Foster gave way to Earl Browder's leadership. A native of Kansas, Browder was better suited to the moderate, collaborationist line initiated by the Third International during the period of the "united front."

The organization of the Communist party during the Twenties and Thirties was built on plans laid down in Moscow. As the American section of the Third International, it represented world communism and was obedient to decisions by the international leaders. Centralization of power, strict discipline of members, ownership of the party press, and orthodox communist doctrine were firmly maintained. A convention of the membership elected the Executive Committee, which, in turn, chose the chairman and all other officers. This was the principle of "democratic centralization," making possible control by a small group.

After 1925 the basic units of the party were small groups called "cells." These were formed secretly in workshops and neighborhoods, and cells in a particular area were grouped together as a sub-section. The sub-sections were main divisions of the Communist party, which in turn was a section of the International. The main source of authority was the international Congress and Executive Committee. Orders passed down directly through the sections, sub-sections, and cells. It was a distinctly military organization, with control from the top.[4]

Perhaps the most interesting feature of communism was its technique of action. Other Marxist groups preached the same general aims and purposes years before the advent of the Third International. But the communists, on the basis of their Russian

---

[4] Oneal, *op. cit.*, 227–228.

achievement, boasted of being masters of the process of revolution. Members of the Communist party in America, taught by the writings of Lenin and others, were proud of their methods and confident of their ultimate success.

The general public, of course, did not have a clear picture of communist techniques. One reason was that the general orders came from Moscow and the other was that the methods were constantly shifting. Opportunism was the key word in communist tactics. All means were subordinated to the final goal of dictatorship of the proletariat, but *any* means to that end was used. As conditions changed, tactics were altered.

Although the party offered candidates for public office, it had no faith in democratic processes. It considered the ballot box useless except as an advertising device. Political methods were not seriously regarded as a means to power; they were just another form of propaganda. Relentless propaganda of every type was the life-blood of the communist effort. The masses had to be " awakened " and influenced to support the party if final victory were to be achieved. Propaganda was spread through books, periodicals, speeches, and demonstrations. That is why the communists fought zealously for civil liberties. They were contemptuous of democracy, but free speech and press were indispensable to the steady flow of revolutionary propaganda.

While propaganda poured out in the most " scientific " fashion, other basic methods of the party were continually changing. The main shift was back and forth from the policy of " dualism " and " co-operation." Wherever and whenever the communists had sufficient following, they came out independently and opposed all other groups, liberal or reactionary. If their following was insignificant, as was usually the case, they submerged their own identity and tried to work with or within other groups, in the hope of ultimately winning them over to communism.

When communism first began in this country, at the close of World War I, the leaders were instructed to be " dualist," or " independent." The air was full of revolution, and it was hoped that a sudden overturn might be forced. In that event the communists did not want the co-operation of moderates or liberals. They felt that by working alone they could make the extreme break, without the necessity of compromise. As conditions became more settled in the 1920's and the prospect of immediate revolution faded, they sought to gain allies through "co-operation" with reformist, liberal, and other sympathetic groups. On February 22, 1922, the Third International ordered communist sections everywhere to follow the line of a "united front" with co-operating organizations. The American section promptly complied.

Since few groups in America during the 1920's would participate in any "united front" with communism, the party had to work secretly. It naturally turned first to the labor unions. If the workers could be won over, the striking power of the organization would be vastly augmented. As early as 1920 the Trade Union Educational League had been formed as a subsidiary for communist efforts within the unions. It was chiefly a propaganda bureau, similar to previous agencies set up by William Z. Foster for winning over conservative workers. As a means of "boring" into the A.F. of L. unions, the League supported all protests made by the rank and file against policies of the leadership. Communist "plants" in various unions, by leading such protests, hoped eventually to be supported as official leaders. That would enable them to subject the unions to communist direction. By 1924 the effort had generally failed, and most of the communists were detected and expelled from the unions. They abandoned the broader effort and concentrated on gaining control of the few unions where they had greater proportionate strength. Those organizations were chiefly in the clothing industry, and progress was achieved toward controlling some of the garment unions.

While the general attempt to capture the labor unions from within was collapsing, efforts were made to win "co-operation" in the political field. One of the most notable examples was the case of the Farmer-Labor party. It had been established in November, 1919, by a group of middle-western unionists. It then attempted to broaden its organization to include farmers and liberals, as well as labor. The communists regarded this as an opportunity for gaining leadership of a rising movement. After careful plans they surprised the original founders of the party by winning control of the Farmer-Labor convention of July 3, 1923. When the original elements quit in disgust, the communists changed the name to Federated Farmer-Labor party and tried to promote it as a " united front " organization. But this first of many similar efforts failed. As soon as the communist stamp was discovered, the " co-operating " groups lost interest. The communists were unable to start an effective political movement although they succeeded in wrecking the original Farmer-Labor party. Many later organizations have been wrecked since then by the same communist technique.

When by 1928 the " boring " and " co-operative " methods seemed futile, the Communist party decided to modify them. The leaders planned to start a rival or " dual " union where there was no hope of capturing the established organization. Four new unions were set up, and in September of 1929, by direction from Moscow, the Trade Union Educational League was transformed into the Trade Union Unity League. It became a central body for the newly developed " dual " unions, while continuing propaganda within many conservative unions. This effort to generate revolutionary unionism outside of the regular labor organizations also failed. Some communist unions were established in the textile, clothing, metal, marine, and lumber fields. But in 1931 the total membership of the Trade Union Unity League was only about 30,000.

After 1932 the Communist party again shifted its methods according to the flow of circumstances. It abandoned " dualism," for the most part, and returned to " boring from within " and building up " united front " organizations. Clubs, leagues, associations, and alliances were established in diverse social fields; as old ones dissolved, new organizations were engineered by the communists. Particularly among youth, efforts were made to capitalize on all protesting forces and convert them to radical ends. The National Student League, succeeded by the American Student Union, was established as a " co-operative " movement of liberal college and university students. Both were controlled by communists. The same was true of the American Youth Congress, which gained wide attention in 1939 and 1940.

Formation of the C.I.O. in 1935 opened new possibilities to

communists in the labor movement. They had proved unable to convert the old and established unions of the A.F. of L., but by performing yeoman service in the organization of new unions, and by camouflaging their true colors, they were able to gain positions of power. By 1940 the communists and their sympathizers had virtual control of several unions in important defense industries.

The rise of the Nazi party in Germany in the late 1930's, with its violent attack on world communism, prompted the Third International to move for stronger co-operation with all democratic forces opposing fascism. The "united front" against fascism was played up by Moscow and its affiliates during the Spanish Civil War and in subsequent European and Asiatic crises. Although collaboration with bourgeois elements was sanctioned for the time being, the International emphasized that the Communist parties must not forget the distinction between them and the democratic groups. During the period of co-operation the communists were to work for positions of control, which could be used to advantage when the capitalist crisis arrived. Meanwhile, they were to praise not the Soviet system, but democracy; not the class struggle, but co-operation.

Communists in the United States and in other countries quickly put the new line into operation, but while in the midst of stirring up hatred of fascism, they were suddenly embarrassed in August, 1939, by announcement of the Russian-German Non-aggression Pact. After momentary shock and bewilderment, communist leaders in the United States quickly soft-pedaled their attack on Hitler. They swallowed former words demanding intervention by the United States against fascism and suddenly proclaimed "The Yanks are *not* coming!" This about-face was, of course, prompted by Moscow in line with the German agreement. But it was disconcerting to American communists who had outdone themselves in building a "united front" against Hitler. The International usually gave advance warning of impending shifts in technique and line. The acrobatic maneuver by American communists in August, 1939, showed some of the difficulties of being tied to an autocratic world organization. When Russia was suddenly invaded by Hitler in

June, 1941, the communists surprised no one by reversing their flip-flop and calling for war against the Nazis.

End of the I.W.W.

The Industrial Workers of the World, with its syndicalist plans for abolition of the wage system through mass strikes, lost its force during World War I. It failed to build a solid and disciplined organization, and when it opposed the government's war effort in 1917 it fell to pieces under counterattack by the government. Activities of I.W.W. leaders in violation of the Espionage and Selective Service acts led to legal charges by the Department of Justice. Government agents raided organization headquarters in all major cities from coast to coast. Even the private homes of the leaders were entered, and records and literature seized. On September 5, 1917, a federal grand jury indicted 166 members of the Industrial Workers.

Trial of the accused began on April 1 of the following year, although only 105 of the total indicted were found and arrested. Judge Kenesaw M. Landis listened to evidence on four conspiracy charges. The trial, held in Chicago, drew nation-wide attention, and in the end nearly all the accused were convicted. Judge Landis on August 30, 1918, gave sentences of from one to twenty years' imprisonment and fines totaling $2,300,000. William D. Haywood was among those found guilty, but the I.W.W. leader escaped punishment and deserted the movement by fleeing to Russia.

Public reaction against the unpatriotic stand of the I.W.W. was displayed locally, as well as by the national government. Meeting halls in many states were closed, leaders placed in jail, and organizers driven out—sometimes with benefit of tar and feathers. The Industrial Workers of the World was smashed by the wave of indignation and temper that rolled over the country. From its peak membership of nearly 100,000 in 1917, the organization fell in numbers to about 7,000 in 1930. Sporadic appearances persisted, but the I.W.W. was no longer a force. Many of its rank-and-file members joined the Communist party.

Achievements of the revolutionary union movement were few indeed. It fell completely short of its fundamental goals and even failed to keep workers enrolled in its unions. It did not become a serious rival of the A.F. of L., although it did anticipate the industrial union structure of the C.I.O. The I.W.W. was never organized for long-term action, but depended upon irregular, guerrilla tactics. Its aims were too extreme to gain broad support, and it finally collapsed under official and public assault.

Radical Movements During World War II

Recalling the effect of World War I upon the socialist movement, leaders of the party in this country viewed the prospect of American involvement in another war with apprehension. The strength of the Socialist party organization had dwindled almost to insignificance by 1940; blows such as those sustained in 1917–1919 could well have destroyed what remained. The basic attitude of the socialists toward the Axis war, however, was somewhat different from its attitude toward World War I. The doctrinal antagonism toward the earlier conflict was predicated on the assumption that all parties to the capitalist-imperialist war were equally guilty. In 1940 the socialists saw the Nazis as the principal threat to be reckoned with and were, therefore, in sympathy with pro-democratic forces.

Notwithstanding their sympathies, the socialists fought hard against intervention by the United States. Norman Thomas, preaching the gospel of neutrality, found responsive audiences during the critical period before Pearl Harbor, when pacifism and isolationism were riding high. Thomas, however, denied any affiliation with the isolationists. His outlook was international, but he was convinced that the United States, by remaining out of the war, could exercise a greater power for world peace and economic reconstruction. Thomas predicted that the struggle between Britain and the Axis would end in stalemate, with Russia emerging as the dominant power of Europe. This view was upset when Hitler turned suddenly on the Soviets in June, 1941, but Thomas continued to oppose American involvement and preparedness. As late as September, 1941, in justifying his opposition to peacetime conscription, he declared that the United States was actually in less danger than a year before. Although there was considerable justification for

Thomas' belief that the United States could exercise a more beneficial influence if allowed to remain at peace, there was a complete lack of realism in his belief that the question of peace or war could be determined by the will of the American people alone.

Thomas' overwhelming obsession was his fear that American participation would mean the suppression of civil liberties and democratic processes at home. This proved to be an unwarranted fear. Moderate policies prevailed after the declaration of war in December, 1941, and the socialists did not suffer from attack or persecution because they did not attempt to obstruct the war effort. Taking a lesson from their experience in World War I, the party leaders gave general support to the war, attempting only to influence its direction and conduct. During the four years of conflict, Thomas called for maintenance of civil liberties, democratic control of the all-out effort, and the establishment of worthy peace objectives, including the elimination of imperialism, intolerance, and the basic causes of war.

The Socialist party did not forget its long-range objectives during the world upheaval. Thomas reiterated the fundamental assumption of his party that the principal problems and forces in the modern world were economic and that the builders of the new society would have to be the workers (in a broad sense) and not the owners of property. Thomas, however, encouraged co-operation between the workers and other groups as the only practical means of attaining socialist objectives. In a direct assault upon communist theory and practice, the socialist leader declared that while Lenin had been correct in many of his ideas, he forgot that men covet power as much as profits. Stalin, Thomas declared, had substituted his own tyranny for that of capitalism; true socialism could be achieved only as a partner of true democracy. The immediate aim of the Socialist party in 1944 was government control of money and banking, natural resources, monopolies, semi-monopolies, and all other exploitive industries.

The general appeal of the Socialist party and its organizational strength continued to dwindle during World War II. In New York City, the principal focus of Socialist strength, a number of party members switched their support to the American Labor Party, an organization supported by various labor and liberal groups in the state. The Social Democratic Federation, which had been formed by a dissident Socialist minority in the 1930's, also backed the American Labor Party for several years, but later withdrew in protest against alleged pro-communist control of the A.L.P. In 1944 the Social Democratic Federation helped to establish a new political splinter, the Liberal party. This organization advocated a mixed economy, involving over-all government planning and private enterprise. Although diverse elements, union and non-union, contributed support to the Liberal party, it represented another socialist off-shoot. These various diversions of socialist strength drained the membership of the national party. In the presidential campaign of 1944, Norman Thomas made a signal effort to unify and expand the support of the Socialist party. He stumped the nation in a strenuous coast-to-coast tour. But although signs of party revival appeared during the course of the campaign, the election outcome proved disappointing. Thomas received but 80,000 votes—a minute fraction of the total balloting. The voting strength of the party had fallen to a point where it was not significantly larger than that of its former rival, the old Socialist Labor party. The S.L.P., its influence restricted almost entirely to New York City, continued to expound the revolutionary doctrines of Daniel De Leon, who had died in 1914. The faithful few, meeting annually to celebrate the anniversary of their prophet's birth, still declared that the workers would eventually win emancipation through De Leonism; but it was clear that they were heard by themselves alone.

Except in the person of Norman Thomas, the Socialist party almost ceased to exist for the majority of Americans during the war years. What attention they gave to radicalism, out of fear or amusement, was directed primarily at the Communist party. The American Reds, whose candidate Earl Browder received only 80,000 votes for president in 1940, were no more potent as an independent political force than were the socialists. But their ceaseless propaganda, their infiltration into labor unions, their veiled influence in many front organizations, and their connection with a great foreign power gave the communists a unique position in the radical movement. During the period of Russo-German collaboration, before June 22, 1941, the communists demonstrated their strength by fomenting strikes in defense industries. It was during this phase of the war that public sentiment became most aroused against the Reds, and the federal government moved to check their power. Earl Browder, their leader, was arrested and convicted for passport fraud; in April, 1941, he began to serve his term of imprisonment in a federal penitentiary.

As soon as Russia was attacked and began to look to the United States for arms, there were no more communist-inspired strikes in war industry. The former obstructionists quickly became super-patriots and warmly supported the Administration's efforts to speed production. This turn of affairs made matters easier for the Administration, which was willing to co-operate with all elements of the country, regardless of political belief, in the interest of winning the war. President Roosevelt also desired, after the United States became a partner in the shooting war, to strengthen the tacit alliance with Russia. As a token of this attitude, Roosevelt commuted Browder's jail sentence in May, 1942. Browder had served fourteen months and would soon have become eligible for parole. The President's action was generally approved by the country since it was felt that the communist leader had already served the normal term for passport fraud, and that his immediate release would promote unity of all elements in the war effort.

The new relationship with Russia and the release of Browder were followed by events which brought the Communist party into unprecedented harmony with the national administration. These happenings in the United States were but part of a world-wide pattern which was cut in Moscow. On May 22, 1943, the Presidium (permanent executive body) of the Comintern proposed a resolution to the constituent Communist parties (sections); it proposed dissolution of the international organization, on the ground that it had outlived its purpose and usefulness. On June 10, after most of the constituent parties had submitted their votes of approval, the Presidium appointed a special committee to close out the affairs of the Comintern and dispose of its property. This sudden, self-imposed end to the work of the Comintern appeared to be an event of singular importance in the history of world communism. The movement, which had started out after the close of the first great war as a world revolutionary effort, was now settling down along nationalistic lines. Dissolution of the Comintern was explained by the communists as proper recognition of the fact that vast differences in economic conditions, social orders, and public consciousness in the various countries required a reorientation of the movement on a national, rather than an international basis.

Whatever were the real reasons lying behind the decision in Moscow to abandon the Comintern, the action was viewed with skepticism in the United States. Some observers thought the move was a natural historical development, a reflection of the growing spirit of nationalism within Russia; others looked upon it as primarily a political maneuver by the Soviets, intended to placate the Allies and thereby to induce greater aid from them during and after the war. Observers familiar with communist tactics were doubtful if the move would have any significance in terms of deeds. The obedience of the various national Communist parties to international direction had always been chiefly in the nature of a voluntary, rather than a forced discipline. It remained to be seen if Moscow would continue to call signals for the national parties and persist in its world-wide anti-capitalist propaganda.

The communists in this country were, as usual, quick to take their cue from Moscow. For several years the party had been asserting that it was no longer a section of the Comintern, that it was, in fact, autonomous. But the dissolution of the international organization was regarded by the communists of this country as a signal to go much further than had been contemplated in the past. In January, 1944, following Browder's " inspired " lead, the national committee of the party announced that its political committee had recommended disbandment of the *party* in favor of an *association*. Browder gave the strongest personal support to this proposal, stating that it was a necessary step in conformity with the Teheran Declaration, signed by the

Big Three leaders in December, 1943. For the succeeding twelve to eighteen months, the Teheran Declaration was the keynote of communist action in the United States; in order to achieve the utmost co-operation among the Big Three in defeating the Axis, the communists willingly submerged their revolutionary ideas in the interest of national unity and harmony. On May 20, 1944, the national party congress accepted the Browder resolution to dissolve the party and simultaneously proclaimed itself the constituent congress of the Communist Political Association. This new, non-partisan organization was pledged to the traditions of the nation's " progressive " forefathers (Washington, Jefferson, Paine, Jackson, and Lincoln) and promised to work through the established two-party system in a manner consistent with American tradition and character.

Browder explained the unprecedented self-denial of the old party as up-to-date Marxism. The faithful, accustomed to swallowing almost anything in the form of official " line," probably gulped a little as Browder told them that Marxists must accept the perspective of a capitalist United States for an indefinite time to come; that an attempt to introduce socialism would violate the national unity in support of Teheran. He declared, further, that the American people were ill-prepared subjectively for a deep-going change toward socialism, and that the post-war period in the United States should call not for a transition from capitalism, but for expanded production and the strengthening of democracy. Expanded production, indeed, had become the chief immediate aim of the communists. Russia, with her great cities and farms laid waste by invasion, needed, more than anything else, to rebuild after the war. Her leaders doubtless hoped that harmony and co-operation, sealed at Teheran, would lead to substantial American aid in Russian reconstruction. Revolutionary agitation in the United States could be postponed; meanwhile, continued harmony was pursued so that uninterrupted production in the United States might provide the materials so desperately needed by the Soviet. Browder argued speciously that he was practicing twentieth-century Marxism, but for the moment he had subordinated doctrinal considerations to the immediate physical needs of

Russia. When, in the spring of 1945, it appeared that American power might be used to check Russian expansion rather than assist Russian reconstruction, the communist line was turned about. In July, 1945, the " revisionist " errors of Browderism were frankly discussed and condemned by the membership; the party was reconstituted; and William Z. Foster, symbol of the old, fighting communism, was raised to leadership. Browder and harmony, having served their temporary usefulness, were discarded.

The Present and Future of American Radicalism

The Socialist party, unlike the Communist, has not undergone violent reversals of aims and methods; free of attachment to a foreign power, it has been guided steadily by consideration of the needs of America in an ever-changing and interdependent world. The Socialist program today is in part the product of the various schools of thought which have preceded it: Marxism, Fabianism, and revisionism; syndicalism, guild socialism, and communism. But modern socialism, as described by one of its leading spokesmen, Harry Laidler, is no longer concerned primarily with dogma; it has grown increasingly pragmatic, practical, and realistic.[5] Although considerable differences of opinion remain within socialist ranks, there is basic agreement on the aim to eliminate waste, insecurity, and the gross inequality of wealth in the United States, while moving toward an industrial order for service instead of profit.

Observation of collective experiments abroad, especially in Russia, led the Socialist party to place emphasis upon objectives and methods beyond nationalization of the means of production. It has become clear that state ownership, of itself, does not produce the millennium; democratic socialism requires more than mere collectivization. In order to prepare the way for successful democratic socialism, the party recognizes the necessity for strengthening such organizations as labor unions, co-operatives, political associations, and educational leagues. It favors closer relations among the working class, middle class, and farmers. It

[5] Harry W. Laidler, *Social-Economic Movements,* pp. 750–751, 642–643. New York: The Thomas Y. Crowell Company, 1944.

recommends development of more effective techniques of local government, an improved system of public administration, and further experimentation with the corporate form of government ownership as a means of decentralizing industrial control. The Socialists wish to preserve free choice by consumers, as well as the civil rights and liberties of citizens.

The Socialist party, notwithstanding its high purposes and manifest reasonableness, has failed to win and hold a substantial following in the United States. Its leaders have hoped that the development of public ownership and control over schools, transportation, water, power, and credit would extend to other areas of economic and social life. They have also believed that the breakdown of traditional property relationships in business, achieved by the giant corporation, would weaken the resistance to socialization. It is probable that public control will continue to expand; but the people of this country will move gradually, and the instrument of change will be the traditional two-party system, not the Socialist party.

Why, then, do the Socialists continue their futile efforts as an independent national political party? Norman Thomas has answered that question by stating that he believed his party will some day supplant either the Republicans or Democrats as one of the two major parties. The Socialist party, by remaining in the political race, " educates " the voters and holds out the hope of an eventual broad alliance of labor and farmer groups. It is most unlikely that Thomas' hopes will be realized. If a strong and durable third party should be formed, it will be led by larger and more powerful elements. The Socialist party might well be absorbed in such a movement, but it could hardly expect to lead it. Socialists have made, and will continue to make, an impression on American literature and thought, but they have ceased to be an actual or potential political force.

The Communist party in the United States has never seriously aspired to independent political power. It is a party in a very different sense—in the sense of a conspiracy aimed at ultimate seizure of control by any available means. The precise relationship of the party to Russian communists has been the subject of much discussion, but the arguments are of little practical significance. It is a clear fact that the party in this country behaves as if its primary loyalty is to Russia rather than America. Whether control be exercised openly through the Comintern, secretly through Russian agents, or by the voluntary submission of native puppets, it is the interest of Russia which is served. The leaders of Moscow are regarded by communists throughout the world as the true apostles of their movement. Party leaders in the United States look toward Russia for guidance and support; Stalin reciprocates by giving his indirect blessing to whatever faction will best serve the shifting policy of the Soviet. Within the party itself, individual members are allowed no freedom to judge or act in an area where the official " line " has been pronounced. Departure from the line leads inevitably to censure and expulsion.

The rigidity of the party system results in a high turn-over of members. The total number of members claimed in 1948 was about 80,000; of this number about ten per cent had belonged to the party for at least fifteen years and were considered permanent. A larger percentage, from thirty to forty per cent, were regarded as fairly stable, with the length of membership ranging from two to ten years. But the remainder, at least fifty per cent, were short-term members. They may join while involved in a strike or some other particular action, but soon lose interest. Many members are also dropped for failure to pay dues or for disagreement with the party line. A great deal is expected of each member; his work for the party must extend into organizational activities, and even into social and personal spheres. Weariness and irritation from the never-ending demands of the party are a common cause for quitting. The quitter is thereafter regarded by the party, of course, as an " enemy of the working class."

In addition to the enrolled members of the Communist party, there is, reputedly, a considerable number of secret members. These people, because of their secret status, cannot be subject to the ordinary party discipline. One purpose behind this special category of membership is the desire to protect certain high-placed individuals whose work for the party would be impossible if their affiliation were known; another reason is to provide a stand-by organizational nucleus, which could continue communist operations underground in the event that the " open " party should be declared illegal.

Loss of members, both secret and enrolled, has frequently resulted from factional disaffection. Although the Communist party is the principal heir of revolutionary Marxism in the United States, it has minority rivals. Probably the most important of these is the Trotskyite group, which was expelled in 1928 for its " left-wing " views. It stands for international revolution as contrasted with the nationalistic trend of Stalinist communism. In 1938 American Trotskyites met with their doctrinal comrades from other countries to form a " Fourth International," which was proclaimed as the legitimate heir of the original " Third International " (Comintern). When the Comintern was dissolved in 1943, the Trotskyites naturally viewed the action as a belated recognition of Stalin's disavowal of true Marxism. At the close of World War II, speaking in this country through the Socialist Workers party, the Fourth International appeared more confident than ever of its mission of world revolution. A faction less influential than the Trotskyites—the Lovestoneites—was expelled from the Communist party in 1929; this group, considered to be " right-wing," included Benjamin Gitlow, who later " confessed " to the American public in a popular autobiography.[6] Whenever factions have broken off from the regular party, a diversion of strength has resulted, and the existence of rival groups constitutes an ever-present threat to the membership of the main stem. It may be anticipated that the process of disaffection and splintering will continue in the future.

The organization of the Communist party is well suited to combat tendencies toward disaffection. The new constitution, adopted in 1945, reinforces the principle of " democratic centralism." Above the party " cells " or clubs, the county, state, and intermediate jurisdictions, is the national committee and national secretariat. Most day-to-day power is concentrated in the secretariat, which consists of the general secretary and two

---

[6] Benjamin Gitlow, *I Confess,* New York: E. P. Dutton & Co., Inc., 1940.

other officials. Between annual meetings of the national party congress, a small circle of men actually makes the policy and issues the communist line to all members. The leadership gets the line from above by means of various devices. The " tip-off " to drop Earl Browder and the co-operation policy was given through Jacques Duclos, leader of the French Communist party. In April, 1945, following a visit to Moscow, Duclos wrote an article in a French magazine; the article criticized Browder and called for a new leader in the American communist movement. As soon as the statement was republished in the *Daily Worker*, it was taken as the source document for a new communist line in this country. Since the dissolution of the Comintern, the French Communist party has been frequently used to transmit new directions from Moscow. However, while the French party may be used today, tomorrow it may be the Bulgarian, Pole, or Hungarian party, or perhaps the recently established international Cominform.

The techniques of action by the communists have changed very little. Propaganda and infiltration are still important methods; special attention has been given to expanding communist influence in labor unions. In 1946 the national chairman of the party, William Z. Foster, started an intensive drive for new members, chiefly in the unions. Under Browder's leadership the party lost some of its strength in labor organizations; Foster, with his experience as a labor organizer and agitator, looked for considerable success in his union drive. The general method of the communists, when they are established in unions, is to work their way into the affairs of the local organizations. If no factions exist, they create them; if issues are lacking, they supply them. The " Commies " spread false rumors about the union leaders, strive to gain control, first, of a faction and then of the local itself. After winning this step, the Communist leaders then work by the same methods to extend their power through the national or international union. Their successes and reverses in the C.I.O. have been discussed in the preceding chapter.

The general line of the Communist party after World War II was to seek power more boldly and openly; this line conformed with the policies of European communists, who were making important political gains. In the national elections of 1948 the communists actively supported Henry Wallace's third-party effort, in the hope of gaining ultimate control of the movement. Long before Wallace announced his candidacy, the communist leadership called for a broad effort to implant in the minds of the masses the idea that the time was ripe for a third party " rooted in the mines and the mills."

It is unlikely that any such bid for political power will succeed, in spite of the aid received from Wallace's break with the Democratic party. For one thing, the anti-radical sentiment of Congress and the public is striking hard blows against the bold new communist attitude. Contempt citations and legal prosecutions may seriously weaken the party leadership and force a modification of its line; it may become necessary for the communists to move more silently for a while, boring " quietly " from within rather than shouting from without. Indeed, it is possible that if their present policy continues to encounter strong opposition, the communists may go completely underground or make a sudden change of face. Earl Browder, expelled from the party in 1946 for " betraying the principles of Marxism-Leninism and deserting to the class enemy," may once again be dusted off and trotted out as the champion of class co-operation and harmony!

The Communist party has achieved none of its basic aims in the United States, and the future of the movement will probably be no more successful than its past. The technological trend in this country is definitely away from the development of a manual, proletarian worker such as Marx described; there is no indication of an intensifying " class struggle." Communism has exerted a considerable influence in some areas of the labor movement, and it has affected currents of thought throughout the United States. But the fact remains that no group advocating revolutionary social change has been able to gain a substantial following in this country. By devious tactics and techniques the communists have gained temporary advantages, but upon exposure of their identity and purpose, the gains have usually been wiped out. They shall doubtless persist in their efforts, however futile they appear. Only in a time of major economic collapse would the communists have a chance of winning substantial support for their program. It is for such a moment that they are waiting. The best safeguard against communism and all other forms of radicalism is a positive development of economic well-being and stability.

ILLUSTRATIVE DOCUMENTS

§16. *'Manifesto of the First Congress of the Communist International,' issued from Moscow in March, 1919.*

PROGRAM

The new era has begun! The era of the downfall of Capitalism— its internal disintegration. The epoch of the proletarian Communist revolution. In some countries, victorious proletarian revolution; increasing revolutionary ferment in other lands; uprising in the colonies; utter incapacity of the ruling classes to control the fate of peoples any longer—that is the picture of world conditions today.

Humanity, whose whole culture now lies in ruins, faces the danger of complete destruction. There is only one power which can save it—the power of the proletariat. The old capitalist " order " can exist no longer. The ultimate result of the capitalist mode of production is chaos—a chaos to be overcome only by the great producing class, the proletariat. It is the proletariat which must establish real order, the order of Communism. It must end the domination of capital, make war impossible, wipe out state boundaries, transform the whole world into one co-operative commonwealth and bring about real human brotherhood and freedom.

World Capitalism is preparing itself for the final battle. Under cover of the " League of Nations " and a deluge of pacifist phrase-mongering a desperate effort is being made to direct its forces against the constantly growing proletarian revolt. This monstrous new conspiracy of the capitalist class must be met by the proletariat by seizure of the political power of the State, turning this power against its class enemies and using it as a lever to set in motion the economic revolution. The final victory of the proletariat of the world means the beginning of the real history of free mankind.[7]

---

[7] *The Communist International. Organ of the Executive Committee,* Petrograd, No. 1, May, 1919, 94–95. Periodical in Library of Congress.

Radical Efforts Since World War I

§17. *'Norman Thomas on Socialism,' written in 1931.*

The days of Adam Smith and the earlier capitalism have gone. Though men still live who were part of the great epic of the pioneers of the covered wagon, that today is a closed chapter in the book of life, a saga almost as remote from the actualities of our time as the stories of the Vikings. For this we chiefly have to thank power-driven machinery. Its development and effective use have made the world one unit. Through it we have the means of conquering man's ancient enemy, Poverty. But his dark kingdoms still are strong, for we have not known how to use the means of our deliverance though they lie at our hand.

Still talking the language of economic individualism we have drifted to a collectivism of great mergers and standardized men. But these mergers have not abolished the wastes and strifes of competition. Nor has the pursuit of profit served the common good. The old dogmas of the economic man who surely knew and served his own interest, of the survival of the fittest through competition, of an automatic, infallible and fool-proof law of supply and demand are exploded, but we have put nothing in their place.

Still talking the language of Jefferson, we have enormously increased the role of government in business and the control of business over government. This has happened within our nation. Among the great nations the strife for profit and power goes relentlessly on. Under these circumstances it is a question no longer of individualism against collectivism but of our capacity to manage and curb collectivism so as to get plenty, maintain peace and release the powers of the individual as a citizen, neither lord nor serf, in industry and the state, and as a person, not a robot, in the enjoyment of life and the search for truth. These things we shall not achieve by any drift. Rather we will be carried, unless we take heed in time, over the rapids of war, made by the very science which might banish poverty, the widest flung catastrophe the human race has ever known.

There are three rational possibilities which offer themselves to intelligent men. One is a development of the so-called new capitalism to a degree where powerful industrialists and financiers, presumably chosen by a precarious sort of natural selection, iron out our tangled affairs and for a reasonable rate of interest manage not nationally but internationally the complex affairs of life. Of that solution we find few signs in a time when great capitalists are so conspicuously failing to grapple with unemployment and tariff wars, the menace of military combat and the intricacies of the fiscal system. Were there far more of the great men about whom H. G. Wells dreams in England and whom former Ambassador Gerard lists as rulers of America, there would still be the question of whether we can ever trust supermen for profit, fixed or indefinite, to rule us without enslaving us.

The second possibility is world Communism. No one can look at Russia and deny the power of Communism or belittle its achievements. It is teaching the world something of the difficulties and possibilities of planned economic control. It is proving that magnificent human energies can be released in industrial life without making profit both God and reward to the individual. But communism in its long transitional period requires a dictatorship and scoffs at civil liberty and grimly awaits the world war or catastrophe through which *alone* it thinks salvation can come. We who do not find reason to reject what democracy we have in the hope through dictatorship of arriving at better, and cannot find proof of the inevitability of war are not ready to hazard everything in America on the desperate communist cure.

The only thing left is the possibility of achieving socialism by democratic processes and without world war. It is a possibility, not a certainty. It must be worked out. To work it out is the greatest task farseeing men have ever undertaken for society. It is a task which requires not a dogmatic creed but a living philosophy of coöperation in owning and managing the things necessary for our common life, a philosophy made beautiful by the hope of plenty, peace and freedom in an interdependent world. . . .[8]

§18. *Earl R. Browder, explaining the American Communist Program after the Declaration of Teheran (December, 1943).*

. . . It is an obvious fact of American life that there is no existing or potential majority now that can be united on a program of action based upon the socialist perspective for our country. Even if we lump together all conflicting concepts of socialism, their adherents constitute a small minority. Therefore, we must state

---

[8] From Norman Thomas, *America's Way Out*, 305–307. Copyright, 1931, and used by permission of The Macmillan Company, publishers.

clearly and definitely that the practical program which can bring together the American majority in support of Teheran will accept the existing economic system as its base of operations and starting point.

It is my considered judgment that the American people are so ill-prepared, subjectively, for any deepgoing change in the direction of socialism that post-war plans with such an aim would not unite the nation but would further divide it. And they would divide and weaken precisely the democratic and progressive camp, at the same time uniting and strengthening the most reactionary forces in the country. In their practical effect they would help the anti-Teheran forces to come to power in the United States.

Adherents of socialism, therefore, in order to function actively as bearers of unity within the broad democratic camp, must make it clear that they will not raise the issue of socialism in such a form and manner as to endanger or weaken that national unity. They must subordinate their socialist convictions, in all practical issues, to the common program of the majority. . . .

Whatever may be the situation in other lands, in the United States the consequence of Teheran means a perspective, in the immediate post-war period and for a long term of years, of expanded production and employment and the strengthening of democracy within the framework of the present system. . . .

Therefore, the policy of Marxists and all adherents of socialism in the United States is to face with all its consequences the perspective of a *capitalist* United States in the period of post-war reconstruction of the world, to evaluate all plans on that basis, and to collaborate actively with the most democratic and progressive majority in the country in a national unity sufficiently broad and effective to realize the policies of Teheran. . . .

The organized Communists, or Marxists, of our country consider that the perspective and tasks which have been opened up by the Teheran accord are so basic and new that as a consequence some important changes are called for in our form of organization and methods of work. . . .

American Communists are relinquishing for an extended period the struggle for partisan advancement for themselves as a separate group, which is the main characteristic of a political party. The Communists foresee that the practical political aims they hold will for a long time be in agreement on all essential points with the aims of a much larger body of non-Communists, and that therefore our political actions will be merged in such larger movements. The existence of a separate political party of Communists, therefore, no longer serves a practical purpose but can be, on the contrary, an obstacle to the larger unity.

The Communists will, therefore, dissolve their separate political party, and find a new and different organizational form and name, corresponding more accurately to the tasks of the day and the political structure through which these tasks must be performed.

There will no longer be a Communist Party in the United States. . . .

The Communists are not joining any existing political party as a group or organization. They are joining the body of independent voters who choose the best candidates from among those put forward by all parties. Individual Communists are at liberty to register under any party designation they see fit, in a way the independent progressives with whom they habitually associate may judge best.

The new organization which the Communists establish for their common non-partisan activities will take over and continue all those educational-political activities formerly carried on by the Communist Party, dropping the party-electoral features which embody the struggle for partisan advancement. . . .

It is true, of course, that this is not an "orthodox" Marxian program in the sense that it reproduces old policies and formulas used by Marxists in the past for different historical situations. No, it is unprecedented and therefore unorthodox. But if we are living in an unprecedented situation, it follows inevitably that a scientifically correct policy for it must be an unprecedented policy. . . .

It is the supreme purpose of Marxism to guide the emergence of unprecedented programs of action. Marxism is not a set of dogmas, and all who try to reduce it to that are trying to destroy Marxism. That is why Karl Marx himself once declared in a moment of impatience with some of his disciples: "I am no Marxist." Marxism produces orthodox programs only for "orthodox" situations. But the most decisive moments of history are the unprecedented ones for which an orthodox program spells failure. . . .

It is a formidable task which American Marxists have undertaken: to educate their country to an understanding that Communists are human beings much like all their fellowmen except that they have found some interesting new methods of thinking.

The task must be accomplished, however difficult it may be, because—above and more immediately than in questions of domestic policy—America will find itself entirely incapable of solving its problems of foreign policy if it is hysterical at the cry of "Communist." The Communists are an inescapable part of the world picture now, and if America is going to play a serious role in this world, we will find it necessary as a nation to deal with Communists of other lands without growing purple in the face, kicking the floor, swooning, or displaying other signs of irrational fear. There is no better place to begin to learn this lesson than right here at home with our own domestic species of Communists. . . .[9]

§19. *Resolution of the National Convention of the Communist Party, U. S. A., adopted July 28, 1945. (Excerpts.)*

We recognize that the future of the labor and the progressive movements and therefore the role of the United States in world affairs will depend to no small extent upon the correctness of our Communist policy, our independent role and influence, our mass activities and organized strength.

That is why today we Communists must not only learn from our achievements in the struggle against fascism and reaction, but also from our weaknesses and errors. In the recent period, especially since January, 1944, these mistakes consisted in drawing a number of erroneous conclusions from the historic significance of the Teheran accord. Among these false conclusions was the concept that after the military defeat of Germany, the decisive sections of big capital would participate in the struggle to complete the destruction of fascism and would cooperate with the working people in the maintenance of postwar international unity. The reactionary class nature of finance capital makes these conclusions illusory. This has been amply demonstrated by recent events revealing the postwar aims of the trusts and cartels which seek imperialist aggrandizement and huge profits at the expense of the people.

This revision of Marxist-Leninist theory regarding the role of monopoly led to other erroneous conclusions, such as to utopian economic perspectives and the possibility of achieving the national liberation of the colonial and dependent countries through arrangements between the great powers. It also led to tendencies to obscure the class nature of bourgeois democracy, to false concepts of social evolution, to revision of the fundamental laws of the class struggle

---

[9] Earl R. Browder, *Teheran,* pp. 67–69, 117, 120, 123, 127. New York: International Publishers, Inc., 1944. Copyright by Earl Browder and quoted by permission of the author.

and to minimizing the independent and leading role of the working class. . . .

Furthermore, the dissolution of the Communist Party and the formation of the Communist Political Association were part and parcel of our revisionist errors, and did in fact constitute the liquidation of the independent and vanguard role of the Communist movement. . . .

The correction of our revisionist errors demands the immediate reconstitution of the Communist Party and guaranteeing the reestablishment of the Marxist content of its program, policies and activities. . . .

Life itself, especially our recent experiences in the struggle against the forces of fascism and reaction on both the foreign and domestic fronts—in the trade unions, in the struggle for Negro rights, in the struggle against the trusts—has fully confirmed the validity of . . . repeated warnings, and has fully exposed the basic revisionist errors of American Communist policy since January, 1944. . . .

We must resolutely strengthen our independent Communist role and mass activities. We must develop a consistent concentration policy and build our Communist organization especially amongst the industrial workers. We must wage a resolute ideological struggle on the theoretical front, enhancing the Marxist understanding of our entire organization and leadership.[10]

---

[10] William Z. Foster, *et al.*, *Marxism-Leninism vs. Revisionism*, 100–104. New York: New Century Publishers, Inc., 1946. Quoted by permission of New Century Publishers, Inc.

CHAPTER SEVEN

Agriculture's Modern Front

THE GREAT farm revolt, which lasted from 1870 to 1896, was ended by the prosperity of the early part of the twentieth century. Since the basic and original complaint was low prices for agricultural commodities, the farmers stopped their agitation when prices and income were restored. They were entering one of the brightest periods in agricultural history. From 1896 to 1914 manufacturing was expanding rapidly. Hundreds of new factories were established, and men were drawn from the farms to work in urban centers. While the domestic demand for agricultural produce was increased, farm overproduction did not develop because people were leaving rural areas for the cities; large-scale mechanization did not reach farming until later. As a result, American farmers found their products being absorbed at fair prices in a home market, with little surplus left for export. The outbreak of the European war in 1914 provided a further boom in the demand for agriculutral goods.

Political Action through the Non-partisan League

Although conditions were relatively good, farmers in some sections believed them to be far from ideal. For a number of years there had been signs of discontent in the upper Mississippi and Missouri valleys. Matters first came to a head in North Dakota. Resentment there was strong against the high interest rates of banks and the excessive charges of "middle-men." Farmers of the state came to believe by 1915 that legislation was necessary to aid their demands. In that year they proposed the establishment of state-owned grain elevators, but the legislature refused. They then turned to a newly formed organization, which promised to take political control from the bankers and corporate interests and give power to the farmers.

The Non-partisan League was started at Bismarck, North Dakota, in February, 1915.[1] The idea of the organization was first presented to the North Dakota Union of the American Society of Equity, a group interested in co-operatives. The Union approved and gave support to the man who "sold" them the idea. Organizers were sent out at once, and by the end of the year the foundations were firmly established.

The man who invented the Non-partisan League, promoted it, and directed its course was Arthur C. Townley. He was an energetic, ambitious man of thirty-five when he began the organization. Born in Minnesota, Townley lived on a farm most of his life. He observed the instability of agricultural income and looked beyond his farm for a solution to the problem. At first he was influenced by the Socialists; joining the party, Townley worked as an organizer in North Dakota. He soon became impatient with the far-off goals of socialism; he wanted action at once, and his contacts in North Dakota convinced him that agrarian sentiment was strong enough to compel reforms. Since no organization in the field was favoring immediate action, he formed one of his own.

Townley's judgment was confirmed in the elections of 1916. His fast-growing League endorsed the Republican primary candidates who approved the farmers' demands, and the league candidates won the governorship and other important state offices. They also gained control of the lower house of the North Dakota Legislature and many seats in the upper house. Townley remained neutral in the campaigns for the United States Senator and President.

Expansion of the League's membership was helped by those election victories. Townley decided to build a national movement, and organizers were sent into Minnesota, South Dakota,

---

[1] Frederick E. Haynes, *Social Politics,* 305. Boston: Houghton Mifflin Company, 1924. This book is the main source used for the Non-partisan League.

Montana, Colorado, and Nebraska. National headquarters were established in St. Paul. In 1918 the League claimed a total of 150,000 members, and it succeeded in electing its candidates to all state offices in North Dakota. The greatest strength was reached in 1920, when nearly 230,000 members were enrolled in thirteen western states. All these except Wisconsin were west of the Mississippi.

The program of the Non-partisan League was not Townley's invention. He merely created the vehicle to place in effect long-standing demands. The League called for state ownership of terminal elevators, flour mills, packing houses, and cold storage plants. Other objectives, aimed at reducing the farmers' costs, were state-owned rural credit banks, exemption of farm improvements from taxation, and state hail insurance. In a bid for labor co-operation, the League stood consistently for traditional workers' aims. It is considered by competent observers as the real starting place of independent farmer-labor politics, which culminated in La Follette's campaign of 1924.[2]

Townley controlled the movement through autocratic devices. The permanent government agencies in the state organization in North Dakota were the executive committee and the president. Townley named himself president and a supporter as vice president. The state organizations outside North Dakota were technically autonomous, each under an executive committee and chairman; the National Non-partisan League, embracing all the state leagues, recognized Townley as president.

Striking power of the League was aided by the large dues collected from members. This organization was different from those of the latter nineteenth century, when farmers were poor. During World War I, with agricultural prices rising, the farmers were able to give substantial financial support to the movement for reform. Annual dues of $2.50, for the year beginning in 1915, were increased to $8.00 by 1920. With a membership of over 200,000 in the latter year, the Non-partisan League had an income of at least $1,500,000.

The principal technique of the League was legislation. Practically all its objectives could be answered only through political

---

[2] Perlman and Taft, op. cit., 525.

action. Propaganda was used, of course, to support ideas and candidates. The chief publication was the *Non-partisan Leader*, begun in September, 1915, as the official organ.

Political action in the states affected was attained through non-partisan methods. The general aim was to capture the primary of the majority party, which was usually the Republican. Precinct, district, and state conventions of the League were held to nominate or endorse candidates for the primary. Mass meetings and all-day outings were arranged to boost nominees. The weight of League support, combined with the ordinary following of endorsed candidates, generally succeeded in securing the party nomination. Victory in the general election followed naturally from the preponderance of the majority party.

Achievements of the Non-partisan League matched Townley's expectations. After gaining control of the North Dakota state government in the elections of 1918, the League put through its entire program in the following year. State-owned elevators, mills, and banks were established. An Industrial Commission, comprising the governor of North Dakota, the secretary of agriculture, and attorney general, was created to supervise all enterprises run by the state. Farm improvements were exempted from taxation and a state income tax was passed. Other accomplishments included state hail insurance, workmen's accident compensation laws, and protective labor legislation for women.

The far-reaching measures of the Non-partisan League in North Dakota were short-lived. Non-farming elements in the state, led by special interest groups, began to react strongly against the complete control of legislation by the agrarian forces. Opposition was consolidated in an Independent Voters' Association, which fostered coalition of Democrats and Republicans against League candidates. The Independent Voters also attacked Townley personally for his mismanagement, extravagance, and dictatorial powers. Members of the League itself resented and mistrusted Townley. Financial difficulties of state-owned enterprises increased popular reaction against the League.

Soon after 1920 the organization began to lose its power. Opponents of the League combined to force the recall of Governor Frazier and the other members of the Industrial Commission on October 28, 1921. The following year, in the face of rising criticism, Arthur C. Townley resigned. Finally, in July, 1923, the *Non-partisan Leader* was suspended. Interest in the League revived spasmodically in later years, but it never reached the strength of 1919 and 1920.

A more enduring effect of the League was felt in Minnesota. In that state supporters of the League joined sympathetic groups to form a state Farmer-Labor party. The idea of uniting the forces of workers and farmers was current in the early 1920's, but the only effective union occurred in Minnesota. In 1922 the Farmer-Labor party elected Henrik Shipstead as United States Senator and Magnus Johnson as Governor. This was the first important third-party victory since the days of the People's party. The Farmer-Labor party reached its height of influence in the state in the mid-1930's, but in the election of 1938 the party was badly beaten by the Republicans. Divided by internal conflicts, the Farmer-Labor group slipped into obscurity by 1943.

The Farm Economic Situation After 1920

The general farm outlook changed sharply after 1920. The period of relative farm prosperity from 1896 to 1920 was ended, and conditions developed that were similar to the distressing period which followed the War Between the States. It was natural to expect that a nation-wide farmers' movement in reaction to the new situation would result.

General stagnation hit agriculture and industry alike after 1920. This stagnation was an inevitable consequence of the price adjustment at the close of the war; sky-high prices of 1918 and 1919 collapsed when huge government and foreign orders were canceled. With artificial wartime demand removed, many enterprisers found themselves with large surpluses on hand. Curtailment was the order of the day, and that meant a decrease in purchasing power.

Industry began to recover during 1922. Businessmen made necessary adjustments quickly, and expanding new fields like radio and automobile production invited unprecedented capital investments. Agriculture, however, remained depressed. Acres of new land had been cultivated to meet the food demand of Allied troops, and by 1920 American output far exceeded domestic requirements. Overseas markets closed rapidly as European soldiers returned to their fields, and fresh competition came from farm lands opened in Australia, South America, and elsewhere.

American farmers faced these new facts with heavier burdens of debt and taxes. During the war boom they had borrowed money to expand output and improve their land; as agricultural prices continued to fall, they borrowed more heavily to meet interest payments and taxes. By 1930 the total farm-mortgage debt in the United States amounted to about forty per cent of the total farm property value, while in the more pleasant pre-war years it was only about twenty-five per cent.[3] With heavy fixed charges, high prices for agricultural supplies, and skidding income, many farmers could not remain solvent. Government before 1933 gave little more than an encouraging smile. Harding, Coolidge, and Hoover professed interest in the farmers' welfare, but refused special assistance. The protective tariff helped some agricultural commodities, but at the same time held up prices on the goods which farmers had to buy. Improved credit was provided and co-operatives encouraged. But the Republican administrations conscientiously believed that direct government help was " un-American "; to take a hand in agriculture would have been to admit that " laissez-faire " didn't work. They called national conferences to soften growing discontent. Investigations and research were promoted, but the only real hope offered was the promise of the eventual return of " normal " conditions. Hoover's financial support of that promise through government purchase of " temporary " surpluses in 1929 ended in a fiasco.

This negative attitude in Washington fostered the farmers' reform movement. The agrarian effort after World War I was an attempt to force changes that would relieve agricultural distress. It revived the old protest against domination by industry and finance. It differed, however, from earlier movements in organization and techniques. Many lessons of the late nineteenth

---

[3] Hacker and Kendrick, *History of the United States,* 631.

century were remembered. Modern farm groups were developed carefully, on a sound financial basis, from local units up to federated national orders. Independent political adventures were shunned for businesslike, "pressure" tactics. Staffs of trained officers and experts were employed to make methods effective. The new organizations were the old farmers' revolt grown efficient and strong. They represented the twentieth-century agricultural front.

Revival of the National Grange

Back in the early 1870's the National Grange of the Patrons of Husbandry was the first organized effort for general improvement of farm conditions. It rapidly lost influence after 1875, and other organizations took its place. But the Grange never died. It revived slowly and rebuilt its strength along social and educational lines. Since World War I it has stood as one of the major forces in farm life.

The National Grange abandoned its early concern with railroad legislation and concentrated mainly on cultural aims. In many farm communities it took a place beside the church and the school as a vital moral force. Educational programs and social opportunities were offered for adults and children through local, state, and regional meetings. Financial aid was given members through Grange-sponsored insurance companies, and many farmers' co-operatives were launched. A broad but conservative legislative program was evolved.

The organization remained a fraternal order, open to men and women engaged in agriculture. New emphasis was placed on the junior granges for young people under fourteen years of age. The local, or "subordinate," granges continued to send delegates to meetings of the state granges, and representatives from the states convened in annual meetings of the National Grange.

The social and educational methods, through literature and discussion groups, followed traditional lines. Grange legislative activities became highly developed. A committee in each local grange worked out proposals to be submitted for consideration by the state grange every year. From these suggestions a committee in each state grange formulated a complete legislative program, which was placed in the hands of state legislators.

National legislative proposals were determined during the annual meetings of the National Grange. Resolutions sent in by the various state granges were considered and a final unified program approved; this program was then placed in the hands of the Grange representative in Washington, D. C. Beginning in 1918, the order maintained a permanent legislative office in the nation's capitol, and this lobbying apparatus employed a trained staff of research and publicity experts. Information was collected there, and numerous publications were issued. The chief regular periodical serving the order's purposes was the *National Grange Monthly*. The Washington office proved a helpful co-ordinating agency for some 8,000 local granges in more than thirty states.

Numerous solid accomplishments were made by the modern Grange in the period between two great wars. Liberalized farm credit, postal savings, rural mail delivery, parcel post, and federal aid for highways were among the aims realized. The Grange also supported pure food and drugs laws and conservation of natural and animal resources. Those achievements indicate the conservative nature of the Granger movement.

Appearance of the American Farm Bureau Federation

The most aggressive effort to solve farm economic problems after World War I was made by a new kind of organization. The National Grange was primarily social and educational; the American Farm Bureau Federation turned special attention to the financial status of agriculture in the nation's economy.

The Farm Bureau Federation, like the earlier farmers' alliance movement, evolved from the ground up. First roots go back to 1906, when state governments in the South began sending out "county agents" to stimulate scientific agricultural methods. Federal farm experts were also sent out to rural counties, and after 1911 the practice was extended to many northern states. With the demand for maximum output during the war years of 1917–1918, government agents were established in every agricultural county.

These " county agents " acted as educators, practical farmers, and organizers. They taught farmers scientific methods through demonstrations and lectures. In order to make their work most effective, the agents made use of existing local farm associations or created new ones. In either case, the organizations through which the agents worked came to be known as county farm councils in the South and farm bureaus in the North. They developed into open, democratic " clubs " of a general nature, and they enlarged their program from scientific education alone to the general improvement of farm life. Reflecting the desires of all farmers, the bureaus remained non-partisan and non-sectarian. They were open to all farm men, women, and children.[4]

A parallel development was the county home bureau. This grew up as an organization around the state home demonstration agent, who was sent into farm counties to give instruction on better household management. Eventually the farm bureaus and home bureaus coalesced as co-ordinate branches of a unified state agricultural program. In New York, for example, the state constitution provided for this. In each rural county a " farm and home bureau association " was established. It was composed of three departments—a farm bureau, a home bureau, and a junior department. The latter grouping was set up for youths between ten and twenty years of age and was generally known as a " 4-H club." [5]

The county associations were semi-private, semi-official. Salaries of the local agents were paid for out of state and federal funds, and their work was closely tied in with government policy. But in 1917 a movement began to unite the farm bureaus into unofficial federations. In February of that year, the New York Farm Bureau Federation was formed by private members of the bureaus. It was composed of the farm bureaus that wished to join and was controlled by their representatives. Practically all the county bureaus became affiliated, and many other state federations were set up on the New York model within a few

---

[4] Haynes, *op. cit.*, 334–335.
[5] Belle Zeller, *Pressure Politics in New York*, 89. New York: Prentice-Hall, Inc., 1937.

years. The chief purpose of state-wide organization was declared to be the advancement of the program of the individual bureaus.

It was not long before the idea expanded into a national organization. In November, 1919, delegates from thirty-three state federations met in Chicago. They founded the American Farm Bureau Federation, which was a kind of central body or alliance for state federations. Organization was started in states where no association had been established. In its second convention at Indianapolis in December, 1920, the Farm Bureau Federation reported an actual membership of over 800,000. Its chief strength was in the Middle-west, but it grew rapidly everywhere. By 1927 it had affiliates in forty-five states with a total membership of nearly 1,500,000.[6]

The objectives of the Farm Bureau Federation were in direct response to the political and economic demands of distressed farmers. They supplemented the educational and social aims of the National Grange. In the drive for legislative relief during the 1920's, the Federation took the lead. Officially, it aimed to strengthen the work of county bureaus and state federations. Its constitution stated the further purpose of protecting the business, social, and educational interests of the whole nation. Special departments were created to study transportation, distribution of farm products, income tax reform, and other matters affecting agriculture. But its legislative department, concerned with promoting laws favorable to farmers, was the most active.

The organization of the Farm Bureau Federation was interesting. The highest governing authority was called the Board of Directors, which was composed of at least one delegate from each state federation and additional representatives according to the number of members in each state. These directors had to be actual farmers and could not at the same time hold public office of any kind. General policy was formulated by the Board of Directors, but during their proceedings they sat with a non-voting House of Delegates, which also represented the state affiliates and was about twice as large. Permanent administrative functions were vested in an Executive Committee chosen

---

[6] Edward M. Sait, *American Parties and Elections*, 134. New York: D. Appleton-Century Company, Inc., 1927.

by the Board. The Committee, with a staff of assistants, carried on important work in the national office at Washington, D. C.

Strong financial backing made possible the securing of expert management. Farm bureau members paid annual dues of $10.00 in the 1920's. The county unit received $6.00, the state $3.50, and the national federation $.50. A membership of nearly 1,500,000 yielded a yearly income of about $15,000,000 to the combined movement. The national organization received about $750,000 of that total, and as a result it was able to pay high-salaried personnel. The president of the American Farm Bureau Federation was paid an annual salary of $15,000 in 1927, and the secretary and chief of the Washington office each received $12,000. Top-level management was not entrusted to " dirt " farmers or political amateurs, but was kept in the hands of qualified professionals.

The methods of the Farm Bureau Federation reflected its scientific and efficient management. Before each session of Congress, a comprehensive legislative program was worked out. This program was mainly the job of the Washington office, and major proposals were usually submitted to a referendum vote of the whole membership before adoption. After final approval of the program it was passed on to Congressmen through experienced lobbyists.

The first outstanding legislative representative of the federation was Gray Silver. He had excellent contacts on Capitol Hill and was familiar with the ins and outs of legislative procedure. One of Silver's neatest accomplishments was the formation of a Congressional " farm bloc " in the spring session of 1921. He hoped to put through the A.F.B.F. legislative program by winning over both Republican and Democratic representatives of farm sections to united action on all agrarian measures. The bi-partisan " farm bloc " was not strong enough to pass legislation by itself, but when there was a close division between the two parties on a bill concerning agriculture, members of the " bloc " could swing the balance. This meant that the Congressmen involved sometimes disobeyed party orders when House or Senate leaders called for a strict party vote. The idea of a

" bloc," with its own leadership and caucus, cut directly across party lines and party responsibility.

Senators Arthur Capper of Kansas and William S. Kenyon of Iowa were the leaders of the " farm bloc " in the upper chamber. They succeeded in converting some twenty of their colleagues—all from farm regions—to the idea. Kenyon was made chairman of the group, and special committees were appointed to study certain types of measures. A similar move was started in the House by Representative L. J. Dickinson of Iowa. These two " blocs " co-operated closely, with guidance from Gray Silver and the A.F.B.F. In the 1921 session of Congress, it was almost wholly successful in enacting the farmers' legislative program.

Party discipline against members of the " blocs " eventually caused their decline, and failure of southern and western farm Congressmen to agree on key issues led to serious reverses in the session of 1924. Federation leaders were then forced to rely upon more conventional pressure techniques. Careful records were preserved of the action and vote of Congressmen on all agricultural measures, and farm constituencies were kept informed of the behavior of their elected representatives in Washington. This form of steady watchfulness held many legislators in line with the program of the A.F.B.F.

A special department of information was established in the Washington office. This agency developed methods for winning popular support of the farmers' demands and for strengthening co-operation among farmers themselves. Divisions on radio, motion pictures, art, posters, form letters, demonstrations, and research were established. A *Weekly News Letter,* containing items of information about agricultural legislation, was sent out from national headquarters to local leaders; it was also distributed to newspapers and magazines as a publicity release, or " clip sheet." The main official publication was the monthly *Bureau Farmer.*

Most of the achievements of the Federation during the Republican administrations were limited to the brief period of " farm bloc " success. In August, 1921, the Packers and Stockyards Act was passed, which made it illegal for packers to combine in the control of prices offered for livestock. Monopolistic practices of that kind were to be stopped by " cease and desist " orders from the Secretary of Agriculture.

The Capper-Volstead Act of February, 1922, exempted agricultural co-operatives from the application of the Sherman Anti-trust Act. They were given the right to process, prepare, handle, and market commodities in interstate commerce without fear of prosecution. The law also provided for enlargement of the statistical services of the Department of Agriculture.

In March, 1923, the " farm bloc " succeeded in securing passage of the Federal Intermediate Credit Act. This provided for the creation of new government-owned banking corporations in the regions served by the Federal Land Banks. They were to supplement the work of the latter by providing short-term credit in agricultural operations.

After the disintegration of the " farm bloc " in 1924, the A.F.B.F. was unsuccessful for a period of years in achieving further important reforms. It tried vainly, with the help of other farm groups, to secure enactment of the McNary-Haugen Bill. This measure provided for the creation of a Federal Farm Board, which was to have broad powers in assisting farmers' co-operatives to control surpluses. Surpluses were to be bought at domestic prices and held for disposal in world markets. The Board was to have authority to collect an " equalization fee " from the growers of each commodity; this would cover the difference between domestic and world prices on the amounts sold abroad. This plan offered farmers the advantage of keeping surpluses off the domestic market and thereby maintaining the prices of crops sold at home. It provided a means of buying up the surplus with a guarantee that the loss in disposing of it would be " equalized " among growers. The bill passed Congress in February, 1927, and again in May, 1928. Each time it was vetoed by President Coolidge.

An alternative measure, called the Export Debenture Plan, proposed that the federal government pay bounties to farm exporters. This payment would hold the domestic price up to the world price, plus the bounty, because farmers would not sell at home for less than they could get by exporting. This measure failed in Congress three times.

When Hoover became President he yielded what he thought was the most that government could give. He supported and approved the Agricultural Marketing Act of June 15, 1929. This law had the backing of the Farm Bureau Federation, which was anxious to gain anything which promised real help. The law rejected the price-fixing feature of the Export Debenture Plan and subsidy features of earlier proposals. It was built on the idea of voluntary self-help by farmers under government supervision. A Federal Farm Board was created to encourage co-operatives and help in the control of surpluses. During the collapse in the fall of 1929, the Board bought up large supplies of commodities to maintain prices. This move, however, gave only temporary relief; prices skidded as soon as the Board stopped its purchases. A few years later, when it disposed of its commodity holdings, the Board forced prices still lower and suffered large financial losses.

None of the measures of the 1920's succeeded in reaching the heart of the " farm problem." Relative overproduction was the underlying difficulty, and none of those laws provided for reduction of acreage. The Administration's hope that agricultural output would be automatically reduced by the " normal " failure and liquidation of surplus producers did not materialize.

The National Farmers' Union

The American Farm Bureau Federation was not alone in the movement for positive government assistance. Another influential organization was the Farmers' Educational and Co-operative Union, commonly called the National Farmers' Union. It was first established in the South in 1902; its founders had been associated with the old granger and farmers' alliance movements. By 1924 the national organization embraced twenty-seven state unions, most of them south of the Mason-Dixon line or west of the Mississippi. It claimed a total membership of over 500,000. The principal aim of this association was the promotion of co-operatives, but it also participated in lobbying. The Union frequently spoke through the National Board of Farm Organizations, a co-ordinating agency for numerous independent agrarian groups.

In spite of strenuous efforts by the National Grange, the Farm Bureau Federation, and the Farmers' Union, no satisfactory reform in agriculture was achieved before 1933. Reform did not come until the farmers were joined by other major groups, who had become roused and fearful for the security of the whole nation. Relief came to farmers after 1933 through a movement larger than that of one economic class alone. It came as part of the general overhauling of American society known as the New Deal.

The sweeping agricultural reforms of the Roosevelt Administration are described in their general setting in the succeeding chapter. Farm organizations, especially the A.F.B.F., were influential in determining the shape of these changes. The over-all program imposed upon American farmers an unprecedented degree of direction, limitations, incentives, subsidies, and financial protection. Although agricultural income was gradually restored after 1933, the traditionally independent-minded farmers grew increasingly resentful of the regimentation to which they were subjected. The farm organizations themselves, in their desire to rescue agriculture from the plight of depression years, had been largely responsible for most of the controls which the New Deal had established. But with the salvage work accomplished and with the prospect of higher farm prices rising in the war clouds abroad, many farmers looked toward removal of controls and free participation in a boom market.

Farm Organizations During World War II

When Hitler invaded Poland in September, 1939, it appeared that the signal had been given for a rise in commodity prices. Farmers recalled the days of World War I, when the Allies placed huge orders for food in the United States, and they expected that the demands of the belligerents in the new war might prove even larger. Prices did go up almost at once, but purchases by foreign countries were limited by their inability to borrow U.S. dollars. The rise in commodity prices, which was caused mainly by speculation, broke suddenly in May, 1940.

The Nazi conquest of the Low Countries and France closed most of continental Europe to American trade; only the United Kingdom, with its dwindling dollar supply, remained in a position to buy goods.

This dark turn of events dimmed the prospect for better farm prices. With hopes of profit in a free market rapidly receding, the growers of various crops fell back once more on government assistance. Tobacco producers were affected most seriously; in order to preserve their dollar balances in this country, the British had switched their tobacco purchases to Turkey. The resulting surplus of American leaf was taken over by the Commodity Credit Corporation, while the growers, acting under the program of the Agricultural Adjustment Administration, agreed to sharp curtailment of future acreage and marketing quotas. In July, 1941, Congress voted to extend the system of price guarantees to other than basic crops; the Secretary of Agriculture was directed to support by purchase, loan, or other expedient, the price of each such commodity at not less than eighty-five per cent of its " parity " price.

The passage of the Lend-Lease Act in March, 1941, and, of course, the formal entry of the United States into the war in December, greatly stimulated the general economic situation. The rise in commodity prices, which had been checked in the summer of 1940, was resumed. The boom anticipated two years earlier appeared to be at hand, but soon after Pearl Harbor the President called for a program of wage-price stabilization. Congress authorized the Office of Price Administration to fix price ceilings on practically all goods; farm commodities were placed in a favored category, which permitted higher ceilings, relative to 1941 prices, than were allowed for non-farm commodities.

But the leading farm organizations were not satisfied with these arrangements. During the war period they worked to raise or break the ceilings on farm products; they fought every effort of the President to hold down food prices; they sought wherever possible to replace farm controls and subsidies with freedom of production and price. As Edward A. O'Neal, president of the A.F.B.F. explained, the farmers believed that government subsidies were tolerable only in time of depression, when demand is inadequate. When consumers have enough purchasing power to pay the "fair" price, as determined by natural supply and demand, government should not limit the price. O'Neal contended that consumers were financially able to pay the "natural" prices for farm products during the war years. The Administration, while not denying the point, held that a sharp rise in food prices would lead to an inflationary spiral, new wage demands, and interference with war production. Roosevelt, indeed, was caught in a vise. While organized labor pressed the Administration to hold the price line and lift the wage freeze, the farmers pressed equally hard to hold wages and lift prices. Had Roosevelt yielded to either pressure, he would have opened the door to economic disruption, social division, and a fatal weakening of the war effort. He held both lines.

The prices received by farmers, even under O.P.A. controls, were high by comparison with previous years. Under the stimulus of these prices, as well as war-time patriotism, American farmers made the greatest production and income record of all time. This was accomplished through longer hours of work and in spite of the loss of over 2,000,000 farm laborers during the war. Net agricultural income, including government subsidies, rose from five and one-half billion dollars in 1940 to nearly fifteen billion in 1945. This increase was the largest proportionate gain of any major economic group during the war. All producers did not participate equally in the increase, and even in 1945 the per capita income of farm families was still below that of non-farm families. However, the boost in income, after many lean years, permitted most farmers to improve substantially their financial situations. Collectively, they paid off over a billion dollars of the total farm-mortgage debt; by the end of 1945 the outstanding debt had been cut to one-half the amount owed in 1930. Some farmers purchased more land to increase their earning potential, and others realized capital gains by selling land in the rising market. In general, farm prosperity was manifested by conservative investment, improvements, and debt retirement. The unwise borrowing and speculation of World War I were fortunately avoided.

The major farm organizations gave their chief attention to raising commodity prices during the war, but they did not neglect other important issues. The American Farm Bureau Federation, which continued to be the most powerful political instrument of commercial agriculture, called for workable plans to control future crop surpluses. It also endorsed the various international economic proposals which were being advanced near the close of the war, and insisted at the same time that the government establish a positive policy toward the regaining of a "fair share" of the world's agricultural markets. The A.F.B.F. attacked many of the federal agencies which had been created before and during the emergency; it was especially critical of the Federal Security Administration. The F.S.A. was one of the "pet" New Deal projects of the 1930's. Its avowed purpose was to aid marginal farmers, by means of loans and technical guidance, to become successful independent farmers. The Farm Bureau, representing the more prosperous agricultural interests, resented what it considered to be a form of state paternalism. It also charged that the F.S.A. agents were often political left-wingers and that they were implanting disturbing ideas among farm tenants and laborers. Fear of the political and social repercussions of the F.S.A. was manifested particularly in the South. A Farm Bureau pamphlet, picked up in one of the southern states, referred to the F.S.A. agents as "modern carpetbaggers"; it alleged that they came to the South with preconceived notions of social reform. The owners of large estates certainly had nothing immediate to gain from the F.S.A. On the contrary, they might be injured if their tenants and farm laborers were converted into independent farmers. The fight against F.S.A. was eventually successful; soon after the war the agency was crippled by curtailment of funds.

The National Grange, while more moderate, generally seconded the legislative policies of the A.F.B.F. With regard to the question of future agricultural surpluses, the Grange favored a two-price system for domestic and export markets. Although opposing many New Deal ideas, it supported the social security program and pressed for its extension to agriculture. It seemed clear, however, that the National Grange, as well as the Farm

Bureau, was no longer seeking broad reforms, either in agriculture or in general.

Demands for social change did come from a third, though less powerful, farm organization. The National Farmers' Union (Farmers' Educational and Cooperative Union) gained increasing public attention during the war. James G. Patton, who became its president in 1940, was young and ambitious and proved to be an able spokesman and organizer. The Farmers' Union stood apart from the major agricultural organizations during the war; Patton supported the Administration's fight against inflation, as well as the system of subsidies and incentive payments. The N.F.U. represented the small farmer and farm labor, rather than the interests of large-scale agriculture. As a means of increasing war-time crop production, Patton urged the federal government to spend up to one billion dollars a year in advancing sums to small farmers for expanding their fields. At the same time he favored converting into a mobile labor force some two million farm families that lacked sufficient equipment for independent farm operations. Patton favored a government program to mobilize, train, and transport these workers as a means of solving the acute shortage of qualified farm hands.

The N.F.U. also called for more agricultural co-operatives to process and market crops, further development of farm credit agencies, a minimum wage rate for farm labor, and improved health services in rural areas. The N.F.U. endorsed the principles of the T.V.A. and advocated its extension to all of the important river valleys of the nation. The philosophy of the N.F.U. could well be called " New Dealish," while the other farm organizations had turned their backs on the New Deal. There was a difference, too, in their attitude toward organized labor. The conservative farmers generally opposed the growing power of labor, but the N.F.U. sought closer relations with the unions. It became increasingly apparent that the aims of the N.F.U. placed it in conflict with the rival farm groups. During the war its co-operative attitude toward the national administration placed it in a position of special favor. But with the war over and public reaction setting in, the prospects for the N.F.U. were none too bright.

The Present and Future of the Farmers' Movement

The outlook for agriculture as a whole is, indeed, uncertain. Boom times, to be sure, continue to prevail, but farmers are apprehensive of an eventual collapse, followed by the bogy of low prices and surpluses. With the end of O.P.A., whose collapse was aided and abetted by the leading farm groups, the sky became the limit on farm commodities. Prices and crop production topped previous highs by the end of 1946; total agricultural income for the year was substantially higher than the record year 1945. Although some commodities, notably cotton and potatoes, declined in price, nearly everything else continued to soar during 1947. In spite of devastating floods and droughts, the total farm income for 1947 exceeded that of any previous year, and the upward trend continued through 1948.

But the farmers remember the price collapse which followed World War I, and they fear that history will repeat. Although the demands of a hungry world are far greater now than they were in 1920, exports could not compensate for a drastic fall in the home market. A major economic setback, with resultant unemployment and loss of purchasing power, would be a serious blow to the farmers as well as to labor. And even if no major depression develops, many observers believe that agriculture faces difficult readjustments in the future. Technological progress has not stood still. Record crops are being produced by fewer workers than were employed in the past; with continuing scientific advance, greater supplies of fertilizer and seed, and increasing numbers of machines, even larger crops appear to be inevitable.

An important effect of the extension of labor-saving devices into agriculture is to force out small producers and to increase the size of the average farm. The more prosperous proprietor, who can purchase machinery, is able to work additional land with the aid of his new equipment; he feels required, furthermore, to expand his production in order to secure a return on the extra investment. Poor farmers, tenants, and hired laborers thus yield their places on the land to the new machines. Within the next generation it will probably be necessary for a population

232

of several million to move from the farms to urban areas; the manufacturing and service trades offer the best possibility of absorbing these workers.

But readjustment of populations does not occur easily or automatically. Before agricultural output is geared to effective demand, it is likely that crop surpluses will develop as they have in the past. The farmers, those who expect to remain on the land, are deeply concerned about a basic solution to the surplus problem. If it is to be solved through export, foreign loans will be required; if it is to be solved through a larger domestic demand, consumer subsidies may be the answer. In any event, American farmers are not ready to abandon government aid, notwithstanding their antagonism toward certain programs and agencies. Shortly after the war the government had to aid potato growers, who had produced a bumper crop. Acting under statutory requirements, the Secretary of Agriculture paid for large quantities of unharvested potatoes, for which there was no natural market. By the end of 1946 the government had spent eighty million dollars to support the price of the potato crop alone. In 1947 various other crops received price support (at ninety per cent of parity), and cotton was given an export subsidy. Existing laws guarantee to farmers, and at higher levels than before, the protection and support initiated by the New Deal. If hard times come and the commercial farmers face trouble, a program of government benefits can be expected which will dwarf the measures of the 1930's.

The farmers themselves are in a stronger financial position than they were after World War I. For the most part they have avoided land speculation and unsound borrowing. The more fortunate proprietors, at least, have paid off debts, improved their plant, and put money in the bank. As a result of this cautious policy, they will be better able to withstand possible economic reverses. The farmers as a whole, in spite of their forebodings, hope for continued high production. One of the features of the New Deal control which they resented most was the imposition of crop limitations. They will accept such measures again if they have to, but they want an economy which permits abundance, not scarcity. So long as people are hungry and cry for

233

the products of the soil, most farmers will resist curtailments of their output. They feel instinctively that the land should produce; that a way should be found to distribute food to the hungry, rather than plough under the crops.

The major farm organizations will use their strength to protect the position and aims of the farmers, but their particular programs will reflect the varying interests of their memberships. The National Grange, oldest of these groups, will doubtless continue along conservative lines. Strongest in the Northeast, the Grange also has a substantial following among middle-class farmers of the Middle-west and Pacific Coast. Its national leader, capable Albert S. Goss, has been influential in holding the organization to a moderate course. The American Farm Bureau Federation is more powerful and aggressive than the Grange. Geographically, the Farm Bureau membership centers in the Middle-west, with important strength in the South; less than one-quarter of its membership lies outside those regions. It represents chiefly the middle- and upper-elements of commercial agriculture, although its membership is by no means closed to small farmers and tenants.

The Farm Bureau has an important organizational advantage over its rivals, because it is intimately associated with state and national governmental agencies. The agricultural extension work, supported by public funds, has been accomplished to a large extent through local farm and home bureaus; there is usually a close relationship between the extension agents and the farm bureau leaders. The Department of Agriculture has frequently depended upon representatives of the A.F.B.F. for advice and assistance, especially in the early days of the New Deal. The influence of the Farm Bureau extends into the federal administration, the land-grant colleges, and the state extension agents.

One of the internal difficulties of the A.F.B.F. is the divergence of interest, on certain issues, between its southern and midwestern elements. The dominant crop interest of the South is cotton, that of the Middle-west is corn. Since the former depends to a considerable degree on export, while the latter is normally consumed in the home market, each is affected differently by foreign trade, tariffs, and export subsidies. The southern growers, since they constitute a minority, are especially sensitive about the balance of power within the A.F.B.F. They felt secure so long as Ed O'Neal, an Alabaman, was president of the national organization; but O'Neal retired in 1947, and the choice of his successor was considered a crucial matter. The southerners opposed Earl Smith, who was perhaps the leading influence in the Farm Bureau, because he was not believed sufficiently interested in cotton. Smith, a " corn " man, had been vice president of the A.F.B.F. since 1936; he was also president of the Illinois Agricultural Association, largest and wealthiest of the constituent state organizations. The man selected as O'Neal's successor was Allan Kline, president of the Iowa Farm Bureau Federation and a leader who was acceptable to the southern group.

Although the A.F.B.F. is concerned with the general position of agriculture, its legislative program centers chiefly upon measures to help the commercial farmer. Some of the constituent state organizations contain strong reform-minded elements, but the national organization will doubtless continue to oppose fundamental changes in the social and economic structure of agriculture. Its principal objectives are to raise the income and protect the interests of farming as a business. The methods used by the A.F.B.F. to further these aims are those of a skillful pressure group. The organization believes in rewarding its legislative friends by giving them support during election campaigns. At the same time it shrewdly refrains from making aggressive campaigns against its legislative opponents, because there is always the danger that the opponents may win. The Farm Bureau representatives have proved especially effective in their appearances before Congressional committees. Their formal presentations of information and views on issues which concern them are markedly superior, and their personal conferences with individual legislators are skillfully conducted. It has been traditional practice for Farm Bureau leaders to support the legislative branch of government in differences with the executive department; this policy has enhanced the popularity of the Farm Bureau with Congress. Leaders of the A.F.B.F. are regarded with respect and appreciation by the majority of members in both legislative houses.

The National Farmers' Union is looked upon more as a new-comer in the halls of Congress. Its organization, based on local, county, and state units, follows conventional lines, but the Farmers' Union differs from its rival agricultural federations in most other respects. The Farmers' Union is deeply concerned with the social structure of American agriculture and wants to curb the growth of large-scale commercial farming. It holds that Congress should re-orient land, marketing, and distribution policies toward encouragement of family-type farming. Since this kind of program has no appeal to the big producers, the Farmers' Union cannot secure the kind of support that the more conservative groups command. Its youthful president, James Patton, is aware of the problems ahead. He has reduced his Washington legislative staff, moved the Union headquarters to the Middle-west, and concentrated upon a " grass roots " membership campaign.

The aims of the Farmers' Union are broader than the field of agriculture alone; in a sense the Union represents a revival of the nineteenth-century agrarian movement. Its objectives call for a positive and helping rôle by government in all social and economic spheres; national planning; resource development; and extension of social security, education, and the comforts of life to all classes. The Farmers' Union favors raising wages of hired hands to the level paid by industry, and it calls also for a closer alliance with organized labor in achieving these progressive goals.

The political methods of the N.F.U. have proved less effective than those of rival farm organizations. Its leaders, for the most part, carry less influence with Congressional leaders; during the war Patton associated himself with the Administration and with organized labor, rather than with the conservative representatives of agriculture in Congress. Following the example of the C.I.O.-P.A.C., the Farmers' Union has proposed to disseminate the voting records of legislators; this practice will not improve its relations with Congressmen. The chief political hope of the organization lies in the election of reform-minded legislators. As it succeeds, through direct action in Congressional districts, in placing such men in office, the Union will find more favorable response to its reform proposals.

While the Farmers' Union looks to a shift in political power, the more conservative agricultural organizations are already in the strongest political position of their history. It became clear in 1946 that a bi-partisan farm group in Congress was successfully blocking the domestic policies of President Truman. The Republican victories in November, 1946, gave the legislators from farm areas outright control of both parties in the House and Senate. These legislators were in almost every instance friendly to the conservative farm organizations. The result of the election also increased the political influence of midwestern agriculture in particular, while diminishing the influence of southern agriculture. Republicans from the central states supplanted southern Democrats in the control of the agricultural committees of both chambers; Congressmen from the cotton states no longer held the balance of voting power. The Republicans, representing midwestern and eastern farmers, could act independently through the strength of their party majorities.

This situation by no means signaled the end of teamwork between growers in the South and Middle-west; both elements realize that over the years their co-operation has been required by their separate interests. The Democrats regained control in 1948, but conservative-minded farmers can still look to Congress with confidence. Although broad social reforms in agriculture cannot be expected, because they are not desired by the dominant elements, Congress will continue to serve the established farm interests for an indefinite time to come.

ILLUSTRATIVE DOCUMENTS

§20. *'Appeal of E. A. O'Neal, President of the American Farm Bureau Federation, to American Farmers,' in portion of address at Ottumwa, Iowa, on July 4, 1932.*

. . . Four years ago both political parties gave solemn pledges to the farmers that they would seek legislation for restoring equality to agriculture to the end that agriculture might prosper. Today those promises stand unredeemed. The inequality of agriculture is far worse than in 1928. Then, agriculture's purchasing power was only 10 per cent below the normal point. Today it is 50 per cent below that parity.

Are farmers going to tamely submit while the leadership whom we have elected to public office openly flout our pleas and callously ignore the desperate plight of agriculture? Are we going to allow our nation to pursue a policy which enriches the creditor class at the expense of the debtor class? A policy which allows middlemen and processors and speculators and market manipulators to fatten their profits even in these times of terrible depression, at the expense of the farmers and consumers; a policy which debases our agriculture to a place of inferiority and contempt, and raises industry to a place of dominance and power?

The time has come for farmers to assert themselves through a war, not of violence but of ballots. It must be a war aimed to send to Congress men who will represent the interests of the farmers, not of campaign contributors. Unless agriculture expresses itself in no uncertain terms there is little hope for us. Our pleas will be ignored and the leaders will be indifferent to our conditions.

George Washington led our forefathers to victory in a momentous struggle for freedom from political oppression. On this anniversary of the day they declared their independence and asserted their right to liberty and equality, let us mobilize and declare with one voice our right to economic freedom and liberty and equality.[7]

§21. *'James G. Patton, President of the National Farmers' Union, on the Need for Farmer-Labor Collaboration.'* A letter to the New Republic, *February 24, 1947.*

The election last November 5 emphasizes with greater force than any other happening in American history the necessity for building unity among the working people who live on the farm and in the cities. Generations of liberals have dreamed about farmer-labor parties and various other joint activities between organized farmers and organized labor. All have fallen short of the mark because neither group had the basic understanding of the other's point of view which is the cement of unity. . . .

If corporate interests in this country are not to take over completely, fresh thinking and major efforts are essential to bring about a thorough understanding of the common interests of both groups.

---

[7] Reprinted by permission of *The New York Times,* July 5, 1932, 27.

Several steps can be taken to bring about unity of interest and action:

First, labor leaders should get over the " pigs-is-pigs " philosophy. Farmers are human beings, and among them there are as many shades of social and economic philosophy as in any other occupational group. Farmers have been at the forefront in this country in past generations in fighting monopoly and the malpractices of corporations. Farmers' attitudes toward labor are by no means hopeless. . . .

When education-information, joint action in cooperatives and exchanging assistance on legislation become widespread in the community, state and nation, then joint political action will come automatically. There is a new Populist revolt, geared to 1952 needs, in the making. This time there must be the understanding—the unity of cause and purpose—between organized working farmers and labor. Then we can build a dynamic, hard-hitting effective people's movement.[8]

---

[8] James G. Patton, " Toward Farmer-Labor Understanding," *New Republic*, 116:2, February 24, 1947, 3, 47. Reprinted by permission of *New Republic*.

CHAPTER EIGHT

The New Deal

THE STOCK-MARKET crash which began in October of 1929 marked the end of an era in the life of the United States. The boom days of easy expansion and unchecked optimism were over. In the sobering months which followed, Americans became convinced that under modern conditions " rugged individualism " led to public disaster.

Collapse of the Laissez-faire Economy

Even before the black days in Wall Street, there were a few observers who saw that all was not well in the national economy. Their warnings, however, were ignored by the great majority of the people. In the 1920's Big Business and *laissez-faire* capitalism reigned supreme. Production and the standard of living rose as never before. Organized labor and the general public bowed before the leadership of business in industry and politics, while suggested reforms were rejected as possible disturbers of the magic prosperity. But the collapse of 1929–1933 brought home the hard truth. Americans learned of the unsoundness of their economic institutions through bank panics, evictions, and bread lines.

Reform had been postponed too long. In the early 1900's the nation awakened tardily to the more glaring abuses in business and government, and the progressive movement, over a period of years, sought to make the necessary adjustments. It was stopped by World War I and the ensuing emotional and moral exhaustion. With the zeal for reform run out, triumphant enterprise took over the direction of national life. Serious cracks developed in the economic foundation, but proposed repairs were neglected in the rush for dollars. It was not until after three years of the worst depression in history that the people expressed their will for reform. Sixteen years of "do-nothing" left a stupendous task in the hands of those chosen to make the needed changes.

So long as the free-and-easy system of the 1920's kept going, no man could say for sure that it was bound to end. Examination of the debris after 1929, however, proved to most Americans that the "boom days" had been inherently unsound. By the winter of 1932–1933, actual conditions intensified the cry for sweeping reform. The total physical output of goods was reduced thirty-seven per cent from the 1929 level, labor income was forty per cent less, and property income was thirty-one per cent less. The income of farmers was cut nearly fifty per cent. Building construction was almost at a stand-still, and close to 15,000,000 men were out of work.[1]

In the midst of deepening gloom, America was afraid. The golden hopes of the 1920's lay shattered, and many predicted the complete overthrow of capitalism. Radical groups hastened to spread the idea that only a revolution could lead the country out of its dilemma. The people looked to the White House for action and relief. But President Hoover stood fast. He was convinced of the basic soundness of *laissez-faire,* and he refused to believe the economic system was stalled indefinitely. His only major step had been the establishment of the Reconstruction Finance Corporation in February, 1932, which made loans to financial institutions and railroads. Hoover regarded that action as a temporary expedient, pending the return of "normalcy." But "normalcy" did not return.

It was impossible to expect President Hoover, who was earnestly devoted to the *laissez-faire* policy, to take the initiative in the needed overhauling of the capitalist system. He was pledged to the ways of the 1920's; the people would not have accepted his leadership even if he had offered it. And by the end of 1932 there was no doubt that only sweeping reforms could revive the American economy.

---

[1] Hacker and Kendrick, *op. cit.,* 672.

A number of powerful factors prevented recovery in the " normal " way of the past. The most important of these factors was the gap between productive capacity and purchasing power. Constant technological advances increased the ability of industry to turn out goods faster than the buying power of the masses could be expanded. A general lowering of prices would have helped consumers to absorb the rising output, but prices were held up by marketing controls in order to maintain profits. As a result, even in 1929 American industry was operating below capacity. During the Depression efficiency was further emphasized and unit production increased. In terms of existing purchasing power, there was no call for plant expansion. The usual recovery stimulus of capital investment in new factories and equipment was almost entirely lacking. Technological progress had thrown the relationship between production and consumption far out of balance.

Labor-saving inventions continued to reduce purchasing power by putting men out of work. In the long run those men might find other places of employment, but the steady impact of job-displacement was a serious brake on consumer spending.

Agriculture, in spite of forecasts that it would return to prosperity, could not rise by its own efforts. The facts of the post-war period proved beyond question that the farmers were caught in a vicious set of circumstances that " rugged individualism " could not cure. And so long as farm buying power remained depressed there could be no adequate market for the products of industry.

The main recovery measure needed was the raising of consumers' purchasing power. " Normal " forces of production and consumption were so far out of balance that something had to be done to bridge the gap. If buying could be increased, production facilities would be enlarged through capital expansion to meet the demand. That, in turn, would provide a market for the investment of idle funds and thereby bring into circulation additional purchasing power.

As Adolph Berle pointed out in a statement on October 29, 1933, the " natural " forces, if left alone long enough, eventually would have produced the required balance. But the American economy had become so interdependent and complicated that those forces were too slow and devastating. Berle said, ". . . they take so long to do it and they crush so many men in the process that the strain on the social system becomes intolerable." [2]

Advent of the New Deal

The American people, in the twilight of 1932, sought new leadership. As in the earlier days of the progressive movement, they did not know what specific reforms were needed. They did know that extensive changes must come, and they were willing to support reasonable proposals. But in 1932 the crisis was more severe than in the early 1900's. The people were therefore ready to go much farther and more quickly than a generation before.

Reaction against the negative stand of the Republicans was the principal force in the election of November, 1932. Probably any Democrat favoring some kind of action would have defeated Hoover. The particular Democratic candidate, however, had a strong, positive appeal. His confidence reassured the voters. His apparent grasp of the complex features of national life marked him as a " natural " for the job of repairing the broken economic and social structure.

Franklin D. Roosevelt was experienced in the ways of politics and government. Having an extraordinary educational and cultural background, he first appeared in politics as a foe of Tammany Hall and was elected to the New York Senate in 1910. Two years later he proved one of the most effective campaigners for Woodrow Wilson. Roosevelt was rewarded for his support by an appointment as Assistant Secretary of the Navy, and his participation in the Wilson administration gave him a strong reformist bent. In 1920 he was nominated by the Democrats for Vice President and made a favorable public impression as Cox's running mate. Stricken with infantile paralysis in 1921, this rising young leader was set back several years. In 1928, however, on the urging of Alfred E. Smith, Roosevelt returned to public life to run for the Governorship of New York. He was

[2] Charles A. Beard and G. Smith, *The Future Comes,* 158, quoting A. A. Berle. New York: The Macmillan Company, 1933.

elected, but Smith, on the same ticket, lost the state to Hoover in the presidential race. For two terms Roosevelt served competently at Albany. When the Democratic National Convention met at Chicago in 1932, he was the leading contender for the presidential nomination.

After winning his party's support, Roosevelt stirred the nation with a whirl-wind campaign. Working with professional advisers in major economic fields, he spoke to an anxious people on every phase of the great problem of Depression. His personal charm, exhibited in a 25,000-mile tour of the country, won the votes of millions.

In the final balloting Roosevelt received nearly 23,000,000 votes to about 16,000,000 for Hoover. His electoral margin was 472 to 59. The Congressional elections also reflected the landslide against the Republicans as heavy Democratic majorities were won in both houses. On March 4, 1933, Franklin Roosevelt was inaugurated. In him were embodied the nation's hopes for reform.

The New Deal, which began on that day, proved to be the most extensive reform achievement in American history. It was the natural successor of the earlier progressive movement, which had made needed adjustments in a rapidly expanding economic system. By 1933 the system had far outgrown those modifications. The progressives found it necessary to try to eliminate only the *abuses* of capitalism, but the New Dealers had to attempt fundamental alterations in the structure itself. But the spirit was the same. Both reform efforts aimed to safeguard and promote the interests of the whole nation in the face of vast industrial changes.

The supporting groups were also the same. As in the progressive movement, the majority of all classes, except the large capitalists, openly recognized the need for adjustment. Organized labor and farmers were strongly behind Roosevelt, and their influence was to be especially important in the drafting of particular reform measures. The decisive backing came again however, from the urban middle class—the great numbers of small businessmen, unorganized workers, government employees retired groups, and professional people, who regard themselve

first as consumers and citizens. They swung the balance in favor
of reform in 1932 and in 1936. Many of them turned away
from the New Deal in 1940, but by that time the essential
features of the new order had been established.

The course of the New Deal, like the progressive movement,
followed its leaders. The progressive effort, however, was spread
over a longer period of time and among a larger number of
leaders. The New Deal was centered almost entirely in one
man—for two reasons: First, the crisis was so intense in 1933
that public pressure compelled immediate action. Second, the
social and economic life of the people had become so interrelated
that a national approach to problems was the only feasible one.

Nature and Aims of the Movement

While the world wondered what sort of revolution would take
place in the United States, the New Deal program quickly
unfolded. Specific objectives were frankly experimental, for no
one knew the ultimate answers in 1933—or knows them yet.
The underlying aims, however, remained the same from the
beginning.

The New Deal was not a revolution. It was not radical. It
took the more difficult path of moderation and rebuilding. It
was a continuation of Theodore Roosevelt's " Square Deal " and
Woodrow Wilson's " New Freedom," as the composite name
" New Deal " suggests. By 1933 Big Business had become overwhelmingly dominant in American industry; Franklin Roosevelt
could not have reversed that fact if he wanted to. He recognized
the huge corporations and mass economy as a fact and tried to
produce the reforms in that economy which the general welfare
required.

That American capitalism needed repair was borne out in the
bitter experience of 1929–1933. It became evident that " natural " forces alone could no longer drive the vast, complicated
machinery. Capitalism had lost its equilibrium. The principal
aim of the New Deal was to restore and maintain balance in the
existing economic order. Private ownership was to continue, but
government was to check practices that might affect the general
equilibrium. Farmers, although they could not improve their

position by their own efforts, were to be given sufficient income to remain solvent and provide a steady market for industry. The unemployed and underprivileged were to be given special protection, in order to conserve human resources and to expand purchasing power. It was recognized that no man any longer lived unto himself alone. Unrestrained self-seeking did not necessarily improve the national welfare. All groups were viewed as parts of an intricate economic machine, and they had to be held in balance to keep the whole machine going. As the President declared on March 5, 1934:

What we seek is balance in our economic system—balance between agriculture and industry and balance between the wage-earner, the employer, and the consumer. We seek also balance that our internal markets be kept rich and large, and that our trade with other nations be increased on both sides of the ledger.[3]

The task of keeping all the major economic forces in balance was perhaps superhuman. It was not enough to regulate just a few important elements, because every action led to repercussions elsewhere. The fundamental aim of the New Deal to enforce balance in the capitalist system implied ultimate control, in varying degrees, of every phase of economic life. It substituted " stabilization " and " security " for free choice and speculation. It meant the building up of a large and expensive staff of regulators. But if the job was difficult, or in the end impossible, it appeared the only way of saving capitalism.

In line with its principal purpose, the New Deal also stood for broad humanitarian measures. It proposed a more equal distribution of wealth and income and protection of the public against swindling and profiteering. It stood for insurance against unemployment, disability, and old-age need. By improving the lot of the " Forgotten Man," Roosevelt hoped to build a healthier and happier united people.

Political reform, which was so important among the progressive aims, was hardly mentioned in 1933. Most of the major

---

[3] Franklin D. Roosevelt, *Public Papers and Addresses,* III, 125. New York: Random House, Inc., 1938.

political changes had been achieved during the earlier period. Economic affairs, moreover, were the dominant consideration of the 1930's. The job of restoring prosperity seemed so large that men could not spare their energies for smaller tasks.

No single, complete statement of all New Deal objectives was ever formulated. The aims grew in the minds of Roosevelt, his advisers, and his supporters in Congress. The program was a fluid one. It was designed for the reconstruction of a social and economic system, and an operation of such magnitude could not be put in final form on blueprints. Many of the objectives appeared first as temporary expedients. Some were abandoned after trial. So broad was the underlying program that particular objectives struck at every part of American life.

Early statements of aims by Roosevelt reflected the connection of the New Deal with the progressive movement. He called for elimination of "special privilege" from control of economic and political affairs, attack on crime and graft, and a check on the growing concentration of wealth.[4] The Democratic platform of 1932, which the presidential candidate pledged to uphold, demanded reform of the banking system, regulation of the stock exchanges, reciprocal trade agreements, federal aid to farmers, reduction of the hours of labor, a "sound" currency, and governmental economy. Roosevelt went to work at once on most of those preliminary proposals.

Special attention was given to the question of control of business. The President wanted such control as was necessary to assure re-employment, shortened work hours, "decent" minimum wages, and no disastrous competition or overproduction. National planning appeared to be the only means to that end. The President hoped that, through some such device as the National Recovery Administration, business and government could co-operate for the desired result. Business was encouraged to work in unison for the welfare of industry and the nation. Roosevelt envisaged the end of old-fashioned competition and the substitution of sincere co-operation among employers, labor, and government.

[4] Franklin D. Roosevelt, *On Our Way,* xi–xii. New York: John Day Co., Inc., 1934.

As he launched the new experiment in industrial control, Roosevelt placed his chief reliance upon business leaders. He urged them to temper the principle of private profit with concern for the public welfare. He declared that the heads of industry, acting as great public servants, were entitled to rich rewards. The President pointed out that " a private (as well as public) office is a public trust." He said: " Business must think less of its own profit and more of the national function it performs." And, finally, to keep the record clear, he stated: " I plead not for a class control but for a true concert of interests." [5]

The New Deal reformers had a ready-made organization with which to put their plans into action. The Democratic party, under Roosevelt's leadership, became the party of the New Deal. The conversion was not accomplished, as some have implied, by corrupt or undemocratic methods. The Democrats under Wilson and Bryan had the same fundamental leanings as those under Franklin Roosevelt; the party always appealed to a large reform element, because the Republicans were traditionally conservative. The Democratic party in 1932 gained overwhelming support because it upheld the idea of a New Deal. Its adoption of the Roosevelt program resulted from natural and democratic processes. With reform in control of the White House and Congress after 1932, organized legislative action was easy for the New Dealers.

Techniques of Action

The methods used by Roosevelt and his advisers to achieve their aims evolved from earlier reform experiences. There were distinct marks of the techniques of Grover Cleveland and the early civil service reformers, as well as those of Theodore Roosevelt and Woodrow Wilson. Added to that was the influence of World War I techniques of mass action. A pseudo-war atmosphere was created in 1933 to make them effective. There was a temporary truce on partisanship, and non-political experts were enlisted for special tasks. Agencies were created on the model of the old Council of National Defense and War Industries Board. Wholesale publicity was launched in an effort to sustain publi

[5] Beard, op. cit., 143–151, 156, quoting Roosevelt.

opinion for the gigantic effort. Probably the most effective single device was the voice of the President himself, whose "fire-side chats" and more formal addresses won the nation's confidence.

An innovation by Roosevelt was his use of professional consultants. Roosevelt recognized the technical nature of the problems confronting the nation and tried to approach them with expert aid. He reached out into the colleges and universities, the legal profession, industry, and finance, seeking sound judgment without reference to party. The President was sometimes criticized for not choosing men recognized as the most capable by their own colleagues; he generally worked only with men whose basic philosophy agreed with his own. Since Roosevelt was alone responsible to the people, he could not give way to others on fundamental principles. He sought technical advisers who would implement his general plans. He was the first president to make broad use of the country's specialized intelligence resources.

The "Brain Trust" was ridiculed by partisan opponents. The traditional, democratic mistrust of experts was shown in thousands of jokes and cartoons. But without trained assistance the New Deal could have accomplished few of its objectives. One of the best known of Roosevelt's "inner group" was Rexford G. Tugwell, who became Assistant Secretary of Agriculture in 1933. He was called variously a philosopher, sociologist, and prophet of the New Deal. Handsome, youthful, and well poised, Tugwell was an early favorite of the President. He was a graduate of the Wharton School of Finance and held three degrees. As a professor at Columbia University, Tugwell had published several textbooks on new-school economics. Although not a radical, Tugwell associated with communists and socialists and had visited Russia; he was doubtless unduly optimistic about the collectivist experiment. His chief limitation, however, was his lack of practical experience in politics. Tugwell became the target of New Deal critics, and the storm at last became so great that he retired to private life. Later, in 1941, Roosevelt appointed him Governor of Puerto Rico, where he attempted to install far-reaching reforms; after some successes as well as disappointments, Tugwell once more resigned from public office.

Probably the most versatile of all the Roosevelt advisers was Adolph A. Berle, Jr. This slender, nervous young man was an expert in many fields and a continuing influence in New Deal legislation. Berle showed early genius, graduating from Harvard at the age of seventeen. He later became a successful lawyer in New York City and joined the faculty of the Columbia University Law School. In 1932 he published, with Gardiner C. Means, *The Modern Corporation and Private Property,* which established him as a first-rate thinker. Berle helped in many departments, but his chief official job was Assistant Secretary of State.

Numerous other advisers were used by the President. " Tommy " Corcoran and Benjamin Cohen, capable New York attorneys, were among the most persistent " back-stage " influences. Some criticized Roosevelt for relying so much upon unofficial counselors. They complained that it was undemocratic to allow such power to political " unknowns." The " Brain Trust " technique had its dangers. But Roosevelt, as the nation's Chief Executive, assumed full responsibility for the ultimate performance of government.

New Deal Accomplishments

Legislation was, of course, the instrument which the other methods served. The nation was given the largest dose of legislative reform in its history, and the quantity was certainly too large to be comfortably swallowed. The people were overwhelmed with new agencies and experiments they did not understand. There were many disappointments and mistakes. That was the price of delaying reform so long that it had to come in a rush.

Since agriculture was the Number One economic problem, it received the most careful attention from Roosevelt. Agrarian groups, notably the American Farm Bureau Federation, were influential in shaping the reforms. But the farm program was primarily a New Deal achievement—by a government concerned with the general welfare.

The basic law was the Agricultural Adjustment Act of May 12, 1933. It struck at the heart of the problem, overproduction, by the only immediate practical means—offers of subsidies for acreage reduction. It also provided for regulated marketing, soil conservation benefits, and higher farm prices. On January 6, 1936, the Supreme Court held most of the A.A.A. unconstitutional.[6] In light of the judicial limitations, a substitute measure, the Soil Conservation and Domestic Allotment Act, was drawn up and passed on February 29. On February 16, 1938, a new and general crop-control law, restoring most of the elements of the original A.A.A., was enacted. It was called the Agricultural Adjustment Act of 1938 and was upheld by a " liberalized " Supreme Court. Additional aid was given to farmers through government commodity loans and crop insurance.

Farm-mortgage relief proved a great help, although most of the foreclosure damage had been done before 1933. The Frazier-Lemke Act, as amended in August, 1935, allowed the mortgagor a three-year moratorium after default, during which time he could remain on the land for a reasonable rental. At the end of that period he had the right to purchase the property at the appraised value. Dispossessed and needy farmers were assisted by the Resettlement Administration, later called the Farm Security Administration. This program aimed at rehabilitation of farm families through resettlement on productive lands.

Control of industry was a major concern of the New Deal. On June 16, 1933, the National Industrial Recovery Act was approved. To combat the tendency toward cut-throat competition, low wages, and long hours, it proposed that each industry adopt a " code of fair competition." These agreements, made by businessmen with the aid of government, had the force of law. They stipulated production quotas, sales methods, pricing, and labor standards in each industry; about 500 separate codes were formulated. The President refrained from using coercive power through licensing and relied upon the public to boycott firms not displaying the Blue Eagle, emblem of compliance. The plan encountered insuperable difficulties. Big business generally dominated the drawing up of the codes, and took

---

[6] United States *vs.* Butler, 297, U. S. 1.

advantage of the situation by raising prices unduly. This action checked recovery by reducing purchasing power. Roosevelt was disillusioned in his effort to achieve reform through employer co-operation as thousands of complaints poured in to Administrator Hugh S. Johnson. To the relief of many, the N.I.R.A. was invalidated by the Supreme Court on May 27, 1935.

Although the general regulation of business was abandoned after the Blue Eagle experiment, public utilities were singled out for extensive government control. Corporate abuses had been most common in that particular field. The Public Utility Holding Company Act of August 26, 1935, placed all interstate operations under regulation by the Federal Power Commission. It required registration of all holding companies and reorganization of their structures. The law aimed to prevent companies which were " holding " the stock of operating firms from draining away the assets of the operating companies. It placed a " death sentence," to be imposed as a final resort, upon utility systems that were not integrated within unified geographical areas.

The Tennessee Valley Authority was established by law on May 18, 1933. This agency, having broad land conservation powers, also served as a test demonstration of cost in the production of hydro-electric power. Several huge dams were built in the Tennessee Valley area, and the project provided a " measuring stick " for public regulation of rates charged by private power companies. One important by-product of this experiment was a general voluntary lowering of rates by private utilities throughout the nation; T.V.A. also introduced scientific methods, equipment, and organization to the farmers of the region.

The Roosevelt administration was more responsive to the wishes of labor than any administration in the nation's history. Some of the main achievements of the New Deal were in the field of labor reform. Organized workers did all they could to improve their own conditions, but their accomplishments were small by comparison with the gains provided by a sympathetic government. The New Deal helped labor as it helped agriculture, not because of group pressure alone, but because it viewed the restoration of workers' purchasing power as indispensable to general recovery.

Section 7a of the National Industrial Recovery Act proved a stimulant to unionization. It provided that all industrial codes must recognize the right of workers to organize and bargain collectively through representatives of their own choosing. It also declared against specific anti-union practices. The American Federation of Labor, encouraged by this support, launched an enthusiastic organizing campaign.

When the N.I.R.A. was declared unconstitutional, Congress passed a law preserving the labor guarantees. This was the controversial National Labor Relations Act of July 5, 1935. It increased government protection for union organizers and established a National Labor Relations Board to hear complaints and issue orders against specified anti-union practices of employers. Although in some cases the Board's decisions worked injustice upon individual employers, it provided practical enforcement of labor's recognized right of collective bargaining. The full consequences of this legislation have been discussed in the preceding chapter on the labor movement.

Workers outside of unions, as well as inside, were benefited by the Fair Labor Standards Act of June, 1938. This law aimed to raise the buying power of the underprivileged by fixing minimum wages and maximum hours of work. An hourly rate of forty cents and a basic forty-hour week were established in businesses involved in interstate commerce. Enforcement of the law was given to a single administrator, who had authority to make standards flexible, according to conditions in each industry or region.

The masses of the nation's earners were further aided by passage of the Social Security Act of August 14, 1935. It provided indirectly for unemployment insurance plans by the separate states and directly for a compulsory old-age annuity system, financed by joint contributions of employers and employees. The law also gave grants-in-aid, on a matching basis, to states which offered allowances to dependent mothers, aged persons, and those physically handicapped. It was only a start on the road to real economic security, but the first step is often the hardest to take.

The broad reform program for workers did not benefit the

millions of unemployed. But they were not neglected. Billions of dollars were spent for direct work relief, and the Works Projects Administration became the principal agency for providing "made-jobs." The concept of responsibility for the unemployed was a new one in Washington. The New Deal, by providing jobs, relieved local governments of the load of direct doles. It maintained the morale of millions of citizens and their children and stimulated business by augmenting purchasing power.

Homes were saved and built by the New Deal. The Home Owners' Loan Act of June 13, 1933, provided needed refinancing, which benefited mortgagors and mortgagees alike. A still more significant reform was embodied in the National Housing Act of June 28, 1934. Building construction had fallen to a record low by 1933. Plenty of credit to finance new homes was available, but banks were afraid to risk it. The Housing Act established a Federal Housing Administration, with power to insure loans for new construction. Guarantees up to ninety per cent of the principal were finally provided, and the F.H.A. had the right in return to fix interest rates, minimum building standards, and provisions for repayment of the loans. Government stepped in where "natural" forces had failed. Hundreds of thousands of homes were built in the years following 1934.

For the "underprivileged" who could not afford better housing the New Deal also provided help. Early in Roosevelt's first term, funds for the Public Works Administration were ear-marked for slum-clearance. On September 1, 1937, the United States Housing Authority was created for the purpose of financing and subsidizing low-cost housing projects for the poor. Because of lack of appropriations and the natural difficulties of the problem, little progress was made. Some examples of what can be done, however, have established a precedent in that field of reform.

Some of the New Deal's disappointments were in the experiments with money, banking, and credit. Roosevelt's "bank holiday" proclamation, which stopped the run on the banks on March 4, 1933, and the Emergency Banking Act of March 9 were expedients to steady the whole financial structure. Reforms began with the Banking Act of June 16, 1933, which provided temporary insurance for bank accounts through the Federal Deposit Insurance Corporation. Later measures strengthened this system, which greatly aided public confidence.

Roosevelt hoped for a time to stimulate recovery and stabilize business at a higher level through monetary manipulation. The theories of Professors George F. Warren of Cornell University and James H. Rogers of Yale supported a plan to devaluate the gold dollar. On January 3, 1934, Congress passed the Gold Reserve Act, which authorized the President to set a new legal definition of the gold content of the dollar. Roosevelt reduced the gold content about forty per cent, hoping thereby to increase prices in terms of dollars a corresponding amount. Although the plan involved purchases of gold wherever offered at an artificially high price of $35.00 an ounce, the policy did not result in raising the general price level. Roosevelt abandoned further manipulation and hope of bringing recovery through the easy device of monetary changes.

On August 23, 1935, another banking act, reorganizing the Federal Reserve System, was approved. It changed the name of the old Reserve Board to the Board of Governors and increased its powers. By purchasing or selling government bonds and by changing the rediscount rates and required reserves of member banks, the Board could greatly influence credit conditions. It thereby had power to turn off the credit valves, as the means of checking a speculative boom, or to open them wide in order to bring business out of the doldrums. This reform paralleled centralized banking arrangements in most other countries.

Long-needed reform in the investment world was brought about by establishment of the Securities and Exchange Commission in June, 1934. The old rule of " let the buyer beware " was set aside, and the federal government assumed responsibility for protection of the investing public. The S.E.C. was given broad power to regulate all securities exchanges. It forbade manipulation of security prices, excessive trading, misrepresentation of stocks or bonds, and other unwholesome practices. It exercised special control over public utility holding companies and their financial operations.

The motor vehicle and the airplane had so disrupted transportation since World War I that drastic reforms were necessary in that field also. The Reconstruction Finance Corporation pumped millions of dollars of loans into the railroads to save them from collapse. Their failure would have seriously affected the life insurance companies and other financial institutions which held railroad securities. An Emergency Railroad Transportation Act of June 16, 1933, provided for release to the roads of funds formerly held in reserve by law. It established a federal co-ordinator, who was to attempt to improve efficiency and consolidation among competing lines. The Act of 1933 was another step in the progression of railway regulation which began in 1887. The Motor Carriers Act of August 9, 1935, went still further in extending the regulatory power of the Interstate Commerce Commission over interstate trucks and buses. The "wringing out" of the overcapitalized transport system was postponed because of the immensity of the task.

Water transportation was directly subsidized. The policy of veiled subsidies through mail contracts was abandoned in the Merchant Marine Act of 1936. The United States Maritime Commission was created with broad powers of regulation and authority to administer grants of money to compensate for cost differentials between American and foreign shipping. "Normal" forces would doubtless have resulted in the disappearance of the nation's merchant fleet. Because ships were essential to commerce and defense, the government intervened to save the situation. The Commission was empowered to build and operate its own ships if necessary, in case private carriers did not respond to financial encouragements.

One of the major dilemmas in the American economy of the 1920's had been the foreign trade situation. High tariffs shut out goods from abroad, so that exports greatly exceeded imports. In the long run Americans could sell more than they bought from other countries only by lending money abroad. That was what they were doing in the boom days, but the practice could not go on indefinitely. When the lending stopped, foreigners had no dollars with which to buy American goods. Exports and a balanced world trade could be revived only by reduction of the tariff.

Any sudden and general lowering of rates would have proved too disrupting to domestic industry. The New Dealers passed the Trade Agreements Act of June, 1934, which empowered the President to negotiate reciprocal agreements with individual nations for reduction of duties. That work was the principal contribution of the Secretary of State, Cordell Hull, to the New Deal reforms. Many agreements were arranged and hundreds of rates cut. Foreign trade gradually recovered, and it was placed on a sounder basis as a result of tariff reform.

Only the outstanding accomplishments of the New Deal have been reviewed here. The over-all program represented a permanent extension of government into every field of economic life. New reforms ceased to be made after 1939 as several forces combined to check them. In the first place, most of the New Deal's basic aims had been accomplished by that time. Secondly, the opposition forces in Congress had become solidified, and finally, the opening guns of World War II drew the attention of the President away from reform to defense of the nation.

Effect of World War II on the New Deal Movement

Although the New Deal was halted as a program of effective action, the momentum of the movement itself was by no means stopped. During the course of World War II, its spokesmen repeatedly called out for further development of New Deal measures. But the tide of events was running against their efforts, and by the end of the war the New Deal movement was spent and broken.

It seemed clear, even to conservative observers, that the fundamental philosophy of the New Deal would not be erased by the war. It was equally clear, however, that the urgency of the conflict, which absorbed the main energies of the nation, militated against additional reform proposals. At war's end the situation was even less favorable to reform ideas, for reconversion and decontrol became the order of the day.

There were many historical markers on the road from reform to reaction. The President himself led part of the way along the road; he sacrificed some reformist aims and individuals in the greater interest of winning the war and insuring the peace. One by one, Roosevelt's advisers and administrators of the New Deal era gave way to more conservative aides. Important among the political casualties was Leon Henderson, able and hard-hitting chief of the O.P.A. Henderson performed a remarkable public service in a tough and thankless job, but he resigned from his post in December, 1942, under pressure from Congressional critics. The opposition stemmed from pressure groups that disliked O.P.A., as well as from individuals who resented Henderson's bluntness and unwillingness to do special favors. His retirement from office, however, was also a part of the general reaction against reform and regulation. The Congressional by-elections of November, 1942, had shown a marked conservative swing; many Democratic party leaders felt that the strong control policies represented by Henderson had to be softened. It was believed, too, that Roosevelt would receive better co-operation from Congress if price administration were to go. Henderson was succeeded by Prentiss Brown, a former United States Senator, whose quiet, unobtrusive manner was more pleasing to the legislators.

In July, 1943, one of the last New Dealers remaining in control of an important war agency was removed. Henry Wallace, after a public squabble with Jesse Jones, was dropped by Roosevelt as head of the Board of Economic Warfare. This move crystallized the mounting resentment in labor and liberal circles and brought forth sharp criticism from the left-wing press. Some New Deal adherents charged that Roosevelt was betraying ideals in order to appease the conservatives in his party and in Congress; they asked themselves if it was not time to seek new leadership. Others, however, did not blame the President. They blamed the weakness of the progressive forces themselves, observing that Roosevelt was simply following the conservative trend of the times. Roosevelt, of course, did not always follow trends, but while concentrating upon the war front, he was unable to fight effectively on the home front as well.

With the election of 1944 approaching, Roosevelt took further steps to align himself with the conservative trend. He took pains to advise the press that the New Deal had long been over and that his administration had shifted its emphasis to " Win the War." Liberal critics again took the President to task for trying to abandon the New Deal as a term or concept; Republican pundits declared that he wished to rid himself of the term only because it had become a political liability. The words " New Deal " had, indeed, lost their appeal of a decade before. The opposition had succeeded in turning the words into a symbol of opprobrium; the fact that the phrase could be so turned was a further reflection of the general public reaction. New Dealers generally, as well as Roosevelt, soon gave up the phrase. They, along with other left-wing elements, gradually began to call themselves " progressives."

In his message to Congress in January, 1944, the President made a strong plea for enactment of an economic " Bill of Rights," which had already been popularized by Henry Wallace. He asked Congress to explore the means of implementing his basic proposal that jobs, food, clothing, housing, recreation, social insurance, and the right to a good education be guaranteed for all. But Congress did nothing, and the President's message, while reassuring to the progressives, did little to check the trend of reaction.

The last concerted effort by the old New Dealers to preserve at least a symbol of their influence took place at Chicago in July, 1944. The progressive elements, spearheaded by Sidney Hillman's P.A.C., worked strenuously for the renomination of Henry Wallace as the Democratic vice-presidential candidate. Their representatives, in and out of the national convention, believed that Wallace was the choice of the rank-and-file of the party. He undoubtedly was, but the convention reflected the more conservative sentiment of the nation as a whole. A majority of the delegates stood fast against Wallace, the bright symbol of the New Deal. Roosevelt alone held the power to force the renomination of the vice president, but he refrained from doing so. He felt a sense of loyalty to Wallace, and expressed publicly his personal preference for him. But Roosevelt also sensed that Wallace would be a political liability as his running mate, and, further, he was unwilling to provoke an open split within his own party. When Roosevelt gave the signal that he would accept an alternative to Wallace, the hopes of the progressives were doomed.

In spite of the setback at Chicago, Wallace and his supporters campaigned vigorously for the Democrats. They accepted Harry Truman, with some reservations, and consoled themselves with the thought that someone less liberal might have been nominated. The victory in November was looked upon by the progressives as a definite check to the conservative trend and a restoration of reformist forces; on election night Wallace made a stirring radio speech, declaring that the outcome was a mandate for the extension of domestic reforms. Wallace and his supporters had misread the signs. The re-election of Roosevelt was, indeed, favorable to their cause by comparison with the alternative. But Roosevelt's victory rested primarily on the public concern over foreign affairs, not domestic reforms. The Democrats increased their majorities in both houses of Congress, but actual control remained in the hands of a conservative coalition.

On April 12, 1945, the heart of the New Deal movement stopped beating. The President's death shocked the world, but it was a mortal blow to the progressives. Although the Roosevelt administration by April, 1945, resembled only remotely its earlier form and appearance, the President had continued to be the personification of the New Deal. His official and popular power, furthermore, was the principal asset still left to the progressives. When Harry Truman took the oath of office on that historic day, it was clear that the remnant of New Deal influence in government was destined to wither away.

The new President had been a supporter of most of the Roosevelt reforms, and he described himself as a little " left of center." Truman officially declared that he would try to follow the program of his predecessor in office. The Roosevelt administration, however, had already moved toward the right, and it was to be expected that Truman, in the process of staffing his own administration, would accentuate the shift. Frances Perkins, Henry Morgenthau, and Harold Ickes were soon to resign. Although Truman from time to time invited former New Dealers to fill minor posts, his more conservative political friends received the high appointments. The President fought courageously but vainly to save O.P.A. during the summer of 1946; in the battle he sacrificed the hard-working liberal, Chester Bowles. Truman was more or less helpless before the conservative Congress, and his attempts to appease the legislative branch won some applause, but little support.

The progressives received mild comfort from the fact that Henry Wallace, who had been appointed Secretary of Commerce by Roosevelt, remained in the Truman cabinet. The President, in deference to the liberal wing of the Democratic party, desired to keep Wallace in his official family. But in October, 1946, the former Vice President forced Truman's hand. He openly criticized the foreign policy of Secretary of State James F. Byrnes, who was then in Paris at a meeting of the Big Three foreign ministers. Byrnes, who could not afford an attack from the rear while negotiating with foreign powers, insisted on Wallace's removal. The Secretary of Commerce, having placed himself in a vulnerable position, resigned on Truman's request. The progressives were thereby deprived of their only strong voice in the President's cabinet.

The Congressional by-elections of 1946 represented the culmination of public reaction against reform. The people were tired of all kinds of restrictions and indulged their desire to have as many controls as possible swept away. They got what they wanted. The Republicans, gaining control of both houses of Congress, strengthened the conservative grip on legislation. The voters were soon to see how the Republicans would interpret the popular mandate.

The Future of Progressive Reform

Only splinters of the original New Deal leadership remain. The death of leaders like Harry Hopkins, the withdrawal of many others to private life, and the loss of Roosevelt as the principal cohesive force undermined the vitality and unity of the reform effort. Individual successors to the movement carry on. Harry Truman, Roosevelt's successor in office, is not a New Dealer, but he stands for many of the objectives endorsed by the progressives. For the most part, Truman lacks originality or imagination and is generally unable to strike the sparks of inspired leadership. His re-election to the presidency in 1948, however, stunned conservatives (as well as the political experts) and revived the hopes of many progressives.

In Congress, Alben Barkley has stood for a continuation of the Roosevelt policies. Barkley, who fought many battles for the President during the New Deal days, did not agree with all the proposed reforms, but as Senate majority leader he rarely failed to give his unstinting support when Roosevelt asked for it. After Roosevelt's death Barkley assumed the defensive in the Senate, protecting the fundamental achievements of the New Deal against efforts to undermine and emasculate them. As Vice-president he is in a position to resume the offensive as a champion of progressive ideas, and Barkley has fresh support from a group of energetic, aggressive young liberals. Veterans of the New Deal in the Senate, like Robert F. Wagner and Claude Pepper, have been joined by a substantial number of new leaders, such as Paul Douglas and Hubert Humphreys. They will attempt to carry on where the New Deal left off.

Outside Congress, several outstanding individuals continue to uphold the New Deal tradition. There is Chester Bowles, who gained more support from the " little people " of the land than perhaps any public figure since Franklin Roosevelt. Bowles' unquestioned zeal for the public good, his modesty and sincerity, and his personal charm are strong political attributes, but he failed to gain the nomination of Connecticut Democrats for United States Senator in 1946. Bowles was a novice in party politics and did not secure the support of the Democratic organization until two years later. In 1948 he became the party's successful candidate for governor, and Bowles should continue to be a strong influence in reform circles.

The Roosevelt family name has not lost its connection with reform ideas. Eleanor Roosevelt still speaks for hundreds of thousands of the underprivileged and their sympathizers; but though she is a leading force among progressives, Mrs. Roosevelt has no personal political ambitions. The Roosevelt having the greatest political potential is undoubtedly Franklin, Jr., who has effectively cultivated the mannerisms and diction of his father.

F.D.R., Jr., a champion of public housing and other measures desired by veterans of World War II, may one day become the focus for a reform revival. He does not appear likely, however, to become an important leader in the near future.

The most controversial spokesman of progressivism is undoubtedly Henry Wallace. As Roosevelt's running mate in 1940, he became the " heir-apparent " of the New Deal, and he so remained in the eyes of his followers, even after the Democrats by-passed him in 1944. Wallace is a man of extraordinary energy, mental capacity, and eloquence. In many of his ventures he has displayed a practical wisdom to match his more visionary idealism. He is the major prophet of the left-wing reformers today, on foreign affairs as well as domestic issues. Wallace, too, has lively mass appeal, although he is handicapped by the lack of political acumen. A more serious limitation appears to be Wallace's reluctance, on some major questions, to face all the facts, his propensity to chart action on the basis of what should be rather than what is. While Roosevelt lived, Wallace followed his leadership and made an important contribution to the New Deal achievements. But with the death of Roosevelt, Wallace lost the steadying influence of his former chief; the effect of his actions and statements, since breaking with the Truman administration, has been to weaken rather than strengthen the general liberal position.

The individual inheritors of the New Deal movement have become associated in two rival groups. Wallace assumed leadership of the Progressive Citizens of America (P.C.A.), formed at the close of 1946 by a merger of the National Citizens' Political Action Committee and the Independent Citizens' Committee of the Arts, Sciences, and Professions. The two committees had actively supported progressive candidates during the 1946 campaign; they chose this new organizational form as a means of carrying on their political program. The P.C.A. calls for a broadening of New Deal policies, and criticizes the Administration's foreign policy, especially toward Russia. It denounces imperialism and fascism, but not communism. Although including originally such names as Henry Wallace, Philip Murray, and Archibald MacLeish, the P.C.A. membership contains substantial communist and pro-communist elements. It favors the union of all left-wing forces, communist or otherwise, against the tide of reaction.

The rival group, Americans for Democratic Action (A.D.A.), is also opposed to reaction, but it differs from the P.C.A. on the issue of communist collaboration. It wants a strong progressive movement, free of the taint of foreign control, in which the American people will repose confidence. The principal leaders of A.D.A. are Eleanor Roosevelt, Leon Henderson, Chester Bowles, Paul Porter, Elmer Davis, and Franklin Roosevelt, Jr. Several A.F. of L. chiefs may also be counted among the leaders, as well as Walter Reuther and James Carey of the C.I.O.

It is clear that the remains of the original New Deal movement no longer represent a unified political force. Their influence has been diminished by the decision of Henry Wallace, backed by the P.C.A., to launch an independent political party, the " Progressive Party." Wallace and his supporters contend that since both major parties are controlled by conservative elements, a third party is required for the achievement of liberal aims. Wallace previously opposed formation of a third party on the ground that such a movement would split the progressive vote and contribute to a conservative victory. He apparently does not expect to win immediate political power, but hopes that the new organization will ultimately displace one of the major parties.

The objectives of the Wallace party were embodied in the political platform of the P.C.A., adopted at Chicago in January, 1948. It called for a reversal of the Truman foreign policy, drastic anti-inflation curbs, general wage increases, and repeal of the Taft-Hartley labor law. The founding convention of the Progressive party, meeting at Philadelphia in July, 1948, repeated those demands and came out for the nationalization of key industries. The major issue between Wallace and the Democrats is on the question of Russian relations and maintenance of world peace, but there are substantial differences in the field of domestic reform. The launching of the third party precipitated a fission between left- and right-wing elements of labor and liberal groups throughout the country. The P.C.A. was the chief sponsor of the new movement; as a result of its action several leading members resigned in protest. One of these individuals was Frank Kingdon, Wallace's biographer and former co-chairman of P.C.A. The A.D.A. announced its opposition to the Wallace candidacy, but the American Labor Party, deserted by all except left-wing members, voiced its strong support. In rapid succession, the divided attitudes of important labor groups became known. The C.I.O. in New York State, by convention vote, formally condemned the third-party effort, but a large minority voted against the resolution. The executive board of the national C.I.O. was divided by a thirty-three to eleven vote on the same issue, with the representatives of the reputedly left-wing unions voting solidly for Wallace. From New York to California the progressive ranks were deeply rent by the Wallace candidacy.

The communists and the Republicans appear to be the main beneficiaries of the third-party movement. The former group hopes to gain ultimate control of any mass movement, such as the new party might become, and the *Daily Worker* and communist leaders were quick to endorse Wallace's bid for the presidency. The Republicans look forward to political benefits in several states, resulting from third-party inroads upon Democratic voting strength. Early political tests suggested the potency of the Wallace campaign; but the third party failed to play a decisive rôle in the presidential election of 1948.

The new Progressive party may affect the balance of American politics, but it is not likely to displace either of the major political organizations. The very fact that the party came into being, with its obvious consequences, was further confirmation of the weak and divided condition of the progressive forces. The momentum of reform, as expressed in the New Deal, had run out. The ideas did not die; they will be passed on, as the progressives of an earlier day passed on their ideas to the New Dealers. A new sweep of reform can be expected within another generation. It will be precipitated by a new set of events, perhaps by an economic crisis. A new progressive movement, springing from the old ideas but molded by a different set of circumstances, will arise as the historic successor to the New Deal.

The New Deal

Illustrative Documents

§22. '*First Inaugural Address of Franklin D. Roosevelt, March 4, 1933.*'

I am certain that my fellow Americans expect that on my induction into the Presidency I will address them with a candor and a decision which the present situation of our Nation impels. This is preeminently the time to speak the truth, the whole truth, frankly and boldly. Nor need we shrink from honestly facing conditions in our country today. This great Nation will endure as it has endured, will revive and will prosper. So, first of all, let me assert my firm belief that the only thing we have to fear is fear itself—nameless, unreasoning, unjustified terror which paralyzes needed efforts to convert retreat into advance. In every dark hour of our national life a leadership of frankness and vigor has met with that understanding and support of the people themselves which is essential to victory. I am convinced that you will again give that support to leadership in these critical days.

In such a spirit on my part and on yours we face our common difficulties. They concern, thank God, only material things. Values have shrunken to fantastic levels; taxes have risen; our ability to pay has fallen; government of all kinds is faced by serious curtailment of income; the means of exchange are frozen in the currents of trade; the withered leaves of industrial enterprise lie on every side; farmers find no markets for their produce; the savings of many years in thousands of families are gone.

More important, a host of unemployed citizens face the grim problem of existence, and an equally great number toil with little return. Only a foolish optimist can deny the dark realities of the moment.

Yet our distress comes from no failure of substance. We are stricken by no plague of locusts. Compared with the perils which our forefathers conquered because they believed and were not afraid, we have still much to be thankful for. Nature still offers her bounty and human efforts have multiplied it. Plenty is at our doorsteps, but a generous use of it languishes in the very sight of the supply. Primarily this is because rulers of the exchange of mankind's goods have failed through their own stubbornness and their own incompetence, have admitted their failure, and have abdicated. Practices of the unscrupulous money changers stand

266

indicted in the court of public opinion, rejected by the hearts and minds of men.

True they have tried, but their efforts have been cast in the pattern of an outworn tradition. Faced by failure of credit they have proposed only the lending of more money. Stripped of the lure of profit by which to induce our people to follow their false leadership, they have resorted to exhortations, pleading tearfully for restored confidence. They know only the rules of a generation of self-seekers. They have no vision, and when there is no vision the people perish.

The money changers have fled from their high seats in the temple of our civilization. We may now restore that temple to the ancient truths. The measure of the restoration lies in the extent to which we apply social values more noble than mere monetary profit.

Happiness lies not in the mere possession of money; it lies in the joy of achievement, in the thrill of creative effort. The joy and moral stimulation of work no longer must be forgotten in the mad chase of evanescent profits. These dark days will be worth all they cost us if they teach us that our true destiny is not to be ministered unto but to minister to ourselves and to our fellow men.

Recognition of the falsity of material wealth as the standard of success goes hand in hand with the abandonment of the false belief that public office and high political position are to be valued only by the standards of pride of place and personal profit; and there must be an end to a conduct in banking and in business which too often has given to a sacred trust the likeness of callous and selfish wrongdoing. Small wonder that confidence languishes, for it thrives only on honesty, on honor, on the sacredness of obligations, on faithful protection, on unselfish performance; without them it cannot live.

Restoration calls, however, not for changes in ethics alone. This Nation asks for action, and action now.

Our greatest primary task is to put people to work. This is no unsolvable problem if we face it wisely and courageously. It can be accomplished in part by direct recruiting by the Government itself, treating the task as we would treat the emergency of a war, but at the same time, through this employment, accomplishing greatly needed projects to stimulate and reorganize the use of our natural resources.

Hand in hand with this we must frankly recognize the over-balance of population in our industrial centers and, by engaging on a national scale in a redistribution, endeavor to provide a better use of the land for those best fitted for the land. The task can be helped by definite efforts to raise the values of agricultural products and with this the power to purchase the output of our cities. It can be helped by preventing realistically the tragedy of the growing loss through foreclosure of our small homes and our farms. It can be helped by insistence that the Federal, State, and local governments act forthwith on the demand that their cost be drastically reduced. It can be helped by the unifying of relief activities which today are often scattered, uneconomical, and unequal. It can be helped by national planning for and supervision of all forms of transportation and of communications and other utilities which have a definitely public character. There are many ways in which it can be helped, but it can never be helped merely by talking about it. We must act and act quickly.

Finally, in our progress toward a resumption of work we require two safeguards against a return of the evils of the old order: there must be a strict supervision of all banking and credits and investments, so that there will be an end to speculation with other people's money; and there must be provision for an adequate but sound currency. . . .

We do not distrust the future of essential democracy. The people of the United States have not failed. In their need they have registered a mandate that they want direct, vigorous action. They have asked for discipline and direction under leadership. They have made me the present instrument of their wishes. In the spirit of the gift I take it.[7]

§23. *'Campaign Address of Franklin D. Roosevelt,' given in New York City on October 31, 1936.*

Tonight I call the roll—the roll of honor of those who stood with us in 1932 and still stand with us today.

Written on it are the names of millions who never had a chance— men at starvation wages, women in sweatshops, children at looms.

Written on it are the names of those who despaired, young men and young women for whom opportunity had become a will-o'- the-wisp.

[7] Franklin D. Roosevelt, *Public Papers and Addresses,* II, 11–13, 15–16. New York: Random House, Inc., 1938. Reprinted by permission.

Written on it are the names of farmers whose acres yielded only bitterness, business men whose books were portents of disaster, home owners who were faced with eviction, frugal citizens whose savings were insecure.

Written there in large letters are the names of countless other Americans of all parties and all faiths, Americans who had eyes to see and hearts to understand, whose consciences were burdened because too many of their fellows were burdened, who looked on these things four years ago and said, " This can be changed. We will change it." . . .

Our vision for the future contains more than promises.

This is our answer to those who, silent about their own plans, ask us to state our objectives.

Of course we will continue to seek to improve working conditions for the workers of America—to reduce hours overlong, to increase wages that spell starvation, to end the labor of children, to wipe out sweatshops. Of course we will continue every effort to end monopoly in business, to support collective bargaining, to stop unfair competition, to abolish dishonorable trade practices. For all these we have only just begun to fight.

Of course we will continue to work for cheaper electricity in the homes and on the farms of America, for better and cheaper transportation, for low interest rates, for sounder home financing, for better banking, for the regulation of security issues, for reciprocal trade among nations, for the wiping out of slums. For all these we have only just begun to fight.

Of course we will continue our efforts in behalf of the farmers of America. With their continued co-operation we will do all in our power to end the piling up of huge surpluses which spelled ruinous prices for their crops. We will persist in successful action for better land use, for reforestation, for the conservation of water all the way from its source to the sea, for drought and flood control, for better marketing facilities for farm commodities, for a definite reduction of farm tenancy, for encouragement of farmer cooperatives, for crop insurance and a stable food supply. For all these we have only just begun to fight. . . .

Of course we will continue our efforts for young men and women so that they may obtain an education and an opportunity to put it to use. Of course we will continue our help for the crippled, for the blind, for the mothers, our insurance for the unemployed, our security for the aged. Of course we will continue to protect the consumer against unnecessary price spreads, against the costs that are added by monopoly and speculation. We will continue our successful efforts to increase his purchasing power and to keep it constant.

For these things, too, and for a multitude of others like them, we have only just begun to fight. . . .[8]

§24. 'Henry A. Wallace on the Challenge of American Life.' Summary statements from 'Sixty Million Jobs' (1945).

We Americans are at our best when we have a hard job to do. The bigger the job is the better we do it—provided that the purpose is clearly defined. When we are thus challenged we plan better, work harder, and produce more than any other people who have ever lived on this earth. Starting with practically an empty arsenal in 1940, we created the most powerful military machine the world has ever seen. In peace, too, we have achieved similar industrial miracles. We must not forget that the genius of America has always been best expressed by the four simple words—"All things are possible." And to me, the greatest miracle of all has always been the casual way we take our miracles for granted.

We went all-out for war. We never faltered. We lived up to our capacities. We "measured ourselves against history." In the peace to come, the American spirit now demands that we go all out to win the People's Peace—that we make full use of all manpower, all natural resources, all technologies, all inventions, and all business-management capacities, to produce the maximum quantity of those things which the American people need and must have year after year. The peace, too, demands that we live up to our capacities.

I am willing to grant that with only 5 million people at work—and with all of the rest of us somehow living upon the slavery of those 5 million—it would be possible to furnish the American people with a higher standard of living than that enjoyed by the Hindus. And I am further willing to grant that with only 50 million people at work, it would be possible for the American people for a time to enjoy a higher standard of living than any other nation in the world—although I wonder how long the Federal debt and our free-enterprise system could stand the forces of economic disintegra-

---

[8] Franklin D. Roosevelt, *Public Papers and Addresses*, V, 566–572. New York: Random House, Inc., 1938. Reprinted by permission.

tion which the continued lack of full employment would bring.
But neither the "poorest" nor the "possibly fair" will suffice when
the "best" can be had. Out of this war must come the determination to work, produce, live, and play abundantly. That applies to
all of us—not to just the few.

The material basis of the fuller life for all which every person
in the United States craves and deserves—if he is willing to work
for it—is the simple basis of food, clothing, shelter, and the opportunity easily and cheaply to move himself and his property from
place to place. Almost on a par with these four fundamentals,
most Americans will put communications—whether by publication,
radio, movie, or wire. Day by day—even hour by hour—we want
to know exactly what is going on in the world. But in order really
to appreciate this material basis to the fullest extent we must have
education to give us a fundamental grasp of the hard realities of
history, geography, economics, and politics. . . .

In the final analysis the full life is a thing of the spirit. It is a
matter of ideas and ideals—of both education and religion. The
purpose of education and religion is to open both to ourselves and
to the next generation the paths of deeper, more thoughtful and
more fruitful living.

Religion contributes to teaching man to take a larger view of
life—to thinking about *why* we do things instead of *how* to do them.
Every great religious leader has worked for the general welfare—
for the issues of social progress in his time, and against those who
"ground down the faces of the poor." Down through the centuries, the basic emphasis on social and human values has remained
as the great contribution of religion.

Education supplements the religious ideal by making us more
efficient in acquiring material, intellectual, and spiritual possessions. Education must give us and our children an understanding
of all the sciences of man, and a background of history, geography,
economics, and government—so that we and our children may live
in harmony among ourselves at home and with all nations abroad.
It is important to educate for the fullest use of our resources and
skills. But it is even more important to educate for character—the
kind of character which enables us to get along in a decent, humane,
and co-operative way.

We must educate our children not only to make a success in life
as competitive individuals—but also, and even more important, to
work together in the service of the general welfare. In recent years,

education has placed so much emphasis on the individual, and so little on the general welfare, that both government and business have become more and more a battleground of selfish pressure groups. The essence of education is striking a balance between these two ends. We want a maximum of the general welfare compatible with the blessings of liberty. We want to unleash all possible creative powers in every child which will give the child liberty of expression. But we don't want that type of liberty which leads to anarchy and violence. . . .

To realize this destiny of ours, we must reconcile political and economic democracy in the service of the full life. Our political parties must stand for something definite in terms of the general welfare and the fuller life for all. Our elections must determine more precisely just how the people's representatives vote on all the fundamental issues of dominating importance for full employment and peace.

The representatives of the people will work more intelligently and more effectively in behalf of the general welfare *only* if the people, themselves, become more intelligent and more effective as an electorate. Constituents who insist that their representatives place undue emphasis on local and special interests are placing an undue burden on those representatives who earnestly strive to stand for the general welfare as well as for the welfare of their constituents. The level of statesmanship in Congress, therefore, directly reflects the level of political and economic education of the voters—and the level of political activity right on down to the precinct. . . .

Politics needs the vigor and freshness of our young men and women. Politics offers to them their only opportunity to help shape the world they want for themselves and their own children. The place to begin is the precinct. The time is today and tomorrow and the next day—not just a few days before an election. Only with the full participation of our youth in politics shall we be able to excel other nations not only in the art of political democracy, but also in the science of reconciling our political freedom with the need for full use of all manpower, all resources, and all technologies in behalf of the general welfare. This demands both political education and a co-operative spirit—the same kind of spirit in peace which we have shown in war.

This is both the challenge and the dilemma of democracy—namely, how to get full production, preserve the fundamental freedoms, and then go forward toward objectives which are worthy

The New Deal

of man's spirit. In all this there can be no compulsion except that
which comes from the earnest search of man's spirit to discover the
divine purpose of the universe. Full employment with abundance
for all is good; but by itself it is not enough. Peace is good, but not
enough. The rights of man are essential; but by themselves, they
are not enough. We cannot attain abundance, peace, and freedom
without recognizing one thing even more basic. And that one thing
is the fatherhood of God and the fundamental decency of man.[9]

---

[9] Henry A. Wallace, *Sixty Million Jobs*, 78–83. New York: Simon &
Schuster, Inc., 1945. Copyright by the Wallace Fund. Reprinted by permission of Simon & Schuster.

CHAPTER NINE

Conclusion: The Pattern of Reform

WHAT can be said about the general pattern of American reform movements? There is no doubt that these efforts have played a vital part in national development. They have helped to bring about fundamental changes in social institutions. The spirit and organization of reform seem to be firmly rooted in the economic, political, and intellectual life of the United States.

Individual reform movements do not follow any fixed pattern. They are as varied as the people who lead and follow them, and they cannot be separated from the complex of forces that makes up the whole of American life. But many significant observations can be made concerning the conditions underlying reform agitation; trends in aims, organization, and techniques; reasons for the disappearance of these movements; and their influence on general social evolution.

Economic distress gave rise to most of the reform efforts which have been examined. Labor's stirring after 1865 was caused by new industrial conditions generally unfavorable to workers and was prompted by the immediate factor of post-war deflation. Insecurity, long hours of work, and bad factory conditions sent labor groping for some means of relief. The same grievances have kept the fires of radicalism burning. Socialists, Communists, and I.W.W. alike have justified overthrow of the existing order by pointing out evils in the existing system.

The farmers before World War I showed the relationship of hard times to reform. Generally conservative in periods of agricultural prosperity, they became extreme in demanding changes during depression. The climax of agitation in the 1890's grew out of successive periods of distress, while returning prosperity after 1900 put an end temporarily to the clamor for reform. An interesting exception to the general pattern was the rise of the Non-partisan League during World War I prosperity. Growing economic strength at that time spurred the farmers on in an attempt to correct long-standing abuses.

Broader movements, involving groups not usually linked together, are nearly always a product of unfavorable conditions. Since they arise more or less spontaneously, general feeling against apparent evils is the chief motivation. The progressive movement and the New Deal are outstanding examples of this kind of reform. The first was an uprising against economic and political abuses. The second, brought on by the Great Depression, continued the attack on weak spots in the social order.

It is interesting to note that distress does not automatically produce a reform movement. It usually takes time and education for those affected to realize their predicament. And, if conditions are too bad, the sufferers may be unable to help themselves. In recent years, for instance, share-croppers and migrant farm workers have faced miserable conditions. But they have been so broken and bewildered that they could not organize effectively for action. Prosperity, on the other hand, sometimes fosters a movement. The farmers' Non-partisan League has already been mentioned as an example. Labor unions have made some of their greatest gains in periods of economic expansion.

A significant shift has taken place in the nature of reform objectives since 1865. Early movements reflected Utopian thinking. The National Labor Union and the Knights of Labor, for instance, envisioned a vague " producers' commonwealth," free from the " wage system." Most of their basic aims ignored the limitations of the world about them. These movements later gave way to the more " practical " American Federation of Labor, and since then organized labor has generally held its demands to realistic day-to-day considerations. Farmers have undergone a similar experience. In the early days of agitation they demanded a new monetary system, producers' co-operatives, and a broad program of government ownership. Recently their main objectives have been modified to deal with more restricted matters—farm prices, transportation costs, and farm credit. A few doctrinaire radical groups, chiefly descendants of Marxism, continue to call for sweeping changes. But even they have come to screen their basic aims with " immediate " proposals of a more limited nature.

This reduction of objectives to " practical " demands is part of a trend in the general nature of reform in America. The idea of reform was originally rooted in humanitarian feeling; movements sprang from a desire to improve the condition of all mankind. But the failure of such broad efforts to gain immediate results led to a narrowing of purposes. Movements that began with commendable idealism often turned toward the " workable," selfish aims of a group or class. The humanitarian appeal of most movements has to a large extent disappeared; their demands now rest upon short-range consideration of their special interests.

Leadership of the movements has reflected the change in objectives. The appealing leader of the nineteenth century was likely to be a man of dreamy, idealistic tendency. Terence V. Powderly of the Knights of Labor was representative of the older type. He may well be contrasted with the realistic advocates of self-interest who have followed in the field of labor—Samuel Gompers, William Green, and John L. Lewis. Farm leaders of the old type have also given way to shrewd organizers and business managers; Gray Silver and Edward O'Neal typified the new order of leadership in agriculture. The radicals, for their part, have become less fiery and wild-eyed. Uncompromising extremists like Daniel De Leon and William Haywood have been succeeded by more thoughtful and " respectable " men—like Norman Thomas and Harry Laidler.

All major reform efforts have shown interesting developments in organization and techniques. Early movements generally tried to embrace many diverse elements. Agitation was taken up as a kind of " crusade " against particular evils, and all sympathetic groups were urged to join the parade. Experience taught that reforms could seldom be gained by parades alone. Careful planning and organization through allied interests were required for success. No matter how desirable a union of all decent forces might be, such an organization was rarely able to agree and work effectively.

Movements like the Knights of Labor, which invited support from all " producer " groups as well as sympathetic non-workers, lacked cohesive membership. It was swamped by a medley of interests and proposals. Skilled and unskilled laborers mingled with farmers, theorists, and radicals. Integration of those elements proved too difficult, and a limited type of organization emerged as the leading power in the field of labor reform. The American Federation of Labor, with its restricted membership and provision for individual union autonomy, was more workable. The narrow composition of the A.F. of L., so often criticized, was the basis of its success in the days before World War I. The Federation was admittedly selfish, rather than broadly humanitarian, but it showed the advantage of cohesive organization in producing immediate results.

Radical efforts in the United States have had to include diverse groups in order to secure a substantial following. The appeal to any one group has never been sufficient to form the basis for a strong movement. As a result the Marxists, for instance, have generally sought support from the skilled and unskilled, middle-class and professional, revolutionary and democratic. This inherent lack of unity in membership seemed unavoidable if the movement were to be kept alive. But it was a weakness that repeatedly has impeded effective action. The communists, recognizing the problem, have tried to keep their organization " pure " while attempting to win converts by " boring " and " united front " tactics. Their approach, however, has not solved this dilemma facing radical movements in America.

Farm groups have followed the trend toward limited, integrated membership. Early organizations proved unwieldy. The inability of the Southern Alliance and Northern Alliance to unite in 1889 was due largely to the divergent forces involved. The regular disappearance of most farm movements whenever prosperity returned gave further indication of structural weakness. Since the close of World War I a more lasting and effective type of organization has been developed. The major agricultural forces of the present are national federations of firmly established local and state-wide units.

Great sweeps of reform, as represented by progressivism and the New Deal, had no organization comparable to that of particular groups. During the period of those movements, the public was so conscious of evils and insistent upon reform that the usual type of organization was not necessary; the ordinary political channels of party and office responded to the demand. It should not be forgotten, however, that even in those cases the persistent work of particular reform groups substantially influenced the outcome.

Practically all early reform movements were ignorant of effective methods to achieve objectives. They seemed to rely upon vague, unseen forces for the accomplishment of what they proclaimed to be desirable. Lacking the guideposts of experience, they floundered into ineffectual and sometimes disastrous courses of action. Most of the older reform programs seemed capable of fulfillment only through legislation, but they lacked specific plans and methods for bringing about the necessary laws. These movements usually drifted into independent political efforts when the established parties failed to respond. The old National Labor Union was swept into this procedure and set up a National Labor and Reform party whose short life has been described. Organized labor, after numerous bitter experiences, abandoned the technique of independent politics. The A.F. of L. has persistently limited itself to non-partisan political activities, except for an unsuccessful venture in the presidential election of 1924. The C.I.O. has leaned toward broader political participation, especially through the instrument of the P.A.C. But majority sentiment within both labor groups is opposed to establishment of a national labor party.

The socialists and communists have not given up the idea of separate political parties, except for the brief interlude of the Communist Political Association. The Marxist movement has generally envisioned direct control of the government as vital to its ultimate ends. Repeated failure at the polls indicates the weakness of this method, and the radicals themselves no longer hope for immediate success this way. They continue independent campaigns chiefly as a medium of propaganda, rather than a direct means to power. The communists supported the Wallace third party, in the hope of developing a "mass movement" which they may come to control. Should control of the new party appear possible, the communists might temporarily abandon their own party name.

Modern farm organizations use non-partisan pressure methods in place of the earlier attempts at independent politics. Their leaders do not wish to repeat the failures of the old National Greenback and People's parties. Today they wield unprecedented influence over both major parties, and their national legislative representatives constitute one of the strongest lobbies in Washington.

Frequent attempts have been made to organize all "liberals" and "progressives" into a single national party. The most impressive bid was made in the campaign of 1912, but in spite of a strong initial showing the Progressive party soon disintegrated. The two major parties have become so deeply entrenched in the national political system that all efforts to build a successful third party seem futile. The most important recent effort has been made by the Progressive party of Henry Wallace, but it will undoubtedly fail, as other third parties have failed, to become an established political power.

It would be wrong to conclude that independent parties have had no significant long-run effects. Although they have not gained political power, they have often forced the major parties to modify their policies. Whenever a new movement has showed a substantial following, either the Republicans or Democrats have borrowed parts of its program. Most of the platform of the People's party was taken up in this way; a large portion of the Socialist program has been likewise absorbed. This result has not only altered the policy of the major parties but has weakened the original appeal of the independents. Perhaps the main obstacle to success for third parties has been the practice of established parties of absorbing their aims.

Reform movements, whether in the shape of independent parties or otherwise, rise up and disappear. The question is often asked, " Why do reform organizations pass out of existence?

What forces bring such movements to an end?" If an analysis be made of this phenomenon, many interesting facts may be discovered.

Internal weakness has sometimes been the cause of collapse. Many early organizations, as already discussed, lacked sufficient cohesion; they went to pieces mainly because the various elements could not reach a common point of view. In some groups, power was too greatly centralized to allow enough local autonomy, while in other cases there was too little co-ordination and control. Associated with this internal factor is the matter of leadership. Ineffective or domineering leaders have sometimes wrecked or helped to wreck an otherwise sound movement. Powderly was a relatively weak leader of the Knights of Labor. De Leon's uncompromising nature repeatedly drove followers away from the old Socialist Labor party. The shortsightedness of rival labor leaders today can seriously handicap their movements, although their organizations are firmly established. Securing and holding public support has become increasingly vital.

Blunders in the field of politics have often undermined reform groups. The fiasco of the National Labor and Reform party destroyed the whole movement of the National Labor Union in 1872. When the farmers' movement turned to politics and the People's party risked all on the silver issue, that effort was temporarily lost in political defeat. Organizations that escaped sudden political disaster sometimes faced slow death; such was the fate of those whose platforms were borrowed by the major parties.

Movements depending upon spontaneous popular support generally stopped when the public lost interest. The progressive movement and the New Deal both lacked a solid and self-sustaining organization; when the zeal for reform ran out, no structure remained to carry on. Such movements are therefore short-lived, because popular excitement cannot be maintained indefinitely. The awakening of a general demand for change results only after the appearance of widespread social evils. But even when awakened, the people become weary of the tension that goes with reform.

Probably the most common cause of the disappearance o.

reform movements was plain failure to achieve results. Early groups usually set objectives far beyond their reach, and persistent inability to carry through generally broke these organizations. That was the chief factor in the collapse of the Knights of Labor, which failed to achieve any major aims, such as the establishment of producers' co-operatives and substitution of arbitration for strikes. The early National Grange declined because of the failure of many of its sponsored co-operatives and the ineffectiveness of its railroad regulation program. "Greenbackism," the "Black International," and countless other movements also suffered collapse through frustration.

But success also has brought an end to some organizations. If a reform group puts its plans into action, there is no longer much excuse for its continuance. The progressive movement and the New Deal stopped partly because of popular relaxation but also because they had reached the end of their major proposals. The decline of interest may be in itself a result of accomplishment. People can seldom remain actively interested in proposals that have been carried into effect.

Another cause of disappearance is the removal of conditions that originally started a movement. Organizations that are born of economic depression frequently die of returned prosperity. This life cycle has been discussed previously in connection with early farmers' groups. Low agricultural prices repeatedly brought forth reform efforts, but when better times came back those efforts evaporated. It should be observed, however, that many recent movements have been so well organized that they have remained intact even after improvements came about. Their original reform nature may have disappeared, but the organisms live on as special-interest groups. It is difficult to ascertain precisely when the transformation takes place in the character of such movements.

How important have reform movements been in American life? Have they brought about necessary social adaptations or would needed changes have been made anyway? No final answers can be given, but it is clear that these movements have had a significant bearing on national development. Whether causal or coincidental, most reform efforts have aimed in the

281

general direction which society has followed. There is good reason to believe that many social changes were at least hastened by these movements, even where no immediate accomplishments can be seen. The effectiveness and pace of the various movements can be roughly determined by reviewing historically the important reform demands and observing the lapse of time from the commencement of agitation until the fulfillment of a particular aim.

Two of the most insistent demands at the close of the War Between the States were the eight-hour day and greenbacks. The National Labor Union first called for these proposals in 1866; later reform elements continued the agitation. Greenbacks have not become a significant part of the monetary system, but the eight-hour day at last became a reality. The federal government put its own employees on this basis in 1868. Private business did not follow the practice until many years later; the year 1916, when the railroads were compelled to adopt the eight-hour day, may be taken as the time when the reform became generally effective. In 1938 it was written into the federal Fair Labor Standards Act along with the forty-hour week. Although the National Labor Union did not live to witness the final achievement, it pointed the way and made a start. Fifty or more years passed between the time when the eight-hour day was first seriously proposed and the time of its general realization. It should be noted that reforms which can be produced through national legislation tend to come sooner than other kinds. Congress passed the law pertaining to federal employees two years after agitation was begun by the National Labor Union. But at that time the Constitution was not interpreted to permit further action by Congress. As a result of that limitation, the eight-hour day for workers in private industry had to be won in slow, piece-meal fashion.

In 1867 the National Grange made the first real demands for railway regulation, a Department of Agriculture, and cooperative farm marketing associations. All these proposals were ultimately successful. Adequate federal regulation of the railroads began with passage of the Interstate Commerce Act in 1887, about twenty years afterward. The Department o

CONCLUSION: THE PATTERN OF REFORM

Agriculture was created about the same time, in 1889. Farm co-operatives developed slowly and were given special exemption from federal anti-trust laws by the Capper-Volstead Act of 1922. The International Workingmen's Association appeared in this country at the same time as the National Grange, but the " International " called for overthrow of the capitalist system. So far this revolution has not occurred in the United States.

The Knights of Labor was the first important organization to propose a widespread system of producers' co-operatives. It established this aim as early as 1878 and at the same time called for the abolition of child labor. Both objectives were supported by many succeeding reformers. A general system of co-operatives never materialized, but prohibition of child labor was eventually accomplished. This reform was long considered to be outside Congressional authority, and amendment of the Constitution proved an impassable barrier. It was not until 1938 that the Supreme Court upheld a federal law, based on implied Congressional powers, which ended most child labor. That law, the Fair Labor Standards Act, answered a demand that had started some sixty years earlier.

Soon after the Knights began their crusade, the farmers raised new proposals. About 1880 the " Southern Alliance " was calling for tariff reduction and a federal income tax. Both of these aims were realized in 1913, some thirty years later. Although the Alliance vainly beat the old drum for greenbacks, in 1889 it endorsed an idea which afterwards succeeded. This was C. A. Macune's scheme for government farm commodity loans. In 1933, over forty years later, they became a part of the New Deal farm program.

The American Federation of Labor can be credited with originating the drive for several important reforms. In 1886 it asked for a national Bureau of Labor Statistics, which was realized nearly thirty years later in the United States Department of Labor. The A.F. of L. also began agitation for immigration restriction; this aim was fulfilled thirty-five years afterward in the restrictive Immigration Act of 1921. Most of the fundamental demands of the national labor unions regarding wages and conditions have been achieved over a period of years.

Conclusion: The Pattern of Reform

In 1892 the People's party initiated a host of reform proposals. Free silver and greenbacks were first on the program. These lost out in the immediate struggle, but credit reconstruction did come some twenty years later in the Federal Reserve Act of 1913. Even silver was to have its day after some forty years of waiting; in 1934 Congress provided for liberal use of that metal in the Silver Purchase Act. Another plank in the People's party platform called for a postal savings system, and this was provided in spite of strong opposition in 1910.

The Socialist party in America has failed to attain its fundamental purpose of abolishing the capitalist system. But most of its " immediate " demands have won remarkable success. In 1901 the party demanded extended government ownership, a system of public works for relief of unemployment, social insurance, and release of private inventions for public use. The last part of the program has not been gained, but government ownership and control have vastly expanded. A Public Works Administration was set up in 1933, about thirty years after the first Socialist demand, and in 1935 the New Deal plans for social security were enacted.

The radical aims announced by the Industrial Workers of the World in 1905 were not so successful. The establishment of the " co-operative commonwealth " along syndicalist lines has not taken place. However, the I.W.W. advocacy of labor organization through industrial, rather than craft unions, was followed thirty years later by the establishment of the C.I.O.

The fundamental aim of democratic control over wealth may not yet be realized, but most of the specific reforms advocated by the progressives were put into effect. In 1901 Theodore Roosevelt demanded conservation, further regulation of big business, and reciprocal tariffs. In the following year Congress passed the Newlands Act as a first step in the program of protecting and developing natural resources; in 1914 the Clayton Anti-trust Act provided a partial answer to the demands regarding business. The tariff idea was not to become a fact until the Trade Agreements Act of 1934. In 1907 Roosevelt asked for laws to protect the investing public and prohibit interstate holding companies. The New Deal, successor to the progressive movement, partially achieved these purposes in the Federal Securities Act of 1933 and the Public Utility Holding Company Act of 1935, nearly thirty years later. Women's suffrage and anti-injunction laws, although subjects of agitation for many years, did not become important issues in national politics until advocated by the Progressive party in 1912. Equal voting rights came eight years later in 1920. Twenty years afterwards, in 1932, Congress passed the Norris-La Guardia Anti-injunction bill.

At the close of World War I, the farmers once more returned to reform activities. In 1919 the newly launched American Farm Bureau Federation called for higher agricultural prices. The " parity " price and income program of the New Deal, beginning in 1933, was government's first adequate reply. A contemporary of the A.F.B.F. was the Communist party, started underground in 1919. Its efforts to erect a revolutionary dictatorship of the proletariat have not succeeded.

The Conference for Progressive Political Action supported a losing candidate, Robert M. La Follette, in the presidential election of 1924, but many of its principles moved forward. Among these was the demand for laws guaranteeing collective bargaining, which resulted nine years later in the protective provisions of the National Industrial Recovery Act. Collective bargaining guarantees were further developed in the National Labor Relations Act of 1935. The Conference failed, however, in its program regarding foreign policy. It called in vain for the abolition of military conscription and a popular referendum on the issue of war.

The Congress of Industrial Organizations, formed in 1935, has seen many of its objectives realized in a remarkably short time. Although most of its aims originated in earlier movements, it was the first organization to give aggressive support to proposed laws for minimum wages and maximum hours. These became fact in the Fair Labor Standards Act of 1938. The C.I.O. has also pressed hard for comprehensive planning by the national government; passage by Congress of the " Full Employment " Act of 1946 represented partial fulfillment of that aim.

The New Deal carried forward most of the principles of the earlier progressives, and its achievements were in large measure the realization of traditional reform objectives. The New Deal also contributed important ideas of its own, and these were first outlined in the Democratic platform of 1932. Among them was the concept of governmental responsibility for maintaining economic balance, within the framework of the capitalist system. As soon as Franklin Roosevelt took office, Congress started work on a vast program of agricultural regulation. In the same year the N.I.R.A. attempted a method of self-regulation for industry. Bank depositors were protected by the Banking Act of 1933, and federal relief for the unemployed was provided. Slum clearance, a New Deal aim, was commenced in 1937 by the United States Housing Authority. Special aid to property owners was given by the Home Owners Loan Act of 1933 and the Federal Farm Mortgage Act of 1935. These were but a few of the many expressions of the newly assumed responsibilities of government. Since most of the New Deal program could be achieved through national legislation, relatively quick results were possible.

The foregoing summary of aims and results has been given to throw light on the general effectiveness of reform movements. Most of the efforts studied have moved in the direction of ultimate national development. Particular demands have been gained in from one year to sixty years, while some have never succeeded. The expanding authority of the federal government appears to provide a growing means of direct and speedy reform action.

A number of important reforms have been realized without the aid of organized movements. The Gold Reserve Act of 1934, for example, provided for manipulation of the gold content of the American dollar. This particular reform had gained the attention of only a small school of economists and advisers of the President. Other reforms likewise may be the work of a limited group, or even one man. But in such cases the particular act is generally a response to some widespread feeling.

The evidence seems to show that most social reforms are closely related to organized movements. However desirable or undesirable this condition might be, it is a fact of American democracy. These movements have assumed a fairly uniform pattern of structure and technique; they constitute established implements of change for today and tomorrow.

Although the public mood following World War II, like that after the first great war, proved unfavorable to reform efforts, there is no reason to believe that strong movements will not persist. Social change continues, at an ever faster pace, and far-reaching institutional adjustments must be expected in the future. It may be hoped that these reforms will not wait upon a crisis and pent-up demand; they may and should come steadily and gradually, through a growing understanding and harmony of interests.

Selected Reading

Introduction: Reform and Democracy

Ellwood, C. A., *An Introduction to Social Psychology,* 1917, Chs. 7–8, 12–13.
Encyclopedia Americana, Article on " Social Reform Movements."
Haynes, F. E., *Social Politics in the United States,* 1924, Ch. 1.
Merriam, C. E., *The Role of Politics in Social Change,* 1936.
Ogburn, W. F., *Social Change,* 1928, Parts IV–V.
Ogburn, W. F., and Nimkoff, M. F., *Sociology,* 1928, Part VII.
Sims, N. L., *The Problem of Social Change,* 1939.

Chapter One: The Workers Organize

Beard, M. R., *A Short History of the American Labor Movement,* 1920, Chs. 7–10.
Carlton, F. T., *History and Problems of Organized Labor,* 1920, Chs. 5–7.
Carroll, M. R., *Labor and Politics,* 1923.
Fine, Nathan, *Labor and Farmer Parties in the United States,* 1928, Chs. 5–7.
Gompers, Samuel, *Seventy Years of Life and Labor,* 2 v., 1925.
Grossman, J. P., *William Sylvis, Pioneer of American Labor,* 1945.
Hacker, L. M., and Kendrick, B. B., *The United States Since 1865,* 1939, Chs. 10, 12.
Haynes, F. E., *Social Politics in the United States,* 1924, Ch. 4.
Kirkland, E. C., *A History of American Economic Life,* 1936, Ch. 13.
Perlman, Selig, *A History of Trade Unionism in the United States,* 1922.
Powderly, T. V., *The Path I Trod,* 1940.
Tarbell, I. M., *The Nationalizing of Business,* 1936, Chs. 1–7, 9–10.
Ware, N. J., *The Labor Movement in the United States, 1860–1895,* 1929.

Chapter Two: Early Radical Efforts

Adamic, Louis, *Dynamite,* 1934.
Encyclopedia of the Social Sciences, Articles on " Anarchism " and " Syndicalism."
Beard, M. R., *A Short History of the American Labor Movement,* 1920, Ch. 11.
Brissenden, P. F., *History of the I. W. W.,* 1920.
Brooks, J. G., *American Syndicalism,* 1913.
Fine, Nathan, *Labor and Farmer Parties in the United States,* 1928, Chs. 6–9.

Haynes, F. E., *Social Politics in the United States*, 1924, Chs. 9–10.
Hillquit, Morris, *Socialism in Theory and Practice*, 1910.
Laidler, Harry, *A History of Socialist Thought*, 1933.
———, *Socialism in Thought and Action*, 1920.
Saposs, D. J., *Left Wing Unionism*, 1926.
Socialist Labor Party, *Daniel De Leon, the Man and His Work*, 1919.

Chapter Three: Farmers in Revolt
Buck, S. J., *The Agrarian Crusade*, 1920.
———, *The Granger Movement*, 1913.
Fine, Nathan, *Labor and Farmer Parties in the United States*, 1928, Ch. 3.
Hacker, L. M., and Kendrick, B. B., *The United States Since 1865*, 1939, Chs. 9, 14, 16.
Haynes, F. E., *Social Politics in the United States*, 1924, Ch. 7.
Hicks, J. D., *The Populist Revolt*, 1931.
Kirkland, E. C., *A History of American Economic Life*, 1936, Ch. 12.
Shannon, F. A., *Farmer's Last Frontier; Agriculture, 1860–1897*, 1945.
Tarbell, I. M., *The Nationalizing of Business*, 1936, Ch. 8.

Chapter Four: The Progressive Movement
Baker, R. S., *Woodrow Wilson*, 4 v., 1927.
Bowers, Claude, *Beveridge and the Progressive Era*, 1932.
Chamberlain, John, *Farewell to Reform*, 1932.
Croly, Herbert, *Progressive Democracy*, 1914.
DeWitt, B. P., *The Progressive Movement*, 1915.
Faulkner, H. U., *The Quest for Social Justice*, 1931.
Hacker, L. M., and Kendrick, B. B., *The United States Since 1865*, 1939, Chs. 20–22, 24.
Haworth, P. I., *America in Ferment*, 1915.
Haynes, F. C., *Social Politics in the United States*, 1924, Ch. 8.
Hechler, K. C., *Insurgency*, 1940.
Howe, F. C., *Confessions of a Reformer*, 1925.
Kirkland, E. C., *A History of American Economic Life*, 1936, Ch. 14.
La Follette, R. M., *Autobiography*, 1913.
Mowry, G. E., *Theodore Roosevelt and the Progressive Movement*, 1946.
Pringle, H. F., *Life and Times of William H. Taft*, 1939.
———, *Theodore Roosevelt*, 1931.
Steffens, Lincoln, *Autobiography*, 1931.
Tarbell, I. M., *All in a Day's Work*, 1939.
———, *The Nationalizing of Business*, 1936, Ch. 12.
White, W. A., *Masks in a Pageant*, 1928.
Wilson, Woodrow, *The New Freedom*, 1913.

Chapter Five: Labor Divides Ranks
Brooks, R. R. R., *When Labor Organizes*, 1937.
Clark, M. R., and Simon, S. F., *The Labor Movement in America*, 1938.
Coleman, McAlister, *Men and Coal*, 1943.

SELECTED READING

Cooke, M. L., and Murray, Philip, *Organized Labor and Production,* 1946.
Fine, Nathan, *Labor and Farmer Parties in the United States,* 1928, Ch. 13.
Hacker, L. M., and Kendrick, B. B., *The United States Since 1865,* 1939, Ch. 31.
Hardman, J. B. S., *American Labor Dynamics,* 1928.
Harris, Herbert, *American Labor,* 1939.
Levenstein, Aaron, *Labor Today and Tomorrow,* 1945.
Levinson, Edward, *Labor on the March,* 1938.
MacDonald, Lois, *Labor Problems and the American Scene,* 1938.
Northrup, H. R., *Organized Labor and the Negro,* 1944.
Peterson, Florence, *American Labor Unions,* 1945.
Slichter, S. H., *Union Policies and Industrial Management,* 1941.
Stolberg, Benjamin, *Story of the C. I. O.,* 1938.
Vorse, M. H., *Labor's New Millions,* 1938.
Wechsler, J. A., *Labor Baron,* 1944.

Chapter Six: Radical Movements Since World War I

Davis, Jerome, *Contemporary Social Movements,* 1930.
Encyclopedia of the Social Sciences, Articles on "Socialism," "Socialist Parties," "Communism," "Communist Party."
Fine, Nathan, *Labor and Farmer Parties in the United States,* 1928, Chs. 10–11.
Gambs, J. S., *The Decline of the I.W.W.,* 1932.
Gitlow, Benjamin, *I Confess,* 1940.
Haynes, F. E., *Social Politics in the United States,* 1924, Ch. 12.
Laidler, Harry, *American Socialism,* 1937.
———, *Socialist Planning and a Socialistic Program,* 1932.
Lyons, Eugene, *Red Decade,* 1941.
Oneal, James, *American Communism,* 1927.
Thomas, Norman, *The Choice before Us,* 1933.
———, *What Is Our Destiny?* 1944.
Westmeyer, R. E., *Modern Economic and Social Systems,* 1940, Chs. 14–29.

Chapter Seven: Agriculture's Modern Front

Abrams, Charles, *Revolution in Land,* 1939.
Capper, Arthur, *Agricultural Bloc,* 1922.
Eliot, Clara, *Farmer's Campaign for Credit,* 1927.
Fine, Nathan, *Labor and Farmer Parties in the United States,* 1928, Ch. 12.
Hacker, L. M., and Kendrick, B. B., *The United States Since 1865,* 1939, Ch. 32.
Haynes, F. E., *Social Politics in the United States,* 1924, Chs. 13–14.
McCune, Wesley, *The Farm Bloc,* 1943.
Moore, A. L., *Farmer and the Rest of Us,* 1945.
Lippincott, Isaac, *What the Farmer Needs,* 1928.
Schmidt, C. T., *American Farmers in the World Crisis,* 1941.
Seligman, E. R. A., *Economics of Farm Relief,* 1929.
Shepherd, G. S., *Agricultural Price Control,* 1945.

291

SELECTED READING

Chapter Eight: The New Deal

Beard, C. A., and Smith, G. H. E., *The Future Comes,* 1933.
———, *The Old Deal and the New,* 1940.
Berle, A. A., *et al., America's Recovery Program,* 1934.
Bowles, Chester, *Tomorrow Without Fear,* 1946.
Dearing, C. L., *The ABC of the NRA,* 1934.
Hacker, L. M., and Kendrick, B. B., *The United States Since 1865,* 1939,
    Chs. 35–38.
Johnson, H. S., *The Blue Eagle from Egg to Earth,* 1935.
MacDonald, William, *The Menace of Recovery,* 1934.
The New Deal, by the editors of the London *Economist,* 1937.
The New Dealers, Anonymous, 1934.
Ogburn, W. F., ed., *Social Change and the New Deal,* 1934.
Rauch, Basil, *History of the New Deal,* 1944.
Roosevelt, F. D., *On Our Way,* 1934.
———, *Rendezvous With Destiny,* 1944.
Soule, George, *The Coming American Revolution,* 1934.
Wallace, H. A., *Sixty Million Jobs,* 1945.
Wecter, Dixon, *The Age of the Great Depression, 1929–1941,* 1948.

Bibliography

Books

Abrams, Charles, *Revolution in Land*, New York, 1939.

Adamic, Louis, *Dynamite: The Story of Class Violence in America*, New York, 1934.

Baker, Ray Stannard, *Woodrow Wilson, Life and Letters*, 8 v., New York, 1927–1939.

Barger, Harold, and Landsberg, Hans H., *American Agriculture, 1899–1939*, Washington, 1942.

Beard, Charles Austin, and Smith, George H. E., *The Future Comes*, New York, 1933.

———, *The Old Deal and the New*, New York, 1940.

Beard, Mary Ritter, *Short History of the American Labor Movement*, New York, 1920.

Berle, Adolf Augustus, *et al.*, *America's Recovery Program*, New York, 1934.

Bizzell, William Bennett, *Green Rising: An Historical Survey of Agrarianism*, New York, 1926.

Black, John Donald, *Agricultural Reform*, New York, 1929.

Bloore, Ella Reeve, *We Are Many*, New York, 1940.

Bowers, Claude, *Beveridge and the Progressive Era*, Boston, 1932.

Bowles, Chester, *Tomorrow Without Fear*, New York, 1946.

Brandt, Karl, *Reconstruction of World Agriculture*, New York, 1945.

Brissenden, Paul Fred, *History of the I. W. W.*, New York, 1920.

Brooks, John Graham, *American Syndicalism: the I.W.W.*, New York, 1913.

Brooks, Robert R. R., *When Labor Organizes*, New Haven, 1937.

Browder, Earl Russell, *Teheran; Our Path in War and Peace*, New York, 1944.

———, *Victory and After*, New York, 1942.

———, *Way Out*, New York, 1941.

Bryan, William Jennings, *The First Battle*, Chicago, 1898.

Buck, Paul Herman, *The Road to Reunion, 1865-1900*, Boston, 1937.

Buck, Solon Justus, *The Agrarian Crusade: a Chronicle of the Farmer in Politics*, New Haven, 1920.

———, *Granger Movement, a Study of Agricultural Organization and Its Political, Economic, and Social Manifestations, 1870–1880*, Cambridge, Mass., 1913.

Budenz, Louis Francis, *This Is My Story*, New York, 1947.

Cannon, James Patrick, *History of American Trotskyism*, New York, 1944.

———, *Struggle for a Proletarian Party*, New York, 1943.

Capper, Arthur, *Agricultural Bloc*, New York, 1922.

BIBLIOGRAPHY

Carlton, Frank Tracy, *The History and Problems of Organized Labor,* Boston, 1920.

Carroll, Mollie Ray, *Labor and Politics; the Attitude of the A. F. L. toward Legislation and Politics,* Boston, 1923.

Carver, Thomas Nixon, *Present Economic Revolution in the United States,* Boston, 1925.

Chamberlain, John, *Farewell to Reform,* New York, 1932.

Childs, John Lawrence, and Counts, George S., *America, Russia, and the Communist Party in the Post-war World,* New York, 1943.

Clark, Marjorie, and Simon, S. Fanny, *The Labor Movement in America,* New York, 1938.

Coleman, McAlister, *Men and Coal,* New York, 1943.

Commons, John R., *et al., Documentary History of American Industrial Society,* 11 v., Cleveland, 1910–1911, IX–XI.

————, *History of Labour in the U. S.,* 2 v., New York, 1918–1926.

————, *Principles of Labor Legislation,* New York, 4th rev. ed., 1936.

Communism in Action, comp. under dir. of Everett M. Dirksen, Washington, 1947.

Congress of Industrial Organizations, Political Action Committee, *Full Employment; Proceedings of the Conference on Full Employment,* Washington, 1944.

Cooke, Morris Llewellyn, and Murray, Philip, *Organized Labor and Production,* New York, 1946.

Croly, Herbert, *Progressive Democracy,* New York, 1914.

Daniels, Josephus, *Wilson Era,* Chapel Hill, N. C., 1946.

Daugherty, Carroll Roop, *Labor Problems in American Industry,* Boston, 1933.

Daniel De Leon, the Man and His Work, New York, 1919.

Davies, Ernest, *American Labour,* London, 1943.

Davis, Jerome, *Contemporary Social Movements,* New York, 1930.

Dearing, Charles Lee, *The ABC of the NRA,* Washington, 1934.

Dennis, Eugene, *What America Faces,* New York, 1946.

Destler, Chester McArthur, *American Radicalism, 1865–1901,* New London, 1946.

DeWitt, B. P., *The Progressive Movement,* New York, 1915.

Eby, Herbert Oscar, *Labor Relations Act in the Courts,* New York, 1943.

Edwards, Gladys Talbot, *Farmers' Union Triangle,* Jamestown, N. D., 1941.

Eliot, Clara, *The Farmer's Campaign for Credit,* New York, 1927.

Ellwood, Charles A., *Introduction to Social Psychology,* New York, 1917.

Encyclopedia Americana, New York, 1928. Article on "Social Reform Movements: Their Historical Development."

Encyclopedia of the Social Sciences, New York, 1930. Articles on "Anarchism," "Syndicalism," "Socialism," "Socialist Parties," "Communism," "Communist Party."

Faulkner, Harold U., *Quest for Social Justice, 1898–1914,* New York, 1931.

Fine, Nathan, *Labor and Farmer Parties in the United States,* New York, 1928.

Fitzpatrick, Bernard H., *Understanding Labor,* New York, 1945.

Fossum, Paul R., *The Agrarian Movement in N. Dakota. Johns Hopkins University Studies,* XLIII, No. 1, Baltimore, 1925.

BIBLIOGRAPHY

Foster, William Zebulon, *Problems of Organized Labor Today*, New York, 1946.
———, *Soviet Trade Unions and Allied Labor Unity*, New York, 1943.
Frederick, Justus George, *New Deal; a People's Capitalism*, New York, 1944.
Galenson, Walter, *Rival Unionism in the United States*, Washington, 1940.
Gambs, J. S., *Decline of the I. W. W.*, New York, 1932.
Gaston, H. E., *The Non-Partisan League*, New York, 1920.
Gitlow, Benjamin, *I Confess*, New York, 1940.
Gompers, Samuel, *Seventy Years of Life and Labor*, 2 v., New York, rev. ed., 1943.
Goodman, Jack, ed., *While You Were Gone*, New York, 1946.
Green, William, *Labor and Democracy*, Princeton, N. J., 1939.
Grossman, Jonathan Phillip, *William Sylvis, Pioneer of American Labor*, New York, 1945.
Hacker, Louis Morton, and Kendrick, Benjamin Burks, *The United States Since 1865*; New York, 3rd rev. ed., 1939.
Hallgren, Mauritz Alfred, *Seeds of Revolt*, New York, 1933.
Hansen, Alvin Harvey, *America's Role in the World Economy*, New York, 1945.
Hardman, Jacob B. S., *American Labor Dynamics*, New York, 1928.
Harris, Abram L., and Spero, Sterling Denhard, *Black Worker: The Negro and the Labor Movement*, New York, 1931.
Harris, Herbert, *American Labor*, New Haven, 1939.
———, *Labor's Civil War*, New York, 1940.
Harris, Seymour Edwin, *Inflation and the American Economy*, New York, 1945.
Harvey, Rowland Hill, *Samuel Gompers, Champion of the Toiling Masses*, Palo Alto, California, 1935.
Haworth, Paul L., *America in Ferment*, Indianapolis, 1915.
Haynes, Frederick Emory, *Social Politics in the United States*, Boston, 1924.
———, *Third Party Movements Since the Civil War*, Iowa City, 1916.
Hechler, Kenneth C., *Insurgency*, New York, 1940.
Hepburn, Alonzo Barton, *A History of Currency in the United States*, New York, rev. ed., 1924.
Hicks, John D., *Populist Revolt: A History of the Farmers' Alliance and the People's Party*, Minneapolis, 1931.
Hillquit, Morris, *Socialism in Theory and Practice*, New York, 1910.
Howe, Frederick C., *The Confessions of a Reformer*, New York, 1925.
Howe, George Frederick, *A General History of the United States Since 1865*, New York, 1939.
Huberman, Leo, *Truth about Unions*, New York, 1946.
Ickes, Harold L., "Who Killed the Progressive Party?" *American Historical Review*, January, 1941, 306–337.
Industrial Workers of the World, *The Immediate Demands of the I. W. W.*, Chicago, 19—.
Johnson, Hugh S., *Blue Eagle from Egg to Earth*, New York, 1935.
Johnston, Eric, *America Unlimited*, Garden City, 1944.
Josephson, Matthew, *The Politicos, 1865–1896*, New York, 1938.
Kendrick, Benjamin Burks, "Agrarian Discontent in the South, 1880–1890," in *American Historical Association Reports*, 1920.
Kingdon, Frank, *Uncommon Man*, New York, 1945.

BIBLIOGRAPHY

Kirkland, Edward C., *A History of American Economic Life,* New York, 1936.

La Follette, Robert Marion, *Autobiography,* Madison, 1913.

Laidler, Harry W., *American Socialism: Its Aims and Practical Program,* New York, 1937.

——, *A History of Socialist Thought,* New York, 1933.

——, *Social-Economic Movements,* New York, 1944.

——, ed., *Socialist Planning and a Socialist Program,* New York, 1932.

——, *Socialism in Thought and Action,* New York, 1920.

——, *Toward a Farmer-Labor Party,* New York, 1938.

Lavine, Harold, *Fifth Column in America,* Garden City, 1940.

League for Industrial Democracy, *Forward March of American Labor,* New York, 1945.

Levenstein, Aaron, *Labor Today and Tomorrow,* New York, 1945.

Levinson, Edward, *Labor on the March,* New York, 1938.

Lewis, Edward R., *A History of American Political Thought from the Civil War to the World War,* New York, 1937.

Lippincott, Isaac, *What the Farmer Needs,* New York, 1928.

Lloyd, Henry Demarest, *Wealth Against Commonwealth,* New York, 1894.

Loeb, Harold Albert, *Full Production Without War,* Princeton, N. J., 1946.

Lombardi, John, *Labor's Voice in the Cabinet,* New York, 1946.

Lyons, Eugene, *Red Decade,* Indianapolis, 1941.

McCabe, James Dabney, *History of the Grange Movement,* Philadelphia, 1874.

McCune, Wesley, *The Farm Bloc,* Garden City, 1943.

MacDonald, Lois, *Labor Problems and the American Scene,* New York, 1938.

MacDonald, William, *The Menace of Recovery,* New York, 1934.

McNaughton, Frank, and Hehmeyer, Walter, *This Man Truman,* New York, 1945.

Manifesto of the Fourth International, New York, 1943.

Merriam, Charles Edward, *American Political Ideas, 1867–1917,* New York, 1920.

——, *The Role of Politics in Social Change,* New York, 1936.

Moore, Arthur L., *Farmer and the Rest of Us,* Boston, 1945.

Mowry, George E., *Theodore Roosevelt and the Progressive Movement,* Madison, 1946.

Myers, James, *Do You Know Labor?* New York, 1943.

Nathan, Robert Roy, *Mobilizing for Abundance,* New York, 1944.

National Citizens Political Action Committee, *Manual of Practical Political Action,* New York, 1946.

The New Deal, An Analysis and Appraisal, by the editors of the London *Economist,* New York, 1937.

The New Dealers, Anonymous, New York, 1934.

Normano, Joao Frederico, *Spirit of American Economics,* New York, 1943.

Northrup, Herbert Roof, *Organized Labor and the Negro,* New York, 1944.

Nourse, Edwin Griswold, *American Agriculture and the European Market,* New York, 1924.

Ogburn, William Fielding, ed., *Social Change and the New Deal,* Chicago, 1934.

Bibliography

———, *Social Change with Respect to Culture and Original Nature,* New York, 1928.

———, and Nimkoff, Meyer F., *Sociology,* Boston, 1940.

Oneal, James, *American Communism,* New York, 1927.

Paxson, Frederic Logan, *Recent History of the United States,* Boston, rev. ed., 1937.

Payne, George Henry, *The Birth of the New Party,* New York, 1912.

Perlman, Selig, *History of Trade Unionism in the United States,* New York, 1922.

———, and Taft, P., *History of Labor in the United States, 1896–1932,* New York, 1935.

Petersen, Arnold, *Daniel DeLeon: Social Architect,* New York, 1941.

———, *Democracy, Past, Present, and Future,* New York, 1940.

Peterson, Elmer Theodore, *Forward to the Land,* Norman, Okla., 1942.

Peterson, Florence, *American Labor Unions,* New York, 1945.

Pettee, George Sawyer, *The Process of Revolution,* New York, 1939.

Pinchot, Gifford, *The Fight for Conservation,* Garden City, 1910.

Post-War Program of the American Federation of Labor, April 12, 1944, Washington, 1944.

Powderly, Terence Vincent, *The Path I Trod,* New York, 1940.

Pringle, Henry F., *The Life and Times of William Howard Taft,* 2 v., New York, 1939.

———, *Theodore Roosevelt,* New York, 1931.

Rauch, Basil, *History of the New Deal, 1933–1938,* New York, 1944.

Raudenbush, David Webb, *Democratic Capitalism,* New York, 1946.

Rice, Stuart A., *Farmers and Workers in American Politics,* New York, 1924.

Roosevelt, Anna Eleanor, *If You Ask Me,* New York, 1946.

Roosevelt, Franklin Delano, *On Our Way,* New York, 1934.

———, *The Public Papers and Addresses,* 5 v., New York, 1938; 4 v., New York, 1941.

———, *Rendezvous With Destiny,* New York, 1944.

Ross, Edward Alsworth, *Social Psychology,* New York, 1908.

Sait, Edward McChesney, *American Parties and Elections,* New York, 1927.

Saposs, David J., *Left-wing Unionism,* New York, 1926.

Schmidt, Carl Theodore, *American Farmers in the World Crisis,* New York, 1941.

Schultz, Theodore William, *Redirecting Farm Policy,* New York, 1943.

Shannon, Fred Albert, *Farmer's Last Frontier; Agriculture, 1860–1897,* New York, 1945.

Shepherd, Geoffrey Seddon, *Agricultural Price Control,* Ames, Iowa, 1945.

Sims, Newell L., *The Problem of Social Change,* New York, 1939.

Slichter, Sumner Huber, *Union Policies and Industrial Management,* Washington, 1941.

Sorokin, Pitirim A., *The Sociology of Revolution,* Philadelphia, 1925.

Soule, George Henry, *The Coming American Revolution,* New York, 1934.

Spargo, John, *Socialism,* New York, rev. ed., 1912.

Stanwood, Edward, *A History of the Presidency,* Boston, 1898.

———, *A History of the Presidency from 1897 to 1916,* 2 v., Boston, rev. ed., 1928.

Steffens, Lincoln, Autobiography of, New York, 1931.

Stein, Emmanuel, *Labor and the New Deal*, New York, 1934.

Stolberg, Benjamin, *Story of the C. I. O.*, New York, 1938.

Sulzberger, Cyrus Leo, *Sit Down with John L. Lewis*, New York, 1938.

Tarbell, Ida M., *All in a Day's Work*, New York, 1939.

——, *The Nationalizing of Business, 1878–1898*, New York, 1936.

Thomas, Norman, *America's Way Out, a Program for Democracy*, New York, 1931.

——, *The Choice before Us*, New York, 1933.

——, *What Is Our Destiny?* Garden City, 1944.

Trotsky, Leon, *First Five Years of the Communist International*, 2 v., New York, 1945.

——, *Revolution Betrayed . . .* , Garden City, 1937.

——, *Stalinism and Bolshevism*, New York, 1937.

Usher, Ellis B., *The Greenback Movement of 1875–1884*, Milwaukee, 1911.

Vorse, Mary Heaton, *Labor's New Millions*, New York, 1938.

Wallace, Henry Agard, *Democracy Reborn*, New York, 1944.

——, *Sixty Million Jobs*, New York, 1945.

Ware, Norman J., *The Labor Movement in the United States, 1860–1895*, New York, 1929.

Wechsler, James Arthur, *Labor Baron*, New York, 1944.

Wecter, Dixon, *The Age of the Great Depression, 1929–1941*, New York, 1948.

Wernette, John Philip, *Financing Full Employment*, Cambridge, Mass., 1945.

Westmeyer, Russell Eugene, *Modern Economic and Social Systems*, New York, 1940.

White, William Allen, *Masks in a Pageant*, New York, 1928.

Wilson, Woodrow, *The New Freedom*, New York, 1913.

——, *Public Papers*, ed. by Ray S. Baker and William E. Dodd, 6 v. in 3, New York, 1927.

Wish, Harvey, *Contemporary America*, New York, 1945.

Wolman, Leo, *The Growth of American Trade Unions, 1880–1923*, New York, 1924.

Woodward, Comer Vann, *Tom Watson, Agrarian Rebel*, New York, 1938.

Zeller, Belle, *Pressure Politics in New York*, New York, 1937.

Periodicals

A listing of the individual magazine articles which have been used in the writing of this book would require an undue amount of space. They have been taken from the following periodicals, whose files for the recent period were thoroughly searched for materials relating to social reform movements:

American Economic Review
American Magazine
American Mercury
American Political Science Review
American Scholar
Annals of the American Academy
of Political and Social Science
Atlantic
Business Week
Canadian Forum
Catholic World
Christian Century
Collier's
Commonweal
Congressional Digest
Contemporary Review
Current History
Foreign Affairs
Fortnightly
Fortune
Harper's
Journal of Political Economy
Life

Monthly Labor Review
Nation
National Education Association
Journal
Nation's Business
New Republic
Newsweek
The New York Times Magazine
Nineteenth Century
Occupations
Political Science Quarterly
Quarterly Journal of Economics
Reader's Digest
Rotarian
Saturday Evening Post
Science Digest
Scholastic
Survey Graphic
Time
Virginia Quarterly Review
Vital Speeches
United States News
Yale Review

Index

INDEX

311